The St. Martin's Guide
to
Teaching Writing

W9-BEC-196

The St. Martin's Guide to
Teaching Writing

Robert Connors
University of New Hampshire

Cheryl Glenn
Ohio State University

St. Martin's Press
New York

For information, write to:

St. Martin's Press, Inc.
175 Fifth Avenue
New York, NY 10010

ISBN: 0-312-02456-8

Exercises from *Notes Toward a New Rhetoric* by Francis Christensen. Copyright © 1967 by Francis Christensen. Reprinted by permission of Harper and Row Publishers, Inc.
Exercises from *Classical Rhetoric for the Modern Student*, Second Edition, by Edward P.J. Corbett. Copyright 1971 by Oxford University Press, Inc. Reprinted by permission.
Excerpt from the Introduction to *Perspectives on Literacy*, by Eugene Kintgen, Barry M. Kroll, and Mike Rose. Copyright 1988 by the Board of Trustees, Southern Illinois University. Reprinted by permission of Publishers.
Excerpt from "Revising the Tagmemics Heuristic: Theoretical and Pedagogical Considerations" by Charles Kneupper. Copyright © 1980 by National Council for the Teachers of English. Reprinted by permission.
Exercises from "A Plan for Teaching Rhetorical Invention," by Richard Larson. Copyright © 1968 by National Council for the Teachers of English. Reprinted by permission.
Excerpt from *Exercises in Style* by Edmund Miller. Copyright © 1980 by Edmund Miller. Reprinted by permission.
Excerpt from *The New Yorker Magazine*. Copyright © 1988 by The New Yorker Magazine, Inc. Reprinted by permission.
Excerpt from *Writing the Natural Way: Using Right-Brain Techniques to Release Your Expressive Powers*, by Gabriele Lusser Rico. Copyright © 1983 by Gabriele Lusser Rico. Reprinted by permission of Jeremy Tarcher Press, Inc.
Excerpt from "The Lives of Albert Goldman" by James Wolcott. Originally published by *Vanity Fair*. Copyright © 1988 By The Conde Nast Publications, Inc. Reprinted by permission of author.

Contents

Introduction

There it is in black and white. You've been assigned to teach a college writing course: first-year English. Sentences, paragraphs, outlines, red ink. "Me—teach writing? I never took a writing course in my life, except first-year English, which I barely remember. What am I going to do?"

That last question, the central concern of every new writing teacher, is the question answered by this book, which was written to tell you what you can do in your writing class to help your students become better writers. The theories, techniques, and methods in the following chapters were not chosen arbitrarily: All are based on classroom practice; all have been classroom tested; and, as a whole, they represent the greater part of our current knowledge—both theory and practice—about teaching writing.

The contents of this book are informed by a three-part thesis. First, writing is teachable, an art that can be learned rather than a mysterious ability that one either has or has not. Second, students learn to write from continuous trial-and-error writing and almost never profit from lectures or "teacher-centered" classes or from studying and memorizing isolated rules. Third, the theories and methods included here were selected according to "what works." Fine authors and important composition and education theories are missing from the following chapters for the simple reason that they don't immediately lend themselves to pragmatic classroom use.

This book is in two parts: Part I, "Practical Issues in Teaching Writing," and Part II, "Theories into Practice." Aimed at the first-time teacher of writing, Part I offers the "nuts and bolts" of teaching composition with chapters ranging from "Preparing for the First Class" to "Responding to and Evaluating Student Essays." If you are a new teacher, you may want to start with Part I and become familiar with the framework: how to prepare for, set up, and teach your first writing course. Then, you can move into Part II.

More experienced teachers may want to begin with Part II, theoretical background and application, which covers the three most important areas of traditional rhetoric (invention, arrangement, and style), and the three most important elements of composition (the sentence, the paragraph, and the sustained piece of discourse). Each of the four chapters consists of a general introduction, followed by discrete units describing specific theories and classroom activities. The classroom activities are structured according to Richard Graves's important teaching model CEHAE—Concept, *Example*, *Highlighting*, *Activity*, *Evaluation*. These activities have been successful for us and for other teachers. We hope they work for you—and that you will help to improve them.

Those teachers and scholars interested in further reading can refer to the *Works Cited* list at the end of each chapter and to the *Suggested Readings* at the end of the book. Though our research cannot do justice to the available literature on composition and rhetoric studies, the sources listed *can* provide you with a useful survey of the history and trends that have informed composition theory.

Works Cited *Introduction*

Graves, Richard. "CEHAE: Five Steps for Teaching Writing." *English Journal* 62 (1972): 696–701.

Part I

Practical Issues in Teaching Writing

Chapter 1

Preparing for the First Class

Finding Out the Nature of the Course

You have been assigned to teach a writing course, but writing courses come in many varieties, even first-year writing courses. Before you can begin to make intelligent and useful teaching plans, you need to find out some of the vital statistics of your course. The course director or director of composition at your school can answer most of the following questions; if there is no composition director you should probably go directly to the chair of the department. Experienced teachers can answer some of the most important questions concerning unwritten practices, but an administrator is a more reliable source for official departmental policy.

First, find out how many credit-hours the course carries and how many times the class meets each week. A three-credit course that meets three hours a week provides far less time for work in reading and writing than does a five-credit, five-hour course; hence, you will want to adjust the number of required writing assignments according to credit hours. Students willing to write ten essays and fifty journal entries for five credits may balk at doing the same amount of work for three credits.

Next, ask how many sections you will be teaching and the number of students you can expect to have in each class. The National Council of Teachers of English recommends that each graduate student teach only one graduate course, and that the maximum number of students for each course be twenty (or fifteen for a basic writing course). Most English departments try to adhere to these recommendations, keeping the numbers within reasonable limits (from twenty to thirty students). Of course, the fewer students you have, the fewer papers you must read and evaluate, the fewer conferences you need to conduct; the fewer students you have, the more time you will have for each student and for class preparation. If you are willing to teach at 8:00 A.M. or at 5:00 P.M., you may get a smaller class than if you teach at a popular time slot, say late morning or early afternoon. The information you gain about the student load will help you organize assignments and plan the syllabus.

Finally, make inquiries about the level of students you will be teaching. If your college or university has open admissions, then the range of student abilities will be wide. Some first-year students are "basic writers," with reading and writing experiences far below those of other students, while other students are strong writers, accomplished and sophisticated products of hard-driving college prep programs. Naturally, you must gear your course preparation—from textbook selection to syllabus design—to the abilities of your students. If you are teaching at an open admissions school, find out if incoming students write English placement essays, and if there is a Basic Writing program, an English as a Second Language program, or a Writing Center. You will also want to know if there are different levels of first-year students, an honors section, perhaps, or if all first-year students are placed in the same course, or if students from all years and levels can be placed in "first-year" English.

If there is a Basic Writing or an English as a Second Language program, you might want to find out their entrance and exit requirements. And while you are discussing these things, try to find out about other adjunct writing programs on campus. Not only will you have a better picture of the entire writing program, but you will know where to send your students for help. Some schools have Writing Centers that provide students help with particular problems and that send representatives into classrooms to give mini-lessons on such topics as the writing process, writer's block, and writing essay exams. You may be surprised at the number of support systems your school offers you and your students. In addition to help with writing, some schools augment student learning with Reading Centers, where reading and comprehension problems can be diagnosed. Often affiliated with the Communications Department, the College of Education, or the College of Allied Medicine is the Learning Disabilities Center, where students can be diagnosed and treated for dyslexia or dysgraphia. By asking questions and talking to representatives of these various programs, you will be much better prepared to guide your students through their writing course. When they have problems that you cannot solve, you will be able to send them to the specialists who can help.

Choosing Texts

After you have discovered all you can about the nature of the courses you are to teach and the kinds of students you can expect, the next step is to investigate the available textbooks. Many writing programs require that certain texts be used by all teachers; others specify a primary text and allow teachers to choose their own supplementary ones, and still others maintain a list of approved texts from which teachers can select their books. The freedom you have in choosing books will depend on your location and program, and on the needs and interests of your students. Begin by finding out what texts others have traditionally used and examining them very carefully. As you work with each text, have your students evaluate it; their responses will make your future choices easier.

Most departments that allow teachers some freedom in textbook selection maintain a small library of texts as samples for teachers to examine. In order to make sense of the books you find there, you can do some background reading on textbooks; several review-articles and bibliographies are available to give new teachers an overview of the world of textbooks.[1]

In addition to background reading, the questions of structure should be kept in mind when examining textbooks: How much do you want the structure of the text or texts to inform the structure of the course? If the text is organized "Invention, Organization, Diction, Style, Paragraphs," will you design your course around that structure and assign a week or two weeks to each chapter, or do you plan to structure your course differently and break up text readings according to a theme or some other personal design? Perhaps you will find a text that presents an organizational schema that is congenial to you; on the other hand, you may have to break up a text to get what you want from it. Remember, the decisions that you make about the text and organization now are decisions that become ironclad contracts once they are written into a syllabus. For the next ten or fifteen weeks you will have to live with your decisions of the next few days. Don't decide hastily.

After teaching with a text, you may want to continue with it, or you may decide to jettison it. Either way, choose your first text carefully, and make certain you get a free desk copy.

Planning the First Two Weeks

The idea of going in and leading a class of college students in a "contentless" course may be a daunting prospect at first. Therefore, it

---

1 For a discussion of composition textbooks see Woods; see also Lindemann.

is best to prepare your classroom time for the two weeks with extra thoroughness. Give yourself a structure for each class that is carefully thought out; it is always better to find yourself carrying some of your plans over to the next class rather than to take a chance that you will be gazing helplessly at the end of your prepared notes with half an hour still left in class.

Though the classroom offers more teaching challenges than you can possibly get around to, dipping into the following chapters can give you an idea of some options available to you. For course structure as a whole, unless you plan to be guided by a text or have some specific plan of your own, you may want to speak to an experienced teacher and adapt a course structure that has been proven successful. After your first term of teaching, you will probably want to revise and experiment with your teaching structure. You may consider changing the text you teach, as well. Before you confront such long term goals, however, you will want to work on a basic strategy for planning and teaching individual lessons.

When drawing up lesson plans, make sure that each lesson contains a section detailing the *goal* or *object* you want to address. If the lesson involves the explanation and exemplification of a method of essay organization, then the goal should be clearly stated: "to familiarize students with basics of three-part organization and show them rudiments of introduction and conclusion form. Examples: one on handout, two from reader." If the lesson involves activities, spell out the purpose of the activities: "to practice introductions and conclusions for three-part arrangement and get students to be able to write thesis statements." Without such goal statements, it is easy to get away from the point of the lesson.

After the goal statement, the amount of actual material in a lesson plan is up to you. Some teachers begin their careers needing full paragraphs and short essays, while experienced teachers can often work from notes made up only of key words. Make certain that you cross-index notes to pages in any text or reader you use. Your lesson plan or activity will prevent you from being left with empty time, or from having to break an activity up before it ends.

Examples 1–1 and 1–2 show two kinds of daily lesson plans. The first one outlines an inquiry activity, one that asks students to respond to pictures, and then to write, share, and rewrite drafts. Notice how the teacher has written the objective in the first sentence: "Look over the rough drafts and see what problems and successes students have had, making brief comments on their drafts where you find it appropriate." Her objective drives her carefully ordered and timed classroom activities.

The second sample lesson is based on an assigned reading, "Who Killed Benny Paret?" If, like this teacher, you are using a reader in your writing course, you will naturally want to draft lesson plans incorporating the reader. In preparation for an upcoming writing assignment, this teacher wanted her students to master the art of writing objective summaries, starting with one on "Who Killed Benny Paret?"

But before her students could begin writing, she wanted to talk with them about the troublesome genre, the trouble lying in the word "objective." So she outlined important points she wanted to hear her students talk about: the central issue of the essay, the writer's point of view, how the progression of the essay relates to the purpose of the essay, and the assumptions on which a writer's views are based.

Then, the class turned to another essay, "Frisbee Golf," and talked through the same points again, discussing the problems with any claim to objectivity. It was only toward the end of class that the teacher specified the practical elements of their summary-writing assignment; she also reiterated the fifth specification in her notes: "Use only the information provided in the original essay. Try hard not to color your summary with your opinions or extra information. An objective summary means you are conveying information and not opinion"—a tough job.

Example 1–1

```
English 110
Inquiry Activity I
Instructions for the Teacher
```

DAY TWO

For today: Look over the rough drafts and see what
problems and successes students have had, making brief
comments on their drafts where you find it appropriate.
(See the Trouble-shooting Sheets for a list of criteria.)
Select one or two examples from your students' writing
for class discussion *OR* use examples provided by the Writing Staff. Run these samples off for use in your class.

1. After having students read the sample narration-
description(s) (one at a time, of course), ask students
from the other groups (the groups that haven't written on
this particular illustration) to identify the dominant impression they get from the written description. Ask them
to identify the aspects of the writing that are making it
easy or difficult to get a "picture" of what is in the illustration. Discuss.

Then show them the actual illustration. Discuss how the
description could have been improved to give a better
"picture" of what is in the illustration. As a part of
your discussion, examine the roles that establishing a
context, using details, and organizing descriptions play
in narrative-descriptive writing. (15–20 minutes)

2. Have them rewrite their drafts. (25–30 minutes)

3. Collect these revised drafts. Make brief comments on
them, especially about their use of details to picture
and support their dominant impression. Return the drafts,
assigning each a check, a check-plus, or a check-minus.

Example 1–2

Objective Summary Writing

—Read "Benny Paret"

1. central issue
2. writer's point of view
3. progression of essay connected to purpose of essay
4. assumptions on which writer's views are based

75–100 words—objective summary

p. 130 *WW* Read "Frisbee Golf"
p. 131
Objective Summary

1. 1/3 length original
2. Main Idea—Thesis Statement?
   key words/phrases
   Supports? How impt. are they?
3. Use your own words
   Plagiarism
4. Follow original organization
5. Only information in original. No opinions, no extra informa-tion. OBJECTIVE SUMMARY means you are conveying infor-mation and not opinion.
6. Give the source. This is for other readers—they may want to find it.

One last bit of advice on class notes: for every concept you explain and exemplify, have two or three other examples in your notes ready to put on the board if more examples are needed. Similarly, while deciding on classroom strategies and on the form of your notes, remember to annotate your texts if you are planning to key class work to them. Do not feel annotation of books is a messy business, best avoided. Instead, occupy the book, underline and mark in it— make your teaching life easier. These texts are some of your raw materials and may be with you for years—make them work for you. Annotate any part of the rhetoric that you feel may need more ex-planation, and mark off the exercises you plan to use. Your marks need be no more than checks or underlinings, but they should be meaningful to you. You should be able to open the book to a page and know immediately what you wish to accomplish on it.

But before you can prepare serious class notes or text annotations, you will need an overview of and a plan for your entire course: the forms your classes will take, the sorts of writing assignments you will require, the order of the material you plan to teach, etc. After you have read this book, talked with your colleagues, and carefully looked over your chosen texts, you should be ready to make a rough draft of your choice. Formalized, this rough draft will be the basis for the central document of your course, the syllabus. Although few teachers adhere absolutely to their syllabus, fewer still depart from it entirely. Writing the syllabus is your next major task.

The Creation of a Syllabus

The syllabus for college courses originated as a list of the books for which every student was to be held responsible; in our day, though, it is usually more encompassing. In writing courses, the syllabus, for all intents and purposes, is a contract between teacher and student; it states, in writing, the responsibilities of the teacher and the students as well as the course standards. Everyone concerned, from your department administrators to the parents of incoming students, may want to know exactly what your plans are. To protect both yourself and your students from potential misunderstanding, then, write a detailed and informative syllabus that spells out your goals and expectations clearly. And such a written contract has other uses: It shows a student who feels ill-used or wants special privileges the clause that has determined your position on the issue in question, whether it be your attendance or due-date policy.

The syllabus is also the public informing structure of the class, explaining what the course will cover, when it will be covered, and what your qualitative and quantitative expectations of students will be. It prevents the teacher from having to repeat countless explanations of course policies, goals, and dates. The syllabus is also the first written impression that students get of the teacher and his or her personality.

Syllabi for writing courses, need to be longer and more detailed than those for literature courses, because students do not have so developed a context of expectations and intentions for composition as they have for their literature courses. If you follow the outline below, you should be able to create a syllabus that fills all of the teacher's major needs and answers all of the students' major questions. This outline does not produce an exhaustive syllabus, but it is a good model for first-time teachers because of its simplicity and schematic development.

1. *Your name, the course number, your office number,* and *your office hours.* The telephone numbers of your office and/or your home are optional. Office hours are those periods when you must be in your office so that students may drop by unscheduled to speak with you. If your department does not require a minimum number of office hours, the rule of thumb seems to be that you should schedule as many office hours as your course has "contact hours"—hours you are actually in the classroom with students. So, if your class meets five hours a week, you might want to set aside five hours a week for your office hours. Teachers can generally choose the time for their office hours, but immediately before and after class times are the most usual. Try to schedule office hours on two successive days, so that students who cannot come in on Monday-Wednesday-Friday or on Tuesday-Thursday have a chance at alternate days. If you include your phone numbers, you need to tell your students between what hours you are willing to speak to them.

2. *Textbook information.* This includes the author, title, edition, and publication information for each text. If you wish students to purchase folders, modules, or supplementary materials, they should be included here.

3. *Course policy.* This section includes your policies on:
   a. attendance—how many absences you allow for each student and what you will do if that number is exceeded. (You'll need to check to see if the department has a policy.)
   b. tardiness—what you will do about students who consistently come to class late.
   c. participation—how much, if any, of the final course grade will depend on classroom participation.
   d. late papers—whether or under what conditions you will accept essays and written assignments after their due dates.
   e. style of papers—what you will demand by way of physical format for graded assignments—double-spaced in pen, typed, etc.

4. *Course requirements.* This section discusses written work and includes:
   a. graded work

   i. Number and length of assigned essays; your policy on revision.

   ii. Requirements of journal and explanation of the journal policy and how or whether the journal will be applied to final grading. (optional section)

  b. Ungraded Work—explanation of policy on ungraded homework, in-class writing assignments, drafts, etc., and how or whether ungraded work will apply to final course grade.

5. *Grading procedures.* This section discusses the procedures that will be followed for evaluation and grading of written work. It does *not* discuss the standards that will be applied; it merely details how assignments will be dealt with in order to arrive at final grades. This includes two specific areas: a listing of the percentage values of each piece of written work as these values apply toward the final grade, and, if you are using a revision option, a detailed review of how it works.[2] This statement needs to be spelled out in detail; otherwise, students will claim confusion as an excuse for not having work done, or for not putting enough importance on a given piece of writing.

6. *Grading standards.* This is an optional section, because many teachers do not like to spell out the standards they will use in any quantitative or prescriptive way. Many departments have created grading standards that must be used by all teachers and may require that they be published in the syllabus. If a grading standards section is included, it can contain:

  a. Standards of form—The maximum number of "serious" syntactic errors—fragments, comma splices, run-ons—that are allowed in a passing essay; the maximum number of lesser errors—spelling, punctuation, usage—allowable in a passing essay.

  b. Standards of content—The levels of semantic and organizational expertise—a clear thesis, support of assertions, coherent paragraph use, development of arguments, etc.—that must be minimally apparent in a passing essay.

7. *Meetings.* This section details how many days per week the course will meet, on which days the meetings will be held, and any special information about specific days that you want students to have; for instance, if workshop group meetings,

---

2   For information on a revision option, see Chapter 3.

in-class writing, or sentence-combining will always fall on specific days of the week, this section announces them.

8. *Course calendar.* Course calendars can be simple or complex. The only absolutely essential element in the calendar is a listing of the due dates for written assignments and call-ins of the journal, but it can contain extremely detailed information on lessons to be prepared, reading to be done, skills to be worked on, goals to be met, and a host of other things. This more detailed material is optional, and whether or not you use it will depend on the degree to which you wish to structure your course beforehand. My advice is not to overstructure your calendar at first—allow yourself the freedom to change plans if the methods you had originally meant to use seem not to be working well.

9. *Course goals.* Whether this is a departmental statement that must be included in every syllabus or a personal definition of the objectives you have in the course, some statement of goals should be included in your syllabus. It should mention the number of graded assignments, basic skills that will be expected of each student by the end of the course, the question of student participation, and the fact that in order to pass the course, each student will have to demonstrate competency in writing. You can also include a personal message of your own about the course and its expectations.

10. *English Department information.* Your department may have special provisions for handling student questions and complaints. If so, you may be required to list the pertinent information on your syllabus: names, office numbers, office hours, official capacity, confidentiality.

These ten points comprise the main elements of a composition syllabus. Other sections can be added, of course, but these are the ones needed for your protection and your students' understanding. We have provided an example of a syllabus that uses a handbook and also focuses on the writing process.

One final bit of advice: Make more copies of the syllabus than there are students on your roster; increase the numbers by one-third. Thus, if you have 24 students on your roster, make 32 copies of the syllabus. Students who drop the class will carry off their syllabi; students who add the class will need copies; and other students will lose theirs and need new ones. Have your syllabus ready for distribution on the first day of class. Be prepared.

Example 1–3

Sample Syllabus

English 110

Section 03
Roger Graves
Room 238 Denny Hall
12:00 MTWRF
Office Hours: Room 515, MW 1:00–3:00

Text: *The St. Martin's Handbook*

Structure of the Course

One of the best ways to learn to write is by writing, and
for that reason students in this course will be asked to
do a lot of inventing, drafting, and revising—that's what
writing is. Sharing work with others, either in peer-
response sessions, writing groups, or collaborative efforts, promotes learning about writing by widening the
response writers get to their work. Finally, guidance
from texts constitutes another important component of
learning to write, by answering questions you may have or
suggesting ways of going about the business of writing.
Because these three approaches operate powerfully in the
classroom, they form the basis of the course schedule outlined below.

To provide practice in writing and the sharing of writings, often the class will be devoted to writing
workshops. These writing workshops will give you the
chance to see how other students have handled writing assignments, to practice editing skills by helping other
students edit their own work, and to draft essays. Many
class days will involve a class discussion of a student
essay that demonstrates how the writing being done might
best be handled. In addition, many classes will open with
a short writing assignment, "freewrite," or writing journal entry. Each week we will read sections from the *St.
Martin's Handbook* that address issues about writing,
guide us in our understanding of those issues, and suggest ways for us to broaden our knowledge and apply that
knowledge to our writing.

Written Assignments

We will write five essays during the term. An "acceptable" draft of each essay must be turned in by the final due date for each essay. At any time during the term, I will assign a final grade to the draft that each student judges to be his or her final effort on each essay. At least one week before the end of the term, students must turn in four of five final drafts for final evaluation. Before the last day of classes, students must turn in the fifth essay for a final grade.

Since you can suspend final evaluation of your progress until the end of the semester, this grading system provides you with the opportunity to have your best work evaluated. (*Type* all final drafts.)

Attendance

Because much of each student's most important work will take place in class, attendance in class is mandatory. (Chronically late students will be warned once; after that, each late appearance will be counted as an absence.)

Final Course Grades

Final course grades will be arrived at by combining grades for the five graded papers, class attendance, participation, and conferences with the teacher in the following manner:

final graded essays (4 times 15):	60%
research essay (fourth essay)	20%
attendance	10%
conferences, journals	10%

Sample Course Schedule[3]

Week	Topics/Focus
1	Introduction: briefly outline the course; identify learning objectives from your perspective and ask the students to add some of their own; present guidelines for grading, plagiarism, late essays, attendance.

3 This course schedule is for the instructor's use; however, it can be modified and handed out to students as well.

Diagnostic writing sample.

Introduction to *The St. Martin's Handbook*.

The writing process (Chapter 1, 2): rewrite diagnostic test to demonstrate drafting, learning through writing.

Assign the first essay: identify the task clearly, provide models of successful attempts, link the assignment to learning objectives, suggest ways for students to use the assignment to learn about something that interests them.

2   Invention techniques: mapping, brainstorming (Chapter 2); research as invention (Chapter 37). Apply invention methods to first assignment.

Draft of first essay due; peer response in class; teacher response: read for overall direction, scope, and suitability for your course and first assignment.

Revising and editing the draft (Chapter 3).

Compare writing-process log entries.

3   Second draft of first essay due; peer response in class; Crafting paragraphs (Chapter 5).

Confer with students individually during either office hours or classroom writing workshops.

Identify specific error patterns you have noticed; conduct mini-lectures for students who share error patterns (the specific chapters you will need to refer to will emerge from the class' needs: see Chapters 6-16 and 27-36); for more guidance, see "Correctness and Patterns of Error in Writing").

4   First essay due.

Assign the second essay: identify the task clearly, provide models of successful attempts, link the assignment to learning objectives, suggest ways for students to use the assignment.

Repeat invention techniques used for the first essay; add Burke's dramatistic pentad.

Freewrite; repeat freewriting sessions and exchange freewrites to share ideas, approaches to the assignment.

5   Draft of the second essay due; peer response in class, teacher response to focus and questions to promote further research or development.

Creating effective prose (Chapter 17); using coordinate and subordinate structures (Chapter 18).

Writing workshop and/or individual conferences.

Second draft of second essay due.

6

Understanding diction (Chapter 24); Strengthening vocabulary (Chapter 26).

Confer with students individually during either office hours or classroom writing workshops.

Identify specific error patterns you have noticed; conduct mini-lectures for students who share error patterns (the specific chapters you will need to refer to will emerge from the needs of the class: see Chapters 6-16 and 27-36).

7   Second essay due.

Assign the third essay: identify the task clearly, provide models of successful attempts, link the assignment to learning objectives, suggest ways for students to use the assignment.

Repeat invention techniques used for the second essay; add tagmemic heuristic or clustering.

Understanding and using arguments (Chapter 4).

8   Draft of the third essay due; peer response in class, teacher response to focus and questions to spur research or development.

Creating parallel sentence structures (Chapter 19);
creating varying sentence structures (Chapter 20).

Confer with students either individually in class
or during office hours.

9   Identify specific error patterns you have noticed;
conduct mini-lectures for students who share error
patterns (the specific chapters you will need to
refer to will emerge from the class' needs: see
Chapters 6-16 and 27-36).

10   Third essay due.

Assign the fourth essay, a research essay: identify
the task clearly, provide models of successful attempts, link the assignment to learning objectives,
suggest ways for students to use the assignment.

Becoming a researcher (Chapter 38); conducting research (Chapter 39); using dictionaries (Chapter
23).

11   Research file due: a list of all sources consulted
so far; notes; photocopies of relevant readings;
summaries; quotations.

Evaluating and using source materials (Chapter 39);
organizing, drafting, and revising a research essay
(Chapter 40).

12   Draft of research essay due; confer individually
with students; devote class time to writing
workshops.

Establishing tone (Chapter 26); creating memorable
prose (Chapter 21).

13   Second draft of research essay due; peer response
in class.

Documenting sources (Chapter 42).

14   Final draft of research essay due.

Fifth assignment: "rewrite or revise an essay from:
1) a course in your major, 2) a discipline that interests you, or 3) this course."

Writing in the different disciplines (Chapter 42);
writing for non-academic audiences (Chapter 45).

Due: a description of the conventions of your discipline; a description of the style of your field.

Due: typed, final drafts of first four papers for
final grading.

15   Draft of the fifth assignment due; peer response in
      class, teacher response through individual conferen-
      ces in class or during office hours; writing
      workshops in class.
      Final draft of fifth essay due.

      Course evaluations

Works Cited *Chapter 1*

Lindemann, Erika. *Longman Bibliography of Composition and Rhetoric.* 2
    vols. to date. White Plains, N.Y.: Longman, 1984–85, 1986.
Woods, William F. "Composition Textbooks and Pedagogical Theory
    1960–1980." *College English* 43 (1981): 393–409.

Chapter 2

The First Few Days of Classes

The First Day of Class

There is nothing like the prospect of teaching your first college class to make you wonder about your own image and how you are perceived by others. The nervousness you feel is completely natural, and every good teacher feels something of it on the first day of every new class. The teaching act is a performance, in the full sense of that word; the teacher is an instructor, coordinator, actor, facilitator, announcer, pedagogue, ringmaster. For the time that you are "on the air" the show is your responsibility, and it will go well or ill depending on how you move it.

Teaching style, the way you carry off your performance, is partially determined by conscious decisions that you make and partially determined by factors within your personality over which you have little control. It is difficult to control the manner and tone with which you naturally address the class as a whole, the way you react to individual students on an intuitive level, the quick responses you make to classroom situations as they come up, and the general personality you exhibit in front of the class. This is not to say that a teacher has no control at all over how he or she appears. Although your essential personality style may not be amenable to change, you can consciously vary all of the other variables. You can control what the class does with its time, the order in which it tackles lessons, the sorts of skills it concentrates on—all of the content-oriented material that is at the heart of every class. You can make an effort toward controlling those aspects of your personal style you want specifically to change or suppress—an unthinking tendency toward sarcasm, for instance, which can turn a bright, outgoing student into a sullen lump. If your personality tends toward condescension or intimidation, you can carefully and consciously wrestle the things you say around so that they come out as encouragement.

More important than anything else, you should try to evince those two most important traits of a good teacher: humanity and competence. If students believe you to *be kind* and to *know your stuff* (and in a writing class, part of your job will be convincing them that there is stuff to know), they will put themselves in your hands and give you a chance to be their teacher. If either side of that duality is missing, you will be perceived either as a tyrant or as a nincompoop. Few teachers possess neither element; many strike a successful balance of the two. However, humanity and competence, cannot be demonstrated by a first-day lecture. They show themselves over time, not by how many jokes you tell in class or how hard you grade, but by the total picture you give students of who you are and how you feel about them and their struggle as beginning writers, and as first-year students. Over time, you and your students will build a common ethos, one you hope is characterized by mutual respect and trust.

It is the first day of classes, an important day for writing classes. Teachers of other classes often distribute syllabi and show the texts; writing teachers, however, have a good deal to get done on the first day. In your office, prepare everything you will take in to class with you. Gather your books, notes, handouts, the class roster, and your pile of syllabi. (For moving materials from floor to floor or room to room within a building, a briefcase or satchel is no affectation.) If you have a tendency toward cotton mouth, get a coffee or a soda—that sort of "prop" can help you through the first day. There's the first bell. Having scouted it out previously, you know where your classroom is. Grab your material, don't spill your drink, and enter the river of students passing through the corridor. There is your classroom. Balancing the cup or can precariously on the edge of the briefcase, you open the door. Twenty pairs of eyes swing up and follow you to the front of the room. You look out at your students. You're on the air.

Bureaucratic Tasks

The university has provided a required and undemanding routine that fills up the first ten minutes of the first class, which are nearly always the hardest. Put your materials down at the front desk and greet those students present. Students will continue to come in, even well into the class hour.

Write your name, office number, and office hours on the blackboard and then arrange your books, notes, handouts, etc., so they are within easy reach. Look up every few seconds, trying to keep eye contact with the students—it is natural to avoid their eyes until you speak to them in an official capacity, but eye contact establishes a friendly connection. Since you will probably want to teach standing up, check to see that the classroom has a lectern that you can use.

Give the stragglers a chance to come in before you call the roll. Introduce yourself, the course, your office number and hours. These first few announcements, routine though they are, are the most difficult. Speak slowly, and remember that you have everything planned, that you are in your element, that you will perform well. Meet the students' eyes as you speak to them, and try to develop the ability to take in large groups of students as you move your gaze about the classroom. You may be surprised at how young some of them look. This is their first college class, and depending on the time of day, you may be their first college teacher.

Announce the add-drop policy of your college or university as preparation for calling the names on the roster. There may be specific policies you are expected to announce; it usually pays to repeat add-drop policy at least one time. Finally, call the roster, marking absences. You will want your students to raise their hands if present and also to tell you if you have mispronounced their names. Try for eye contact with each student as you call the roll; if you have a poor memory for names, try to connect their names with their faces as soon as possible.

After you have called the roll, ask for a show of hands of those whose name you did not call. There will always be a few. Now is the time to repeat the add-drop policy and to announce that after class you will talk to those students with approved add or change forms. After class, then, you can attend to them and make decisions on whether you can handle more students in your class. The ultimate decision about accepting more students may be yours.

Explaining the Syllabus

Hand out copies of the syllabus. After everyone has a copy, read through the important parts of it aloud. On this first reading, stress the texts—bring your copies to class and display them so your students will know what to look for at the book store. Discuss attendance and lateness policies, the paper style policy (typed, double-spaced; handwritten, every other line), number and length of required papers, journal policy. If you are using a revision policy, go over it in detail, giving examples of how it might be used. There is inevitably confusion about a revision policy and how it works; you may as well try to dispel it. Some students will think of revision as punishment, or simply as the production of a prettier copy of the same words. Go over the calendar of assignment due dates and mention the grading standards you will be applying. After you have gone through it, ask if there are any questions about the syllabus.

Finally, you will want to tell students about the Diagnostic Essay that you have scheduled for the second day of class. If yours is a school that offers a Basic Writing or an ESL program, then the Diagnostic Essay serves to alert you to the students who can best be helped by those particular writing courses. If your school has a Writing Center or one for Learning Disabilities, you have backup resources for your own efforts with particular students. The best helped and treated writers are those who have received a diagnosis—fast.

Dismissal

There is little left to do on the first day. You can pad the class with lecture, but it may not be worth the effort. Instead, ask your students to answer a few questions—about general goals, academic likes and dislikes, what they most want to learn, etc. Make your assignments, including the reading of the syllabus. Then ask your students to write down questions they come up with about course policies that they want to talk about during the next class. If there are no final questions, dismiss them.

You will immediately be surrounded by the "post-class swirl" of students wishing to talk to you—students who only a moment ago had no questions. Some will want to add the course—send them to the correct office. Some will have completed add or change-or-section forms—sign them up on your roster. Some will have questions they were too shy to ask in class—speak to them. As each situation is resolved, the crowd will diminish, and eventually the door will close after the last petitioner. It may not have been a smashing success, this first day of class, but you did it.

The Second Class

You will still be nervous on the second day, but the worst of it will have passed. There are still some bureaucratic tasks to be cleared away—you will need to call the roll again (remember eye contact and see if you can remember specific name-face relationships) and perhaps give your short add-drop policy speech again. If you have new students, as you probably will on the second and perhaps the third day, give them syllabi and ask them to speak to you after class. Ask the class for questions on the syllabus and course policies; go over those that may be confusing one last time.

Because you want to find out, as quickly as possible, your students' strengths and weaknesses as writers, you will want to assign the diagnostic essay today. As its name suggests, this exercise gives you an idea of how healthy students are as writers. Very simply, ask the students to take out paper and pen and write for twenty to thirty minutes on an assigned topic that allows for narrative or descriptive personal responses. The best topics for the diagnostic exercises are those that can be answered in a single short essay and that ask students to rely on their own experiences. Master diagnostician Edward White offers the following option:

> Describe as clearly as you can a person you knew well when you were a child. Your object is to use enough detail so that we as readers can picture him or her clearly from the child's perspective and, at the same time, to make us understand from the tone of your description the way you felt about the person you describe (White 8).

Two other options are as follows:

> In a short essay, discuss the reasons why your best (or worst) high school teacher was effective (or ineffective).

> In a short essay, discuss the best, most worthwhile and valid, advice you received about adjusting to college life.

Introduce the diagnostic essay to the class for what it is—an exercise that will give you an idea of how well they are writing *now*. Stress the fact that it will not be given a letter grade, and it will have no effect on the final class grade. But remind them that you will be looking at both form and content, at their ability to organize a piece of writing and to develop it with specific examples. You might want to spend some time talking with them, helping them see the difference between general and specific detail. They should try to write as finished a piece of work as possible in the time allowed. Make certain that they put their names on the papers and that they make a note if they have already taken Basic Writing or ESL courses. (You can bring paper and pass it out if you object to the appearance of paper torn from spiral notebooks.) Put the diagnostic assignment on the blackboard—and then give them the rest of the hour to think and write. Call out a few time checks during the hour so that no one runs short on time. At the bell, collect the essays.

Work to Do That Night

You will have several tasks to accomplish after class or that night, the most important of which is evaluating and marking the diagnostic essays. The first task you must consider, even before you look at the pile of diagnostics, is that of preparing yourself psychologically for what you will find. Many freshmen may write at what will at first seem to you an appallingly low level of skill. If you plunge into a set of diagnostic essays "cold," you may be brought up short by the apparently overwhelming number of errors and problems you see. As Mina Shaughnessy points out, some teachers of underprepared students initially cannot help feeling that their students might be retarded; certain pervasive error patterns are so severe and look so damaging on a paper that they can be shocking. (Shaughnessy 2–3). This problem is particularly likely if you teach at an open-admissions college without a basic writing program. With luck, your students' essays will not evidence any irreparable problems, but you should be prepared.

Having prepared yourself, plunge into the pile of essays. Most will be short, two or three pages. Aside from some nearly illegible handwriting and inventive misspellings, most essays should be readable. In reading diagnostics, it is a good idea first to read quickly over each essay, trying to get a sense of the writing as a purposeful whole. Then, in a second reading, begin to mark the paper, looking for the following three specific areas of skill, listed in order of importance:

1. Knowledge of and ability to use paragraph form, including topic sentence, specific details and examples to develop, support and organize the controlling idea
2. Ability to write a variety of grammatically correct and interesting sentences
3. Ability to use the language in a relatively standard fashion, including grammar, verb forms, usage, punctuation, and spelling

To get a sense of these three skill levels, you may sometimes have to read each essay two or three times, but since they are not very long, this is not as time-consuming as it sounds. By the bottom of the pile, you should be spending around ten minutes on each diagnostic, including writing comments on each skill level and a terminal comment.

You may want to make up a notebook or card file for your class, with a page or a card for each student; thus, you can chart the strengths and weaknesses of the students as they show in each major piece of writing he or she turns in. The first entry will cover this diagnostic exercise. Note whether the student grasps organization, can use sentences, has control of usage. A short three-to-five–sentence description of each student's strengths and problems, consulted and added to at the time of each new writing assignment, can be of great help in setting individualized goals for students and in discovering what sort of particular practice in writing each may need. Also, these progress cards will be helpful to you when you confer individually with your students. During your readings of the diagnostic, look especially for *patterns* of errors—a continuing inability to use commas correctly, a continuing confusion about verb endings, a continuing tendency to begin fragments with relative pronouns. Chart such patterns carefully, for they will be your concern in the future, and they will provide important information for the tutors at the Writing Center.

These diagnostic essays and the way that you respond to them will shape the perception that your students have of you as much as your classroom attitude does. As always in grading and evaluation, take the time to consider how the students will feel upon reading your comments. Will they come away with the feeling that they have problems that can be dealt with, or will they be overwhelmed by your criticism? Try to balance criticism with encouragement; treat errors and problems in papers as signposts pointing to needed work, not as dead-end signs.

After you have read the diagnostics, marked them, and noted each in your records, you can put them aside and turn to the other task of the evening: planning the next day's classes. The next class will be your first "real" class, the first class that will demand a prepared lesson plan. Be certain that you know what you want to introduce and accomplish.

Before the next class, you must decide if any of your students might benefit from the specific programs available on your campus. You want your students to thrive under your guidance, not merely survive. If you feel that a student should be enrolled in the Basic Writing or ESL program instead of first-year writing, now is the time to make the necessary arrangements through either the Director of Composition or the Director of one of these programs. If you feel a student would benefit from the services of the Writing Center, for example, perhaps you ought to talk to one of the tutors about how to get your students enrolled and how the Center can best help a student who is taking a writing course. The diagnostic essay can also provide pleasant news for especially good students: Some schools have provisions for strong writers to be exempted from first-year writing courses. If that is the case at your school and you have a student who deserves to be exempted, make the necessary arrangements.

The Third Class

Although you have information about the diagnostic essays, announce to students that you will talk to them about their status at the end of the hour.

Today will be your first day of "real" teaching. You will want to state the goals of and introduce your first lesson, which may be based on material from the substantive chapters of this book. Whether you want to start by teaching Invention or the Sentence, today's class is where you begin. You may decide to connect the work you begin today with the first writing assignment, but maybe not. You are the teacher; the choice is yours. Because students may not yet have been able to get the texts, you may want to begin with a handout.

With ten minutes or so to go before the end of class, make your assignments for reading and homework exercises and prepare to return the diagnostic essays. Pass them back, but before you dismiss the class, call out the names of the students with whom you need to speak. Giving marked papers back at the end rather than at the beginning of class is a good policy; that way the student's reactions to them, good or bad, do not color the class period. Students who have the option to exempt your course should be moved out. Those who should move to Basic Writing or ESL should be spoken to privately. Ask them to confer with you as soon as possible. Those students who need to work with the Writing Center while they take your course should be encouraged to schedule an appointment with a tutor, and to take their diagnostic essays with them to the appointment.

Works Cited *Chapter 2*

Shaughnessy, Mina. *Errors and Expectations: A Guide for the Teacher of Basic Writing.* New York: Oxford UP, 1977.

White, Edward M. *The St. Martin's Evaluation Manual.* New York: St. Martin's, 1989.

Chapter 3

Everyday Activities

Discipline

The most common discipline problem in college classes has nothing to do with classroom order. It is absenteeism. The temptation to skip classes is great, especially among freshmen, who may for the first time in their lives be in a situation in which no one is forcing them to attend classes. In dealing with absenteeism, teachers must first consider that this *is* college, not high school, and that they have no "big stick" that can compel attendance. Before the term even begins, you should be familiar with your school's policy on class attendance and should work with it as best you can. In general, unless your department has a specific written policy, teachers are not allowed to use grades to compel attendance in writing courses; in other words, some schools will not allow you to fail a student who never comes to class but who writes the assigned papers. You can, of course, make class participation a part of the final grade; those not in class cannot participate. In addition, brief in-class writings and group work on a project will encourage steady attendance. Often, the best way to deal with absenteeism is to plan the course to discourage it. Try this: Give information about graded assignments on one class day, have your editing workshops on another class day, have graded papers due on yet another class day—fill up your week with days that provide meaningful progress toward a goal. If a day is missed, the goal becomes harder to attain; the tasks at hand become more difficult. If a student skips an editing day and then receives a poor grade because of sentence fragments her editing group would have caught, she quickly becomes aware that the advantages of being in class are quite concrete.

Another problem you may have is the student who consistently shows up for class five, ten, even fifteen minutes late. Here again, your school may have a policy, but usually this is a matter best settled privately between student and teacher. Speak to the student after class or in conference, and find out if there is a valid reason for the lateness. Surprisingly often, students do have good excuses—a long campus walk, an unreasonable teacher in the previous class, personal responsibilities of different sorts—but just as often the lateness is a result of late rising, poor planning, or careless habits.

If the student's reasons for lateness simply do not seem valid, state politely but seriously that students are not welcome in your classroom unless they are there by "the final bell." The personal interest you show in each case can have a good deal of effect; after these discussions, students usually begin to appear on time. This may not be the best solution to the problem, but it does circumvent the tiresome institutional coercion that seems to be the only other alternative.

Late essays—written assignments handed in (often under the office door or secretly in your office mailbox) after their due dates—can be another problem, but only if you allow them to become one. State in your syllabus that you will not accept late essays. Then, when the inevitable requests for extensions appear, or the late papers show up, you can adjust that policy as seems fit and humane. It is often better to announce a harsh and unyielding policy initially and then adjust it than it is to announce a liberal policy, see it abused, and then try to establish a harder line.

Plagiarism in the classroom—students presenting others' work as their own—is a serious problem for writing teachers. Plagiarism ranges in severity from a single, uncited news magazine quotation to a carefully retyped fraternity file version of an "A" research paper. It can be as crude as a long passage from Bertrand Russell amidst a jumble of sentence fragments and misspellings, or as sophisticated as an artfully worked-in introduction lifted directly from a sociology text. Whatever the degree, it is bad news for both student and teacher. Hence, you will want to approach the problem of plagiarism with both subtlety and caution.

Instead of railing against plagiarism, you might better serve your students by explaining to them the ethical advantages of giving full credit to their sources. Crediting sources as fully as possible is an important element in establishing their ethos. First, by acknowledging their sources, they will be better able to critically examine their own research and thinking. How timely and reliable are their sources? Have they used them accurately? Secondly, crediting sources helps readers by placing each student's work into a *context* of other thinking and writing; it shows in what ways that student's work is part of a textual conversation and helps readers see exactly what the student is contributing to that conversation. Finally, crediting sources allows a student to thank those whose work she has built on and thus avoid the charges of plagiarism. Crediting sources fully and generously, then, provides a means of establishing *ethos* as a writer, of establishing credibility. Failure to credit sources corrupts the textual conversation and misleads readers; it can easily destroy the credibility of both the writer and the work.

The best policy for dealing with plagiarism is not to invite it in the first place. You won't want to use writing assignments that lend themselves to easy answers from general sources; nor will you want to rely on paper topics that have been around your department for years. If you can make certain that all student essays have gone through several revisions and that all the early drafts are turned in with the typed copies, you can be pretty sure that your students have written their own papers. Good assignment planning and classroom management can make plagiarism difficult—more difficult, in fact, than writing the paper. And if your department has rules or a statement on plagiarism, be sure to read it aloud and discuss it with your class.

The final disciplinary issue is that of classroom order. "Order," of course, is a relative term; very often an "orderly" writing class is abuzz with discussions of choices and options, editing points, and correctness. Order does not mean silence. It does, though, signify a progress of meaningful activity, one that can be disrupted in a number of ways. Whether the class is discussing something as a whole or is broken into groups or is listening to you explain something, certain protocols should be observed. One of your functions is to represent those protocols by accepting the responsibility for running the class.

Rare is the classroom order problem that can not be solved by serious words to the right person—in private. College students are anxious to prove their maturity and usually will not continue behavior that you have spoken to them about. If students are disruptive, ask them to see you and speak plainly to them. They will nearly always straighten out. Occasionally—very occasionally—a truly disturbed student may appear in a class and resist all rationality, every effort to keep order and even to help. If you find one of these people in your class, go immediately for help from your program or department, and get the student out of your class if the disruptive behavior continues. You owe it to the other students in the class. Once again, though, nearly all classroom discipline problems can be settled on an adult level, and students appreciate being approached on that level.

Student Conferences

The student-teacher conference has a number of functions, but the primary ones have to do with getting to know your students better as individuals, lessening the distance between student and teacher, and letting your students know that you care about how they are doing. The student conference can allow you to explain writing strategies to students, discuss their problems, strengths, and weaknesses, set goals, plan and examine future work together, and in general establish the coach/athlete or editor/author relationship that is our ideal of teacher-student interaction.

Unfortunately, in spite of all these desirable goals and profitable possibilities, you may very well find yourself sitting lonely with your office door open during your office hours, seldom seeing a student. The hard fact about office hours is that students, by and large, cannot make the time to drop by the office; they simply do not know how valuable a resource the teacher can be, even the teacher who has made it clear that students are welcome.

Instituting a system of conferences with students, held either in the office or the classroom, is probably the best way to ensure personal contact and to effect useful help with revision. Mandatory conferences need to be specified as such, from the beginning of the course, preferably on the syllabus itself. The number of conferences you have with your students is up to you. Some teachers specify only three conferences per term; others ask their students to meet with them weekly or biweekly for very close personal supervision.

To arrange the conferences, specify a range of possible times on a sign-up sheet and send it around the class during the week preceding the conferences; make the range of time broad enough (usually covering two consecutive days to allow most students to find a possible time). Depending on what is to be discussed, allow ten- or fifteen-minute conferences for every student. If students need more time than that, you can make appointments with them.

There are two schools of thought about student conferencing: the Donald Murray approach, in place at the University of New Hampshire, in which students come to the teacher's office, and the Roger Garrison approach, in which all conferencing is done in the classroom and forms the backbone of the course. While Garrison's method has been shown to work well, it is a radical departure from traditional classroom activities, and, unfortunately, cannot be well explained in the space allotted here. Discussed instead will be conferences held in the teacher's office, which function as supports to regular classroom activities.

Handling office conferences requires forethought and planning. If you try to "wing it" in a conference, your students will know quickly that you have nothing specific to tell them and will lose interest. The whole purpose of a student conference is to establish understandings about work that is to be done or problems that are to be solved, and you should make your plans with those tasks in mind. Your talk should be future-oriented, not past-oriented. If a conference merely becomes a post-mortem on a bad paper or an oration on a concept the student cannot easily grasp, it will quickly produce a student who avoids eye contact with you, agrees feverishly in monosyllables with everything you say, and escapes as soon as possible.

Each conference must have a purpose that may draw on the past but is essentially directed toward future work. Conferences work best when they have one of the following purposes:

1. Discussion of an outline, plan, or draft of an upcoming assignment
2. Discussion of content revisions of a paper already evaluated
3. Discussion ot the success and direction of any long-term ongoing project (like a research paper)
4. Planning and discussion of exercises or activities meant to deal with *specific* and *identified* form problems: syntactic errors, verb endings, etc. The key word here is specific. If you don't try to create a hierarchy of error patterns that can be worked on one by one, the student may just assume perpetual inferiority, and despair. Error problems must be made to seem soluble to the student by presenting them as step-by-step procedures.

Each successful conference, then, should have a "backbone" of written work that the student is expected to bring, even if it is only an outline or an invention-list. Each should end with at least a tacit "task assignment," in which you make your expectations known (Arbur 338–42). During the conference itself, you may have specific questions and bits of advice ready—advice that is always listened to closely because it is given personally. You may want to refer to that index card on which you've recorded the student's progress. Although you may say the same thing to each student, to that student it is personal advice. Before you let each student go, ask him if there are any questions that he wishes to discuss, and if not, call in the next. Many of these conferences will be similar, and you will be tired after a morning of them. They will, however, bring you closer to your students, allow you to critique and assist them on a more individual basis, and ideally, make them more willing to seek you out in the future.

Conferences about drafts and papers may be demanding, but they are much more efficient ways to help students understand content and organization questions than the marking up of papers. Conferences are *dialogue:* Students can ask questions, explain themselves, react to suggestions. The bond between writer and reader becomes real and personal. The more conferencing you do with your students, the better they will come to understand the concept of an audience and the better you will come to know them as individuals.

Classroom Routines

Most new teachers of writing are used to certain sorts of classroom routines. They are those we grew up with: lecture by the teacher or directed discussion by the class. These routines are what we know best, and the temptation is to rely on them completely in writing classes as we have in literature classes. Unfortunately, they cannot be used as the only methods of classroom instruction in writing courses; in fact, they cannot even hold center stage. The writing teacher must use a much larger array of classroom activities, an array that brings student *writing*—not student talking, student listening, or student note-taking—to center stage.

Let's deal with the old standbys. Classroom discussion is probably the method most congenial to new writing teachers, familiar as it is to both teachers and students. The teacher in a discussion does not "lead" the class in any authoritarian way; instead he or she guides the discussion, and everyone has a chance to contribute. Inexperienced teachers of composition usually envision themselves as using discussion, but the essential component of discussion—*content*—is simply not available in a composition course as it is in history, biology, or psychology courses. The content of a composition class is often theoretical and is best discussed in practical, student-writing terms or as it applies to a short story, a poem, a piece of literature.

This is the hard truth about discussion in writing classes: It cannot be practiced without content, and the content to be discussed should be the content of the students' individual pieces of writing; otherwise, the writing class will concern itself with easy-to-isolate form. It is hard to get an exciting discussion going about sentence fragments or three-part organization, unless the discussion is hooked into the students' writing. Students tend to be uninterested in discussing formal questions unless those questions can be presented concretely or can be applied to their own work; therefore, to be useful and interesting, such discussion must be carefully planned and directed (see the descriptions in some of the following chapters). A teacher can, of course, assign essays in the reader and then spend all the class time discussing the content of the essays: ecology and bigotry and love and death, all fascinating subjects. Such use of class time, though, is appropriate to a course in the appreciation of nonfiction, not to a writing course—unless the teacher successfully manages to connect the reading of literature with the students' development as writers. Discussion in writing classrooms, then, cannot be the central routine it is in literature classrooms. Discussion does have a place in the teaching of composition, however, and can be used for two main purposes. The first is a relatively traditional use: Classroom discussion of an object, idea, or situation is a prewriting activity that can give students ideas about content that they might wish to use in writing. This sort of discussion needs to be limited and used carefully, because it can easily take up more class time than it is worth. It should not be used in place of the invention activities described in Chapter 6, but as a supplement to them. The second use of discussion, described in Chapters 6, 7, and 8, involves classroom conversations about different stylistic and organizational options available within sentences and paragraphs. Such discussion can be a valuable element in helping students make formal and stylistic choices in their writing. However, any discussion of form must focus on concrete examples of stylistic choices; otherwise, students will engage in arguments over abstract concepts but will not be able to contextualize their ideas.

As the thesis of this book has suggested, students simply do not learn to write—do not learn to control any art—by studying abstract principles. As the philosopher Michael Polanyi writes,

> The aim of a skillful performance is achieved by the observance of a set of rules which are not known as such to the person following them. . . . Rules of art can be useful, but they do not determine the practice of art; they are maxims, which can serve as a guide to an art only if they can be integrated into the practical knowledge of the art (49–50).

In this case, the "practical knowledge" of writing cannot be gained by listening to lectures on the rules and protocols of writing, but only by actual writing and writing-based activities. Lectures provide none of these useful activities; in fact, a lecture usually functions as a placebo, assuring students and teacher alike that academic activity is in fact going on in the classroom.

Again, this is not meant to suggest that you cannot tell your students anything or that a teacher explaining material to students is somehow invalid. The very act of teaching is predicated, it seems, on the assumptions that one person can know more than another and that knowledge or skill can be transmitted. Every chapter of this book contains material that must be explained to students. Such explanations, thought, are but the preludes to writing or a writing-based activity. After explaining, exemplifying, and pointing out the major components of a skill, you as the teacher must set up a learning situation and let the students practice the skill. Rather than announcing rules, you will be describing behavior, and when the students practice that behavior enough, they will inductively come to grasp the rules that govern it. This is the only way that "lectures" in a writing class are truly beneficial to students.

Other classroom activities peculiar to the writing classroom take different forms, but all have one thing in common: they all involve students practicing writing or editing skills. You can ask your students to spend the larger part of their classroom time writing and talking, to you and to other students, about the choices and options thta make up the writing process. Most of the classroom material in the following chapters is based on this sort of classroom approach, which can take the form of students writing or working alone, or of two students working together, or of students confederating into groups. It may take you some time to get used to the meaningful chaos of a writing classroom as it works; at first, the writing centered classroom can seem appallingly disoriented, accustomed as we all are to the teacher-centered atmosphere, especially in literature classes, of our own educations.

In-class writing, an important part of the writing-centered classroom, can be in form of pattern practices of sentences or paragraphs, short essays written on the instructions of the teacher, or editing sessions following specific guidelines. What use you make of writing-based activities will depend on what skills you are trying to teach at the time. There are, though, some activities not based in any one specific pedagogy that can be used with excellent results.

David Jones has developed one such successful activity that can be easily adapted to the writing class. On the first day of class, tell the students that they will each be responsible for assigning and grading a short essay. This essay will be written by all the members of the class in response to an assignment created by a student; it will then be evaluated by the person who made the assignment. Send around a sign-up sheet and have each student pick a date, telling them to have a short writing assignment prepared on that date. On the day the student has signed up for, she is to put the assignment on the blackboard at the beginning of class; the only stipulation is that the topic be simple enough that a coherent response can be written in ten minutes. For the first ten minutes, the class does nothing but write silently. (You might write the assignments too. It produces a sense of solidarity, and the students feel that the task is thus dignified.)

Each student usually produces three-quarters of a page to a page of longhand. At the end of ten minutes, collect the essays and give them to the student who created the assignment. He or she then has one week in which to evaluate and grade them, yours included, and then return them to you for checking. Then you can return them to the writers. Before each group of essays is returned to you, though, ask the assigner to read aloud to the class her favorite response to the assignment. This gives the writer of the "winning" essay satisfaction and allows other students to hear their peers' work. Although not necessarily brilliant, those essays do represent valuable practice.

Evaluation of these short essays can be a problem. Because students are such tentative graders, peer evaluation usually produces a disproportionate number of B's and bland, generally approving comments. A more guided evaluation procedure is more helpful to the student writers and readers. You may want to implement the following six questions that the student "grader" must address for each paper. Under this system, each evaluation must have a sentence responding to each of the following questions:

1. What is the most successful content element?
2. What is the least successful content element?
3. What is the main idea, and is it well supported?
4. If you see a formal or mechanical problem, what is it?
5. How well did this essay answer the assignment, and why?
6. Give a grade of A, C, or F, using the evaluation system described on the syllabus.

The grades do not, of course, count toward the students' final grades, but they do give class members an idea of how their writing is perceived by their peer group. Evaluating these essays also gives students some small idea of what we as teachers have to go through in order to evaluate student papers.

Workshop Groups

Workshop groups are groups of from three to nine students, initially chosen and assembled by the teacher, which meet together during class time to accomplish specific tasks. These tasks can include a brainstorming discussion of a topic for writing, a discussion of how an upcoming assignments might best be done, editorial work on one another's drafts, mutual advising about problem areas, division of research tasks, and other mutual-aid endeavors. The workshop group provides a peer group for each student within a class, a group smaller and more manageable than the class as a whole, a group whose members become familiar and trustworthy over the course of a term.

One important task of workshop groups has been to provide a forum for nonthreatening peer editing and evaluation of written work. Students are initially unwilling to critique one another's work, but workshop groups quickly make it evident to them that they are acting as mutual defenders. As they learn that problems left uncorrected in a group member's paper will be pounced upon by the teacher, they become very serious about checking each other's work. Every mark or notation that the group makes on a rough draft will be one that the teacher does not have to make on the final version. By seeing different stages in each others' essays, they will get a sense of the plasticity of prose, and how changes to be made really can help. Peer judgment makes the teacher's judgment seem less arbitrary.

Workshop groups, then, give students a sense of solidarity, a sense of peer accomplishment, and a critical sense as well. Carefully set up, they are not difficult to use. First of all, they demand chairs or desks that can be moved around into circles. The size of the groups you form—and they should be created by the second week, if possible—is up to you, but they seem to work best when the number of students in each group does not exceed five. Above that number it is likely that an "in-crowd" will form within the group and exclude one or more members. Do *not* allow students to form their own "affinity workshop groups" of friends; that sort of group almost guarantees that such exclusion will take place, as friends band together against outsiders. As a matter of fact, by waiting until the second week of class to form groups, you will have the opportunity to see who the friends are in class, who knows whom, which students always enter class together or sit together or leave together; then you can assign them to different groups. When forming groups, try to include at least one student who obviously writes well in each group and try to balance the groups in terms of race and sex. Then, encourage the members in each group to swap names, addresses, and phone numbers so that they can continue their mutual support system after class hours.

Though workshop groups are capable of many tasks, their primary week-to-week use lies most clearly in editing practice. Several days a week, usually the week before a written assignment is due, have students bring to class "rough drafts" of the assignment. The workshop groups then meet to pass the drafts around the circle of the group and to edit and critique what they read. Better than the "buddy editing" system, in which two students merely trade drafts, in the group editing system each draft gets critiqued by at least three and usually four other people. Problems not spotted by one group member are usually caught by others. Group editing also has the advantage of allowing better writers to assist poorer ones and giving all students an idea of how others are approaching the assignment.

Rather than giving students a free rein in this editing practice, you may want to specify a process of editing or other areas that you want investigated, often elements relating to the rhetorical skill being dealt with in class that week. Some weeks you might ask students to dissect sentences; another week, paragraphs, arrangements, breadth of inventive coverage of the subject, etc. Such direction gives structure to student critiques, which can have a tendency to wander. The following list of questions compiled by Mary Beaven provides a general structure for student critiques:

1. Identify the best section of the composition and describe what makes it effective.
2. Identify a sentence, a group of sentences, or a paragraph that needs revision, and revise it as a group, writing the final version on the back of the paper.
3. Identify one or two things the writer can do to improve his or her next piece of writing. Write these goals on the first page at the top.
4. (After the first evaluation, the following question should come first.) What were the goals the writer was working on? Were they reached? If not, identify those passages that need improvement and as a group revise those sections, writing final versions on the back of the paper. If revisions are necessary, set up the same goals for the next paper and delete question. (149)

Students do not respond to these questions by writing on the draft; instead they write their answers on a separate sheet of paper and clip it to the draft. Each writer should have several written evaluations of his draft by the end of the period.

The following "workshop sheet," taken from Chapter 3 of *The St. Martin's Handbook*, sometimes takes students twenty-five or thirty minutes to work through when peer-editing a paper, but the time is well spent. The descriptive rather than directly evaluative nature of the elicited response allows students to be more honest with one another than many workshop procedures do. Following are some questions that might serve as guidelines for evaluating a draft. Students can use them to respond to each other's drafts or to evaluate their own.

Questions for Reviewing a Draft

1. Introduction: What does the opening accomplish? How does it catch the reader's attention? How else might the essay begin? Can you suggest some better way of opening?
2. Thesis: Paraphrase the thesis of the essay in the form of a promise: "In this paper, I will . . . ." Does the draft fulfill the promise made by the thesis? Why, or why not?
3. Supporting points: List the main points made in the draft, in order of presentation. Then number them in order of interest to you, noting particularly parts that were *not* interesting to you or material that seemed unnecessary or added on for no reason. Review the main points one by one. Do any need to be explained more fully or less fully? Should any be eliminated? Are any confusing or boring to you? Do any make you want to know more?
4. Organization: What kind of overall organizational plan is used—spatial, chronological, or logical? Are the points presented in the most useful order? What, if anything, might be moved, deleted, or added? Can you suggest ways to make connections between paragraphs clearer and easier to follow?
5. Paragraphs: Which paragraphs are clearest and most interesting to read, and why? Which ones are well developed, and how are they developed? Which paragraphs need further development? What kinds of information seems to be missing?
6. Sentences: Number each sentence. Then reread the draft, and choose the three to five sentences you consider the most interesting or the best written because they are stylistically effective, entertaining, or memorable for some other reason. Then choose the three to five sentences you see as weakest, whether boring, bland, or simply uninspired. Are sentences varied in length, in structure, and in their openings?
7. Words: Mark words that are particularly effective—those that draw vivid pictures or provoke strong responses. Then mark words that are confusing or unclear. Do any words need to be defined? Are verbs active and vivid?
8. Tone: How does the writer come across in the draft—as serious, humorous, satiric, persuasive, passionately committed, highly objective? Mark specific places in the draft where the writer's voice comes through most clearly. Is the

tone appropriate to the topic and the audience? Is the tone consistent throughout the essay? If not, is there a reason for varying the tone?

9. Conclusion: Does the essay conclude in a memorable way, or does it seem to end abruptly or trail off into vagueness? If you like the conclusion, tell why. How else might the essay end?

10. Final thoughts: What are the main strengths and weaknesses in the draft? What surprised you, and why? What was the single most important thing said? (40–41)

Remember that responses to workshop protocols like this are more useful if they are written down and clipped to the original draft than if they are just talked about.

During these workshop group meetings, as during writing activities in class, don't sit back and watch. Instead, drift from group to group, sitting in on each for a few minutes, talking, listening. Be ready to answer questions, to settle debates on choices and conventions, to read papers or passages of papers. Do not act merely as "the judge," but rather as a resource person who can help students find their own ways. Be friendly and informal, and try to draw students who seem shy or withdrawn into the life of the group. Most important, be supportive of the activity; only if you show that you think workshop meetings are important will students come to believe in them.

One final activity that workshop groups can engage in is the selection and reading aloud of final versions of essays in class. You may want to spend half a period every several weeks on this. Give each workshop group five minutes to meet and choose an essay and a reader on the day that final versions of essays are due. This division between essay and reader—no one ever reads his or her own essay—will allow you to critique the essay without publicly embarrassing the writer, who can remain anonymous. After each reading (and there are usually four essays read, one from each workshop group), try to make a comment or two in which you point out the strengths of the essay read. If it has severe problems, mention them only in order not to give the rest of the class the idea that bad writing is good. In general, though, try to say only positive things, and then ask the class for their impressions. The stipulation about this in-class reading is that the choice of reader and essay must rotate each week, so that by the end of the course every student will have had his essay read and will have been a reader.

Successful Writing Assignments

Making and evaluating writing assignments are at the heart of a composition teacher's job, and the life of a writing teacher has often been described as a perpetual search for good topics for writing assignments. All good writing teachers, no matter how "finished" their courses seem, are on the lookout for better assignments.

This book makes the assumption that the course you are teaching is "straight composition"—a course in which the *content* of literature plays at most a minor role. Therefore, the assignments here discussed do not include the whole large genre of assignments that asks writers to respond to literature. This is not to say that such literary topics are unimportant; they are, however, more applicable to literature courses, which have a critical-semantic emphasis, than to composition courses, which have a generative-formal emphasis.

Establish the number and length of essays you will ask for. Next, decide whether you will "sequence" them in any way or try to correlate written assignments with the work going on in class in any given week. Detailed correlation of assignments and lessons has both good and bad aspects; on the one hand, it can make the lesson and its related activities more involving for students and can make them work harder at learning it, but on the other hand, it can also turn your class into a completely grade-directed exercise. Students may want you to spend the time teaching nothing but "how to do this week's assignment." But such activity will not help them in the long run. For this reason alone, you may not want to tie graded assignments tightly to classroom work.

This is not to say that assignments should never or will never correlate with taught skills. Of course they will; it is impossible they should not. But such correlations should be made in the students' own minds and not in the plan of the course. The assignments can then be sequenced according to a separate plan, one created by the teacher.

The most common sequence for writing assignments is the one based on the work of Alexander Bain. A Scottish logician, Bain divided all writing into four *modes of discourse:* narration, description, exposition, and argumentation (118–21). The first two modes, which are more concrete, are the bases for the earlier assignments in the course; they allow students to draw on their own experiences and observations for subject matter, seldom forcing any higher-level generalizations or deductions. The second two modes, which are more abstract, are left for later assignments, when students will be able to better handle nonpersonal manipulation of ideas and concepts in expository or persuasive fashion.

The supposition of this sequence of assignment is that students gain confidence in their writing by first using the more concrete and personal modes of narration and description; they then are better able to use the abstract modes. Unfortunately, narrative and descriptive skills do not seem to carry over easily into exposition and argumentations; students who are confident and even entertaining when narrating experiences and describing known quantities sometimes flounder suddenly when asked to generalize, organize, or argue for abstract concepts. Bain's modes of discourse are far from the realities of the writing process. As James Kinneavy and James Moffett, among others, have pointed out, modes are not aims, and uses of the modes today must contain an element of awareness of their limitations.[1]

However you decide to design your course, one thing is certain: When structuring the sequence of assignments, it is important to connect each assignment to the others. In creating the sequence, you must always consider "the activities and operations of mind in which the student must engage if he is to cope with the assignment," as Richard Larson says, and arrange assignments so that they inform one another (212). Asking a student for a "five-part argument" between a "comparison-contrast essay" and a "process-analysis essay" is simply not logical because the progression is unclear. Try to connect each assignment to skills that have been practiced previously and to those that will come after.[2]

After you have decided on length, number, and sequence of types of assignments, you can get down to the actual business of creating each individual one. You will want to write down *all* assignments beforehand and pass them out to your students, not only allowing you to be as specific as you need to be but also helping to prevent any misunderstanding on the part of the students. Each word in an assignment, no matter how small, is extremely important because the

---

1 In *Teaching the Universe of Discourse* (Boston: Houghton, 1968), Moffett posits a highly schematic representation of the whole spectrum of discourse, one that acknowledges the limitations of beginning discoursers. Kinneavy's *A Theory of Discourse* talks about increasingly complex communicative acts. Beginners build on "interior dialogue" to move on to "conversation," "correspondence," "public narrative," and finally, "public generalization or inference." Moffett would have students begin with "drama" before moving to "narration," "exposition," and "argumentation."

2 For discussions of assignment sequencing see Coles; see also Bartholomae and Petrosky.

assignment wording is the seed from which oak or dendelion will grow. When you distribute an assignment, tell your students to pay close attention to the wording, to what is being asked, before all else.

In fact, you may want to take some time to go over "wording" with your students. They need to know, for *all* their classes, that certain words like "analyze," "describe," and "explain" tell them what logical strategy to use and often help set the form of their response. The following adapted list, from *The St. Martin's Handbook* (Chapters 2 and 5) defines the most commonly used strategy terms:

Analyze= divide an event, idea, or theory into its component elements and examine each one in turn. [Example:] Analyze the American way of death, according to Jessica Mitford.

Compare and/or demonstrate similarities of dissimilarities between
Contrast= two or more events or topics. [Example:] Compare the portrayal of women in "In Search of Our Mothers' Gardens" and "I Want a Wife."

Define= identify and state the essential traits or characteristics of something, differentiating them clearly from other things. [Example:] Define first-year student.

Describe= tell about an event, person, or process *in detail* creating a clear and vivid image of it. [Example:] Describe the dress of the "typical" college professor.

Evaluate= assess the value or significance of the topic. [Example]: Evaluate the contributions of black musicians to the development of an American musical tradition.

Explain= make a topic as clear and understandable as possible by offering reasons, examples, etc. [Example:] Explain the functioning of resident advisors.

Summarize= state the major points concisely and comprehensively. [Example:] Summarize the major arguments *against* surrogate parenthood.

Strategy words give your students important clues for the thesis of their essays. Once they understand what the strategy words asks them to do, they need only understand the meaning of all the content words in their assignment.

So what *is* a good assignment? Edmund J. Farrell (220–24) tells us what a good assignment is *not*. A good assignment is *not* an assignment that can be answered with a simple "true-false" or "yes-no" answer: "Do the SAT exams have too much power over students' lives?" Such assignments do not offer a writer enough purpose or give enough direction, and students are often at a loss for a place to go after they have formulated their simple answers.

A good assignment is *not* one which leads to too-short answers or unfocused answers: "How do you feel about the ozone layer?" or "Is inflation a serious problem?" These kinds of assignments invite poor writing from inexperienced writers.

A good assignment is *not* one which is vague nor one which assumes too much student knowledge: "What are the good and bad points of U.S. foreign policy?" or "Is America decaying like the Roman Empire did?" Not only are such assignments far too broad, but even a minimal answer to either one would require students to do considerable reading and research.

A good assignment is *not* one which poses too many questions in its attempt to get students to write specifically: "In the popular television show *The Prisoner*, why is the Prisoner kept in The Village? Has he committed a crime? Is he evil? Why or why not? Why do we never see Number One? What might that mean to the Prisoner's guilt? Can he ever really escape?" This sort of assignment means to help students by supplying them with many possibilities, but can often provoke panic as inexperienced writers scramble to try to deal with each question discretely.

A good assignment, finally, is *not* one which asks students for too personal an answer: "Has there ever been a time in your life when you just couldn't go on?" or "What was the most exciting thing that ever happened to you?" Some students will be put off by these sorts of questions and not wish to answer them, while others will revel in the chance to advertise their adolescent angst or detail their trip to Las Vegas. Either way you are likely to get bad writings, filled with either evasions or cliches.

If good assignments are not any of these things, then, what are they? William Irmscher has listed a number of useful criteria in *Teaching Expository Writing* (69–71). First of all, a good assignment has to have a purpose. If you ask students to write a meaningless exercise, that is exactly what you will get. An assignment like "Describe your dorm room in specific detail" has no purpose but to make the student write; the response to such an assignment is meaningless as communication. If we extend the assignment a bit, though, to "Describe your dorm room and explain how various details in it reflect your personality and habits," we have made it a rhetorical problem. The answer to the assignment now has a purpose, a reason for saying what it says.

Irmscher tells us that a good assignment is also meaningful within the student's experience. "Meaningful" here does not necessarily mean "completely personal," but you must keep in mind the fact that your students do not usually have access to as wide a world of opinion, fact, or experience as do you. Though you can perhaps discourse coherently on the Aswan Dam or the civil rights struggle of the sixties, for 17- and 18-year-olds these subjects may serve as topics for research. The subjects that students can be expected to write well about without research are those that fall within their own ranges of experience—the civil-rights struggle as seen in the bussing program at their high schools, or the drug problem as it relates to their circle of acquaintance.

A good assignment, continues Irmscher, also asks for writing about specific and immediate situations rather than abstract and theoretical ones. "Discuss the problem of sexism" will not elicit the good, specific writing that an assignment more tied to concrete reality will: "Discuss how you first became aware of sexism and how it has affected the way you deal with other men and women." If you pose a hypothetical situation in an assignment, make certain it is one within students' conceptual abilities. "If you had been Abraham Lincoln in 1861..." is the sort of assignment opening that will only invite wearying and uninformed fantasy, while "The Board of Trustees has voted to raise tuition by $100 per year. Write a letter to them explaining why they should reconsider their decision," is a hypothetical situation that students can approach in an informed and realistic manner.

A good assignment should suggest a single major question to which the thesis statement of the essay is the answer. "Is smoking marijuana harmful, and should the marijuana laws be changed?" Asks for several different, though related, theses. It is better to stay with a single question whose ramifications can then be explored: "Discuss why marijuana should or should not be legalized, supporting your argument with details from your own experience or experiences of people you know."

A good assignment should be neither too long nor too short. It should certainly not be longer than a single paragraph unless it includes "content" information such as a table, graph, quotation, or evidence of some sort which must be responded to as part of the essay. Too short an assignment fails to give enough guidance, but too long and complex an assignment will frustrate and confuse students.

A good assignment, then, must be many things. It should ideally help students work on specific stylistic and organizational skills. It should furnish at least minimal data for the student to start from and should evoke a response that is the product of discovery concerning those data. It should encourage the student to do his best writing and should give the teacher her best chance to help the student.

One final word on assignments: do not be reluctant to change assignments or to jettison those that do not work out. As mentioned earlier, every writing teacher is always on the lookout for new and better topics, not because the old ones were necessarily bad, but because good teachers always search for better ways of teaching. You may also find that you get tired of reading students' responses, even good responses, to an old assignment. When you find this creeping boredom setting in it is time to change assignments, as much for the sake of your students as for your own sake.

Revision of Student Essays

As the sample syllabus in Chapter 1 suggests, the revision of student essays before they are finally graded should be an important element in college writing courses. The inclusion of a revision option in your course is up to you, of course (unless your department requires or forbids one), but most experienced writing teachers are committed supporters of the revision option; the reasons for allowing revision seem to far outweigh any inconveniences.

Revision of essays is an important component of writing courses because it allows teachers to escape from the necessity of having to grade all writing done by students. At the same time, it removes the constant threat of grade pressure from the writing situation and allows students to concentrate on writing rather than on "getting the grade." In other words, it provides a new and less judgmental relationship between teacher and student, one in which the teacher can be a "writing coach," rather than the "hanging judge" whose only function is to give grades.

Revision allows students an insight into the editing process that is difficult to achieve if all writing is graded and filed without any chance to change or reexamine it. Studies of the composing process have shown that many students sit down and write a paper with little planning, make no notes, grind out the minimum number of words necessary, and type up what they have written with few changes. Writing is seen as a one-shot, make-or-break process. For these students, the very idea of large-scale revision is alien, and providing a revision option allows them to approach the task of editing in a new way: as re-seeing their writing. They need to learn what an important element self-correction is in producing quality writing.

A revision option can work in several different ways, but all of them involve the same general idea: The teacher collects student essays and evaluates them, then returns them to the writers, who have the option of rewriting their essays for a higher grade. The mechanics of turning in essays and of grading them differ from system to system, but all have in common this "second-chance" element.

The following is just one example of a successfully implemented revision routine: On the due date for Essay A, each student must turn it in. Essay A either will be marked "DRAFT" at the top, which indicates that the writer wants the paper evaluated but not graded, or it will be unmarked, which indicates that the writer wants the paper evaluated and graded.

The teacher goes through the stack of essays at home, evaluating all of them but grading only those not designed as draft. The papers marked "DRAFT" are to be approached differently from those to be graded. First of all, do not edit drafts for formal errors; if you do students will be tempted to retype their papers without those marked errors, rather than really to revise them. The terminal comments you will make on drafts contain far more specific suggestions and criticisms than the ones you will put on graded essays; the terminal comments on drafts must act as the blueprints for revision, while those on graded essays must, by the very nature of the grading process, be more concerned with justifying the grade than with suggestions for changes.

The next week, pass back both drafts and graded papers; students who passed in drafts then have ten days or so—until the next week's due date—to revise their papers, which must then be turned in for final grading. If a draft is very good, as occasionally happens, the student might just pass it back unchanged and take a grade on it, but 90 percent of students rewrite their papers. When final versions are passed in, ask that the original draft be clipped to the revision so that you can see what changes have been made. On this second sweep through Essay A, you will grade it, mark the formal errors (usually with checkmarks), write a short comment on the success of the revision effort and the general quality of the essay, and return it to the writer for the last time. During the intervening week, rough drafts of the next assignment, Essay B, come in, and perhaps a few early revisions of Essay A. By the time you get all the final versions of Essay A, you will be seeing the rough drafts of Essay C as well. So during any given week, you may be evaluating or grading as many as three separate assignments. It is not so confusing as it sounds. Here is a diagram:

Week Two:

Monday   Friday
                                         Essay A due in draft form

Week Three:

Monday   Friday
Essay A returned   Essay B due in draft form (Some
                                         revised A's turned in)

Week Four:

Monday   Friday
B's and A's returned   Essay C due in draft form. Essay A
                                         due in final form (Some revised B's
                                         turned in)

Week Five:

Monday   Friday
C's, B's, and A's returned

Some teachers find that other permutations of the revision system work better for them. They allow their students all term to revise their drafts, asking for all revisions during "revision week" at the end of the quarter or semester. This system allows students more time to revise, bit it does result in a great influx of papers to read and grade during that final hectic week. Other teachers grade all papers as they come in, and then re-grade those that students choose to revise. This system gives students an idea of how they are doing in terms of grades, but it also tends to make the teacher work harder at grading, especially since the terminal comment of a graded paper is expected to justify the letter grade rather than make suggestions for revision.

The most common objection voiced against the revision option is that it creates more work for the teacher. And it does. In a class of twenty-four students that demands six graded essays from each student, the teacher must evaluate and grade 144 essays. If revision is allowed, the number of papers to be looked at rises to around 240.

But it is not as much extra work as it might first appear. The revision option places more of the added responsibility on the student than on the teacher. Reading for evaluation takes less time than reading for evaluation *and* grading; final reading and grading of the revision takes up less time than either. Once you "get the system down," you should be able to read for evaluation and write a terminal comment in between five and seven minutes. Grading the revised version takes around five minutes, because you will know enough about the writer's purpose to grade more meaningfully. In neither reading should you give the attention to small formal errors that you would in a single reading; in the first reading, mark no errors at all, though you may want to mention serious error patterns in your terminal comment. In the second reading, errors get only a checkmark. The very act of revision means that there are fewer formal problems.

Without a revision option, you can go through a stack of essays, evaluating them, marking all the errors, writing complete marginal and terminal comments, and then justifying your grade, in about three-and-one-half or four hours. With a revision option, the weekly stack, which is larger, takes four to four-and-one-half hours. Although the revision makes grading take a bit longer, you will feel better about the act of evaluation and about yourself as a more effective teacher. Since so many students are willing to do the extra work implied by revision, you probably ought to be willing as well.

This paean to the revision option should not obscure the fact that it can present problems. The most obvious one is the temptation on the students' parts to use the teacher only as editor. Do not mark all of the formal errors on each rough draft as well as evaluating the drafts for content. Not only will it prolong the time spent grading, but doing so will lead your students to believe that they need do no more revision than a simple re-typing, incorporating your formal corrections. Too many students already see "revision" as meaning nothing but pencil work and formal correction, and to edit their drafts for them only allows them to continue in this error. If you want to mark errors in drafts, do so with a simple checkmark over the error, which the student must then identify and correct.

The second major danger revision presents is a psychological one: the fact that students tend to believe that the act of revising a paper will automatically earn them a higher grade. It is the "A-for-effort" misconception. If you get a draft that would be worth a D and the revision moves it up to a C, the student often has a hard time understanding why, with all those changes, the paper is not worth a B or an A. Part of the problem might be due to the students' tendencies to see any paper without serious formal errors as A or B work, even if its content is vacuous or its organization incoherent. Some students, used to grade inflation, simply cannot get used to their work receiving C's or lower grades, especially if it is formally perfect. One way to get around this expectation is to assign no grades at all until after at least one revision or until you can declare the essay "acceptable" (usually the equivalent of a passing grade or a C).

Revision of written work is of great help to students. No longer is an essay a "do-or-die" proposition, to be created in fear and trembling because of the knowledge that it must soar or crash on its maiden voyage. Revision allows students to reflect on their writing and to see writing for what it is: a continuing process of re-seeing a subject, a process that never has to be completed until the writer is ready to say, "I can do no more."

Research Papers

Thus far we have been discussing the teaching of writing in general; we will now focus on a specific writing assignment for students: the research paper.

The research paper is a extended essay, usually of at least 1000 words, and demands that the student master not only essay-writing skills but also the skills of library research and of citation and bibliography form. Research papers are generally done in response to topics assigned by the teacher and may be worth a larger percentage of the final grade than the shorter essays written for the course. They tend to be long-range tasks, requiring from three to five weeks; and may work better in a semester-long rather than a quarter-long course. Many accomplished writing teachers require a research paper of 1000 to 1200 words from their students each semester, and they have very good results from the assignment. The reservation commonly expressed about research papers is that they too easily become "literature surveys" without a clear thesis. You can circumvent that reservation by specifically assigning an argumentative research paper, one that asks students to use researched material to support a central argumentative position, which you then assign. This "argumentative edge" gives a point to the whole assignment that it would not otherwise have. Some successful topics might include these:

Nuclear Power Generation: Yes or No?
Deficit Spending: Good or Bad Policy?
Socialized Medicine in America: Pro or Con?
Euthanasia: Yes or No?

Your students may come up with their own topics. In assigning sides for the argument, always let students choose the side they feel strongly about; one always argues better for truly held beliefs.

If you elect to use the research paper assignment, you will have to spend a few class periods teaching research and citation skills. A library tour might be a good idea; for many students, it is the first introduction to the computerized search, card catalogs, serial files, reference room and reference librarians. You will want, at least, to explain the basics of research procedure; how to search a subject, how to expand a search by use of indexes and bibliographies, how to use notecards, what sorts of notes are most useful, etc. Encourage students to do research together and to share findings with other class members who have chosen the same topic, so that no student is left without help or a place from which to begin. Ask students who have found particularly useful sources to bring them to class and share them.

Along with research skills, you will want to give some time to citation skills for although some students have written research papers in high school, their skills are usually rusty by the time you see them. They need to be taught the use, form, and properties of footnotes, bibliographies, and lists of references—research and citation information you can find in *The St. Martin's Handbook.* Many writing teachers are more comfortable teaching only MLA form for footnotes and bibliography, but with the explosion of interest in the sciences, you may want to teach APA form as well.

Students usually need at least several days' practice working with citation form. You can use the blackboard to explain the major forms for citation of books and journals and then give a homework assignment asking students to translate raw titles and authors into proper footnote, bibliography, and list of reference forms. At the next class meeting, ask volunteers to put their answers on the board, and then ask other students to translate them from note to bibliography form or vice versa. Students need to master the different citation forms in order to do a proper job on a research paper.

You will also want to explain other elements of the research paper: how to use quotations, how to fit quotations into sentences, what sorts of material needs to be footnoted, what sort of physical format you expect. If you have any trouble answering any of these questions, you can consult Chapter 42, "Documenting Sources," in *The St. Martin's Handbook.* Those handbooks which cover the research paper often do it extremely well; it is in this sort of formal instruction that handbooks come closest to fulfilling their promise.

Although the persuasive nature of the research paper described here makes it a livelier assignment than a mere literature survey might be, you cannot expect exhaustive researching, high-level argumentation, or sophisticated research methods from your students, who have just entered the process of becoming college-level writers.

Many teachers find that they must specify a minimum number of footnotes, sources cited, bibliography entries, and lines of arguments, for these papers are usually done under time pressure and are first attempts, practice runs. You may, however, elicit interesting papers and enthusiastic research as soon as your students begin to feel drawn into the conversation surrounding their area of inquiry. They may enjoy serious researching and becoming genuine experts; one student may gradually become someone who knows more than anyone else on campus about Joseph McCarthy's political affiliations, or Wordsworth's "Lucy" poems, or new uses of metal hybrids, or Jackie Robinson's contributions to sports history. You can assure your students that they will be truly knowledgeable and will be able to add their knowledge to the conversation of educated people that goes on all about them, not only in college but in the media, in community groups, and in workplaces.

Works Cited *Chapter 3*

Arbus, Rosemarie. "The Student-Teacher Conference." CCC 28 (1977): 338–42.*

Bain, Alexander. *English Composition and Rhetoric.* London: Longmans, 1877.

Bartholomae, David, and Anthony R. Petrosky. *Facts, Artifacts, and Counterfacts.* Upper Montclair, NJ: Boynton/Cook, 1986.

Beaven, Mary H. "Individualized Goal Setting, Self Evaluation, and Peer Evaluation." *Evaluating Writing: Describing, Measuring, Judging.* Ed. Charles R. Cooper and Lee Odell. Urbana, IL: NCTE, 1977. 135–56.

Coles, William E., Jr. *The Plural I: The Teaching of Writing.* New York: Holt, 1978.

Farrell, Edmund J. "The Beginning Begets: Making Composition Assignments." *Rhetoric and Composition: A Sourcebook for Teachers.* Ed. Richard L. Graves. Rochelle Park, NJ: Hayden, 1976. 220–224.

Garrison, Roger. "One–to–One: Tutorial Instruction in Freshman Composition." *New Directions for Community Colleges* 2 (1974): 55–84.

Irmscher, William F. *Teaching Expository Writing.* New York: Holt, 1972.

Jones, David. "The Five-Minute Writing." CCC 28 (1977): 194–96.

*Full names for abbreviated periodicals and organizations are given in the "Invitation to Further Study" at the end of this book.

Kinneavy, James L. *A Theory of Discourse.* 1971. New York: Norton, 1980.

Larson, Richard. "Teaching Before We Judge: Planning Assignments in Composition." *Teaching High-School Composition.* Ed. Gary Tate and Edward P.J. Corbett. New York: Oxford UP, 1970. 207–18.

Lunsford, Andrea, and Robert Conners. *The St. Martin's Handbook.* New York: St.Martin's, 1989.

Moffett, James. *Teaching the Universe of Discourse.* Boston: Houghton, 1968.

Murray, Donald. "The Listening Eye: Reflections on the Writing Conference." *College English* 41 (1979): 13–18.

Polanyi, Michael. *Personal Knowledge: Towards a Post-Critical Philosophy.* New York: Harper, 1964.

Chapter 4

Responding to and Evaluating Student Essays

In a real sense, it is unfortunate that we have to grade student papers at all. If we could limit our responses to advice and evaluation, without leaving a grade, we could create a supportive rather than a competitive or judgmental atmosphere. But if taken seriously and approached cautiously, the evaluation of student papers can serve to encourage and help students achieve their goals of the writing tasks.

The first thing you need to know about evaluation and grading (which from now on will be called "evaluation" for the sake of brevity) is that there are two major methods of evaluation: personal and group. We all know about personal evaluation; it is the system in which the teacher sits down alone at his desk and carefully reads, marks, evaluates, and grades a piece of student writing without advice from anyone else. Group evaluation, on the other hand, usually involves *holistic marking,* in which groups of trained "raters" quickly read many pieces of student writing in organized sessions. Charles R. Cooper, a leading theorist of holistic evaluation, describes it thus:

> Holistic evaluation of writing is a guided procedure for sorting or ranking written pieces. The rater takes the piece of writing and either (1) matches it with another piece in a graded series of pieces or (2) scores it for the prominence of certain features important to that kind of writing or (3) assigns it a letter or number grade. The placing, scoring, or grading occurs quickly, impressionistically, after the rater has practiced the procedure with other raters. The rater does not make corrections or revisions in the paper. Holistic evaluation is usually guided by a holistic scoring guide which describes each feature and identifies high, middle, and low levels for each feature. ("Holistic Evaluation" 3)

Which sort of evaluation, personal or group, is better? If the desired end of evaluation is to let students know how well they *really* write, the evaluation must be *reliable,* that is, it must eliminate random personal biases and somehow stabilize measurement. Personal grading cannot do this with any degree of success, as was proved by a study done in 1961 by the Educational Testing Service of Princeton. In this study 300 student papers were rated on a scale of 1 to 9 by 53 members of professional groups—editors, lawyers, teachers. Of the 300 papers, 101 received every grade from 1 to 9, and no paper received fewer than five different grades. It was a pathetic testament to the reliability of personal grading (Diederich 3). Even assuming that the sense of intuitive agreement about grading among teachers of freshman English might be higher than that among professionals in general, this test showed that the degree of grade variation due to personal bias is huge. Teachers simply do not share values about what constitutes good writing to the degree they need to to achieve respectable consensus, and as a result, personal grading, which produces a percentage of agreement ranging between 30 and 50 percent, is not very reliable.

Holistic rating by trained raters, on the other hand, can produce an agreement rate of over 90 percent and can also cut down appreciably on the amount of time that teachers spend on evaluation of papers. Holistic grading is more reliable than personal grading, promotes better student-teacher relations, takes less time to accomplish, and produces students who no longer tremble under pressure of weekly grading. However, holistic evaluation requires a level of organization, coordination, and training that is not generally available to new teachers of composition, or, for that matter to any teachers. Programs that incorporate holistic grading must make sure that the essays to be rated are written for the same assignment and share a certain physical format. Raters must assemble at a neutral location at a certain time, and agree on what analytic scale to use. They must be trained, directed, and checked by persons familiar with holistic analysis. Unless the decision to use holistic methods is made and enforced by the director of a writing program or the chairman of a department, it is very difficult to organize. This difficulty, however, does not detract from the superiority of holistic methods.[1] For now, though, we must leave holistic evaluation and return to the method used by most teachers: personal evaluation.

In preparing to grade and evaluate your first stack of student essays you must consider some questions. First, are you expected to enforce departmental grading standards? If your department has them, you must be prepared to work within them, for in all probability they are taken very seriously as an attempt to reduce grade inflation within the composition program. Usually this question of enforcing

---

1 Teachers interested in organizing holistic evaluation methods for their departments should consult Diederich, *Measuring Growth in English;* Cooper and Odell, *Evaluating Writing;* White, *Teaching and Assessing Writing.*

standards gets down to a practical question, one you will have to answer for yourself even if you have no departmental guidelines to follow: Will you assume that every student paper starts out in your mind as a potential A, and then gradually discredits itself (if it does) into a B, a C, etc.? Or will you assume that each paper begins as a C, an average, competent paper, and then rises or falls from that middle ground? Much of the answer to that question will necessarily depend on the ethos of the program you're teaching in.

Teachers who begin with the first assumption, that all papers are A's until proved otherwise, have a tendency to view a student essay only in terms of what is wrong with it. On the other hand, those who start from the position that all papers are C's are perhaps overly willing to see all student work as average C work. Teachers who begin with the C assumption are grudging with their A's. This may not necessarily be wrong, but it can be discouraging for students who struggle but never rise above C level.

Whichever position you start from, you will have to reach some decision about one other question: Will improvement, which is presumably the goal of a writing course, be taken into consideration during final grading? Should a student who starts out in September writing at C level and works up to B level by December be given a B, even if her mathematical average is a C+? This question can be answered in one of two ways, assuming that you do want to somehow take improvement into consideration.

The first method of considering improvement is to set up your schedule of written assignments so that later assignments are worth a larger percentage of the final course grade, thus weighting that final grade toward improvement late in the course. The second method is to toughen your grading standards or to assign "tougher" topics as the course progresses, so that a paper that might have received a B during the second week will get only a C during the eighth week. The first method works better for newer teachers—the process of tightening standards over time can easily become arbitrary, and personal grading is already arbitrary enough.

So you have your stack of paper, ready to be graded. Let's begin.

General Routine for Evaluation

An efficient general procedure for handling papers is that suggested by Richard Larson (152–55), as follows.

First, read over the paper quickly, making no marks, but instead trying to get a sense of the flow of the organization and of the general nature of what is being said. Try to decide during this reading what you like about the paper and also what elements of it need work.

Next, re-read the paper more slowly, marking it for errors and writing marginal comments. You may read it paragraph by paragraph this time, thinking less about overall organization.

Finally, re-read the paper quickly one last time, this time taking into consideration the overall purpose of the paper, its good and bad features, the number of formal errors it shows, *and* your marginal notes and comments. After this reading, you will write your terminal comment on the paper and grade it.

After you have finished evaluating and grading the paper, make a note of it in your student file. Compare its successes and failures to those of past papers, and if you see improvement (or decline), note it. You might at this point add a sentence or two to your terminal comment concerning the paper's success compared to previous efforts. After this, you can put the paper in the OUT basket and take up another.

There are other evaluation procedures, of course. Some teachers use evaluation sheets detailing areas of content, organization, and style: These sheets are filled out by the teacher and clipped to the student papers in place of written comments on the papers. Other teachers have experimented successfully with tape-recording their comments on cassettes and returning each student paper along with a cassette of comments on it. Both of these methods are useful, but both require more set-up than the technique described here and in most ways are merely permutations of it.

The final act, of course, is to return the students' papers (at the *end* of a class). You should return student papers as quickly as possible— no doubt you can remember the agony of waiting for your own teachers to get papers back to you.

Marginal Comments

A good number of the marks you make on a student paper will be in the form of marginal comments on specific words, sentences, and paragraphs. Making comments in the margin of a paper allows you to be specific in your approbation or criticism; you can call attention to strengths or weaknesses where they occur. Marginal comments include comments on substantive matters and notes that will make the student aware of other options he had in particular places.

When you are writing marginal comments, you will want to balance your advice and criticism with praise. Try to avoid the temptation to comment only on form, to do nothing but point out errors. You can and should use conventional editing symbols, but do not let them become your only marginal effort. Do not use a mere question mark if you have a problem understanding a section—spell out what your problem is. If reasoning is faulty, do not merely write "LOGIC" or "COH?"—let the students know what is wrong and try to give them some direction for revision.

What sorts of marginal comments are effective? First of all, a comment of praise is always welcome. If students say something or make stylistic points that seem effective or appeal to you, do not be afraid to tell them. A simple "Good!" or "Yes!" next to a sentence can mean a great deal to a struggling writer, as you may recall from your own voyages on seas of red ink. Simple questions like, "Evidence?" or "Does this follow?" or "Proof of this?" or "Seems obvious. Is it true?" can cause a student to question an assertion more effectively than a page of rhetorical injunctions.

Mary Beaven mentions three sorts of marginal comments that she has found particularly helpful:

1. Asking for more information on a point that the student has made.
2. Mirroring, reflecting, or rephrasing the student's ideas, perceptions, or feelings in a non-judgmental way.
3. Sharing personal information about times when you, the teacher, have felt or thought similarly (139).

All of these sorts of comments are "text specific"; they will make students feel as if the teacher is genuinely interested in what they have written.

Marginal comments are nearly always short—single sentences or even phrases. As Nancy Sommers has noted (151), marginal comments tend to "freeze" students onto the present draft, while terminal comments often invite a new draft—so it is best to keep the number of marginal comments down when evaluating first drafts. Students can be put off if you write a response to everything they say in a paper (not to mention the work it takes), so three or four marginal comments per page seems to be the upper limit that is worthwhile, at least for actual multiword "comments." Richard Haswell goes one step further, or perhaps one step backward, in his marginal comments. In "Minimal Marking" (601), he writes that "all surface mistakes in a student's paper are left totally unmarked within the text. These are unquestionable errors in spelling, punctuation, capitalization and grammar . . . . Each of these mistakes is indicated only with a check in the margin by the line in which it occurs."

Purely formal marginal or interlinear comments on errors are another area entirely. You must decide yourself on a system for making note of formal errors. (See the section on Formal Standards in this chapter.) Two different teachers might see a page of student writing in two completely different ways; one might mark a fragment, a comma splice, and three misspellings while another might mark those errors, plus four misuses of the comma, three awkward phrasings, a misplaced modifier, and five bad word choices. Much will depend on your philosophy. Those members of the Minimalist school of error marking point out major errors but leave minor faults alone (unless they are the only errors). The sight of papers that have been bled to death by well-meaning teachers and of papers whose margins are completely filled with criticisms can make any writer despair.

After the term has run for a few weeks and students have been alerted to their error patterns, you will no longer need to use the usual code for errors—FRAG, CS, RUNON, AWK, CAP, SP, S-V AGREE. Instead, you can gradually shift to a system of check marks, placing a check mark over each error. This forces students to discover for themselves what they have done wrong, and saves you from having to continue as editor. Because check marks are also considerably faster to apply, you can devote your time, instead, to real comments and to a more attentive reading of the paper.

Terminal Comments

Terminal or general comments are probably the most important message you give students about their papers, even more important than the grades. Terminal comments must do a great deal in a short space; they must tell students why they did well or ill, let them know whether they responded well to your assignment, help create a psychological environment in which the students are willing to revise or write again, encourage some writing behaviors and discourage others, and set future goals that you think the students can meet.

There are, of course, different types of terminal comments, and the general message of a terminal comment will depend on whether it is justifying a grade or making revision suggestions. Justifying a grade will often force the terminal comment to focus in a closed way on errors, problems, and things not done well, while revision advice can look to the future and deal with error patterns in a more positive way. Both sorts of terminal comments share certain components, though, and the difference between them is more a matter of percentages of these components than of anything else.

First, every terminal comment should focus on general qualities, presenting your impression of the paper as a whole. A good terminal comment devotes a large part of its content to an evaluation of the thesis of the paper under examination, and on how well that thesis is supported. How well does the thesis respond to the assignment? If a thesis is a sort of promise of what the paper will include, how well does the paper keep this promise? The answers to these questions must take in content, organization, and style, and must concentrate all of this information in a short space.

Next, the terminal comment should maintain a serious yet interested tone; no humor at the expense of the writer is allowable unless you are giving the paper an A. It should include praise for the well-done elements of the paper as well as mention of the elements that need work. It should point out improvements made and encourage more. It should not concern itself with formal errors, except perhaps to mention one or two important patterns of error that you feel need to be identified. It should not go over material already covered in marginal comments, nor should it be any sort of compendium of marginal comments. It should not be overly long—certainly no more than 150 words.

Meeting all these goals is not as difficult as you might think. After an entire afternoon of constant grading, you will have a real sense of your class as a continuum of writing abilities. Even when fatigue sets in and the temptation grows stronger merely to scrawl, "This is miserable and you've got a lot of gall to insult me with it," you will see how *each* paper compares to the ones that came before and to those of the rest of the class this time. But if you are uncertain about your abilities to write good comments or want to look at examples of the sorts of comments good teachers use, your colleagues and office mates are a natural resource. Ask around about teachers in the department who are highly respected *as teachers,* and ask them if they would check your paper annotations and show you theirs. Colleagues constantly help each other with revision of larger pieces, and it is natural to seek help in the same way when wishing to improve your writing of terminal comments. Also consider the most worthwhile and helpful comments you have received on your own papers.

In conclusion and reiteration: Terminal comments should show the students that you have read their work carefully, that you care about improving their writing, and that you know enough about your subject to be able to tell them what they did well and how to improve those things they did poorly. Once again, as in all aspects of teaching, your terminal comments will only be useful to students if they demonstrate humanity and competence.

The Grade

The comments you make in the margins and at the end of a paper
are the truly important responses that a student gets from you about
her writing, but the grade, the simple letter, remains the first thing a
student looks for. Although personal grading can be difficult, it can
be made easier for you and for other new teachers if you can organize
a grading seminar among writing teachers in your department. Such
a seminar will bring together new and experienced teachers to discuss and practice grading. This group need not meet more than once
or twice and need not be large, but in one afternoon the experienced
teachers can share many of their techniques and standards with the
new teachers and learn from each other as well.

If you succeed in organizing such a seminar, ask each teacher attending to bring copies of several unmarked student essays, enough
so that everyone attending can get one. Each teacher should mark
and grade his or her copy of the essay separately, and then contribute
to the discussion following the marking session. Out of these discussions of what problems and strengths each paper shows will come a
stronger sense of context and unity for both new teachers and old.
Though they can be difficult to organize, such seminars are extremely
useful—they can give new teachers a sense of how to grade papers
beyond the ability of this or any other book, beyond the expertise of
any one teacher.

If you have to proceed alone, make certain that your grading system corresponds to that used by your school. It will be extremely
troublesome to you if you unthinkingly use a system you are familiar
with, finding out only at the end of the term that you must adapt it
somehow. Find out before you grade your first paper whether your
school uses a four- or five-point system and whether or not you can
give plus/minus grades. Also, be alert for the "B fallacy": the temptation to overuse the grade of B. B does, after all, seem like such a nice
compromise; the work is not really all that good, so A is not indicated, but to give it a C would be so cruel. To many new teachers, and
not a few experienced ones, a C seems such a negative judgment, a
condemnation. Why not a B? If you seem to be giving too many B's
and are vaguely dissatisfied with yourself for it, you can often get
back on the track by coldly asking yourself, each time you are
tempted to give a B, what elements in the essay deserve a B. What, in
short, makes this paper better than average? Is it word choice? Organization? Ideation? If you can honestly point to a specific area in
which the paper is better than most others you've seen, it may

deserve the B. If you can find no specific area in which the paper excels, draw a deep breath and give it the C it does in truth deserve.

Formal Standards

As all experienced writing teachers are aware, formal standards are by far the easiest to mark, recognize, and enforce. They are largely standards of convention and correctness, and you will find that going through a paper marking formal errors is rather a mechanical job. You mark a spelling error here, a sentence fragment there, and it takes time and judgement. There is a natural feeling after having marked a paper for formal errors that you have done a solid, creditable job of telling the student what is wrong with the paper.

That sense of fulfillment, of having completed a job, makes formal evaluation seductive. Because of it, teachers are often tempted to base most of their grade on the formal qualities of the paper and not enough on the content. It is easy to see why: Formal evaluation is concrete and quantitative. It demands few complex judgment calls, which are at the heart of content evaluation. If a teacher produces a student essay dripping with red marks, he or she has obviously done a careful reading of it; so, why do more? It is a relief to be able to tell students they got a D because of three fragments and nine misspelled words and not have to deal with the complex, sometimes arbitrary world of content: thesis statements, patterns of development, assertions.

Yes, it is tempting to weight a grade to the formal qualities of the paper, but doing so is profoundly wrong. A piece of writing consists of far more than its comma use and punctuation, and if we stress nothing but formal grading, we will become mere pedants, obsessed with correctness to the detriment of meaning. We cannot fail to mark formal errors. As Mina Shaughnessy says, they are "unintentional and unprofitable intrusions upon the consciousness of the reader" which "demand energy without giving any return," but neither should we give them more than their due (12).

Andrea Lunsford and Robert Connors recently attempted to determine which errors are the most prevalent in student writing. In surveying over 21,000 student essays, they identified the twenty errors most often committed by student writers today. Here, in order of occurrence, is Lunsford and Connor's list of the twenty most common error patterns:

1. Missing comma after an introductory element
2. Vague pronoun reference
3. Missing comma in a compound sentence
4. Wrong word
5. Missing comma(s) with a nonrestrictive element
6. Wrong or missing verb ending
7. Wrong or missing preposition
8. Comma splice
9. Missing or misplaced possessive apostrophe
10. Unnecessary shift in tense
11. Unnecessary shift in pronoun
12. Sentence fragment
13. Wrong tense or verb form
14. Lack of agreement between subject and verb
15. Missing comma in a series
16. Lack of agreement between pronoun and antecedent
17. Unnecessary comma(s) with a restrictive element
18. Fused sentence
19. Dangling or misplaced modifier
20. *Its/it's* confusion

(*The St. Martin's Handbook* xxxvii)

Within any such group of serious errors, many teacher make a further distinction, one between *syntactic errors,* including sentence fragments, fused sentences, and comma splices, that take place on the sentence level, and *word-level errors.* Syntactic errors are much more serious than word-level errors, because they often present the reader with a situation in which it is impossible to know what the writer meant to say. If teachers quantitatively count errors, they nearly always count syntactic errors and word-level errors separately.

Standards of Content

The evaluation of formal correctness, as has been noted, is comfortable for teachers because it deals with conventions that are so completely agreed upon; a comma splice is a comma splice. Content grading is a much more abstract business, and despite the fact that content is at least as important as form, writing teachers in general are less confident about their ability to judge ideation and organization, and are therefore tempted to give these things less than their due when grading. To do so, though, is a serious error. Yes, it is more of a judgment call to say that a thesis is vague than it is to identify a tense shift, but we must take the responsibility. The teacher must make serious content judgments, and they must inform the evaluation or grade of the paper.

Content grades are usually assigned on the basis of how successful the paper seems to be in four specific areas, which we will follow Paul Diederich in calling *Ideas, Organization, Wording,* and *Flavor* (55–57).

The area of *Ideas* concerns the following questions:

1. How well does the essay respond to the assignment?
2. How novel, original, or well presented is the thesis of the essay?
3. Are the arguments or main points of the essay well supported by explanatory or exemplary material?
4. Is the thesis carried to its logical conclusion?

The area of *Organization* deals with material that is a step lower on the scale of abstraction. It concerns these questions:

1. Does the essay have a coherent plan?
2. Is the plan followed out completely and logically?
3. Is the plan balanced, and does it serve the purpose of the essay?
4. Are the paragraphs within the essay well developed?

The area of *Wording* sometimes impinges on the formal level of grading; but with respect to content, it is more concerned with word choices than with grammatical correctness. It addresses these questions:

1. Does the essay use words precisely?
2. Does the essay use words in any delightful or original fashion?

Finally, there is the level of *Flavor,* which is the term Diederich uses for what other might call "style." The questions asked in this area are:

1. Is the writing pleasing to the reader?
2. Does the writer come across as someone the reader should like and trust?
3. Does the writer sound intelligent and knowledgeable?

These guidelines may help you to grade content, but short of reprinting one-hundred graded student essays along with analyses of their content quality, there is little more this book can do to make your task easier. It is you who must ultimately decide whether an essay says something significant, has a strong central idea, adheres to standards of logic in development, and supports its contentions with facts. All teachers know the uncomfortable sense of final responsibility that goes with the territory of teaching; if it becomes overwhelming you can always share your problems with fellow teachers. Asking colleagues to give second opinions on papers is a common and useful practice. You are not really out on the edge alone.

Works Cited *Chapter 4*

Beaven, Mary H. "Individualized Goal Setting, Self Evaluation, and Peer Evaluation." Cooper and Odell 135–156.

Cooper, Charles R. "Holistic Evaluation of Writing." Cooper and Odell 3–32.

Cooper, Charles R. and Lee Odell, eds. *Evaluating Writing: Describing, Measuring, Judging.* Urbana IL.: NCTE, 1977.

Diederich, Paul B. *Measuring Growth in English.* Urbana, IL: NCTE, 1974.

Haswell, Richard. "Minimal Marking." *CE* 45 (1983): 600–04.

Larson, Richard. "Training New Teachers of Composition in the Writing of Comments on Themes." *CCC* 17 (1966): 152–55.

Lunsford, Andrea, and Robert Connors. *The St. Martin's Handbook.* New York: St. Martin's, 1989.

Shaughnessy, Mina P. *Errors and Expectations: A Guide for the Teacher of Basic Writing.* New York: Oxford UP, 1977.

Sommers, Nancy. "Responding to Student Writing." *CCC* 33 (1982): 148–56.

White, Edward M. *Teaching And Assessing Writing.* San Francisco: Jossey-Bass, 1986.

Appendix to Chapter 4

The End of the Term

Final Course Grading

That final A, B, or D next to a student's name represents your ultimate judgment on that student, usually the only judgment he or she will carry away from your class. It is both a difficult task and a relief, a closure, to mark down that letter.

You have, of course, since before the first day been preparing a system that would allow you to judge each student's individual performance. In front of you is evidence concerning the following factors:

1. Grades for each written essay
2. Weight of each assignment (5%, 10% . . .)
3. Test grades
4. Amount of class participation
5. Faithfulness of homework and journal (if required)
6. Amount of perceived improvement in writing ability

Of these five factors, only the first two are amenable to a mathematical solution. To arrive at a mathematical "raw score" for a student is a bit time-consuming but not difficult. If each essay and test is weighted alike, you need only convert the letter grade into its numerical equivalent, add those numbers, divide by the number of assignments, and then convert that result back into a letter grade. For example: Student X's grades: B-/C/B+/D/C+/C+/B-/C-

Conversion chart: (this example assumes a 4–point system)

$$
\begin{aligned}
A\ \ &= 4 \\
A\text{-} &= 3.7 \\
B\text{+} &= 3.3 \\
B\ \ &= 3 \\
B\text{-} &= 2.7 \\
C\text{+} &= 2.3 \\
C\ \ &= 2 \\
C\text{-} &= 1.7 \\
D\text{+} &= 1.3 \\
D\ \ &= 1 \\
F\ \ \ &= 0
\end{aligned}
$$

The student's grades thus convert to

```
3.7
2.0
3.3
1.0
2.3
2.3
2.7
1.7
```
For a total of: 18.0

The next step is to divide this product by the number of assignments.

$$\frac{18.0}{8} = 2.25$$

The result can then be converted back into a grade or left in the form of a GPA. If you convert to a grade, you must establish your own cutoff points. In this case, a 2.25 GPA is obviously closer to a C+ than to a C, but the cutoff problem becomes more difficult when the GPA is 2.50 or 2.85. You must make those decisions yourself.

If your assignments are not all weighted the same, the final mathematical raw score is more complex to work out. Let's assume, for instance, that you use nine assignments, which are weighted like this:

```
Assignment #1   5% of raw score
           2   10%
           3   15%
           4    5%
           5   10%
           6   10%
           7   15%
           8   10%
           9   20%
```

You obviously can't merely convert, add, divide, and convert. You must figure the weighting of each assignment into the final raw score. The table on the next page can help you in adding up weighted assignments:

	5%	10%	15%	20%	25%
A	5.0	10.0	15.0	20.0	25.0
A-	4.75	9.5	14.25	18.4	23.75
B+	4.5	9.0	13.5	17.6	23.0
B	4.25	8.5	12.75	17.0	21.25
B-	4.1	8.2	12.3	16.4	20.5
C+	3.9	7.8	11.7	15.6	19.5
C	3.75	7.5	11.25	15.0	18.75
C-	3.6	7.2	10.8	14.4	18.0
D+	3.4	6.8	10.2	13.6	17.0
D	3.25	6.5	9.75	13.0	16.25
D-	3.0	6.2	9.3	12.4	15.5
F	2.5	5.0	7.5	10.0	12.5

Using this table is not difficult. Simply find the value of each grade according to the percentage value indicated for each column, and add up the values for all asssignments. The score for assignments that are all A's would be 100, that for all F's, 50. If you wish to convert the final numerical score into a grade, you can use this chart:

A = 96–100
A- = 92–95
B+ = 88–91
B = 85–87
B- = 82–84
C+ = 78–81

C = 75–77
C- = 72–74
D+ = 68–71
D = 65–67
D- = 62–64
F = 50–61

To give an example of this system in action, let's evaluate another student's grades.

Student Y's grades: C+/D+/B-/A-/C-/C-/B/C+/C-

Given the weighting of the grades previously mentioned, Student Y's addition would be:

Assignment #1	(5%)	C+	=	3.9
#2	(10%)	D+	=	6.8
#3	(15%)	B-	=	12.3
#4	(5%)	A-	=	4.75
#5	(10%)	C-	=	7.2
#6	(10%)	C-	=	7.2
#7	(15%)	B	=	12.75
#8	(10%)	C+	=	7.8
#9	(20%)	C-	=	14.4
		Total Score:		77.10

The score of 77.1 equals either a C or a C+ on the grade scale. Once again you will have to establish your own cutoff points. To simplify, you might move 0.5 and above up the next number and below 0.5 down; therefore, a rating of 77.1 would mean a raw score of C.

Mathematical systems can aid us in figuring a final grade, but they are not all that goes into it. The writing grades that go into the final numerical score will certainly be by far the most important elements determining the final grade, but to that raw score that the numbers give us we must add the judgments of our sensibilities, our senses of many different, subtle qualities that fall under the heading of class participation. How much did the student care? How hard did he try? How serious was he? How willing was she to help others? How was her workshop-group performance? How much time did she give to journal entries? These and other considerations must go into the process of turning that raw mathematical score into a final grade. And ultimately, as with individual paper grades, this grading decision is one that you, the teacher, must make alone.

The question of failing a student is painful and real, especially if you know that the student has been trying hard to pass. It is not so difficult to write down the F for a student who has given up coming to class, or who seems not to care. But that desperate, struggling one, is hard to fail.

You won't want to fail such students. If a student looks as if he or she is in danger, recommend dropping the course, seeking outside writing help, and picking it up again when he or she is able to pass. Most do drop if they see that there is no hope, but sometimes no advice helps; the student cannot or does not drop, and you are forced to write down that damning F.

Do we do it? Yes. To be fair to the other students, we must. Being able to force ourselves to do it is one of the meanings of the word "professional."

Evaluating Yourself

The teacher has to make final judgments about the students in the form of grades, but their judgments about you and your course, important as they are, are usually optional. Not all departments demand that teachers use student evaluation forms in their courses. Even if yours does not, however, you will learn a great deal about your course and your teaching by developing a form and asking students to take time to complete it. Student evaluation forms should be filled out anonymously either as required homework or during class time on the last day of classes. You may want to collect them all—unread— seal them in an envelope and ask one of your students to keep them until after you have turned in your grades.

You can choose appropriate questions from and add to the following.

Evaluation Form

(space questions to leave room for student response)

1. How would you improve the content of the course?
2. What was the most useful assignment in the course? Explain.
3. The least useful assignment? Explain.
4. In what way in particular was the textbook helpful? For which assignment? What are the weaknesses of our textbook? Do you recommend that it be used again?
5. What seemed helpful or useless to you in the way of teacher responses and comments to your written work? What specific advice do you have for the teacher?
6. How has the revision policy affected the way you do your writing? Do you have any suggestions that might improve that policy?
7. Do you feel that the course requirements were fair? Why?
8. Did the group work sessions help you edit your work? How might they be improved?
9. Did the instructor accomplish his or her objectives for the course? Did you know what those objectives were?
10. How would you recommend the instructor change his or her in-class presentations to make them more effective?
11. What did you gain from the research paper assignment? The ability to do research? to marshal evidence? work in a group? speak publicly?
12. Was the grading policy clear to you? Was it fair?
13. How helpful were the conferences? Would more or fewer be better?
14. General comments: amplify above answers or address unasked questions.

Afterword

Your evaluations are read and digested; your grade cards are marked, signed, and turned in. Nothing remains but the stack of student Theme Folders and your faithful gradebook, filled with red and green and black hieroglyphs where previously only blank squares existed. Your first writing course is a memory; you will henceforth see those students only occasionally, accidentally, except for the few who will come back and report to you their triumphs and failures in other courses. The hardest part of it is over for you, and now, a seasoned veteran, you will soon be able to tell the nervous new teachers of next year not to worry, that they'll do fine. You have just entered the most vital and exciting field in the teaching of English. Welcome.

Part II

Theories into Practice

Chapter 5

Teaching Invention

With some solid teaching experience behind you, you are ready to explore more fully the discipline of composition and rhetoric. The following chapters will guide you in that exploration, focusing first on the teaching of invention.

Invention, which in rhetoric traditionally meant a systematic search for arguments, has become a much broader term in composition classes today. Invention has become the writer's search for the *thesis*, or central informing idea for a piece of writing, and all of the *supporting material* that will illustrate, exemplify, or prove the validity of that thesis. Invention is the central, indispensable canon of rhetoric. Without content material, there can be no effective communication, and invention is the process that supplies writers and speakers with their content material.

Invention is particularly important in college writing courses, because it helps students to *generate* and *select from* material that they must write about (Lauer, *Invention* 3). This process is often difficult for students, who may have had little practice at such activity. When faced with a writing assignment, many students are troubled not by the lack of a subject or topic (often, one is supplied) but rather by a seeming lack of anything important or coherent to say about it. Invention comes into play here, providing processes by which the student writer can analyze the assigned or chosen subject in order to discover things to say about it.

Most serious and experienced writers have incorporated some system of invention that they use to plan and carry out their writing. For many, then, this is a subconscious process; theories of and suggestions for teaching invention, making it a conscious activity, may seem artificial. The discomfort with artificial systems is not new. The history of rhetoric is characterized by a continuing disagreement about the usefulness of systems and topics; it seems to be an argument as old as rhetoric itself.[1] On the one hand we have the idealists, those rhetorical theorists who believed that there could be no meaningful communication unless the speaker or writer was broadly educated, trained in philosophy, morals, ethics, and politics, and of great

---

1   For a useful survey of rhetorical invention throughout history, see Harrington.

natural intellectual ability. For a person of this order, systems and topics might be secondarily useful, but subject matter would flow primarily from individual meditations and wisdom rather than from any artificial system of discovery. On the other hand, the realists, whose greatest spokesman was Aristotle, were aware that not everyone who needed to communicate had the broad educational background necessary to produce subject matter from personal resources. Many people needed an external system to consult in order to probe their subjects and discover subject matter and arguments.

The systems of invention in this chapter try to provide that assistance. Most incoming freshmen have had very little opportunity to practice serious, extended, coherent writing, and a no longer surprising very few of them can name two books they have read in the past year. Clearly, many of our students are in need of training in invention; without some introduction to the techniques of discovering subject matter and arguments, they might flounder in a morass of vague assertions and unsupported, ill-thought-out papers all term. They need a system to buoy them until they can swim by themselves.

The revival of rhetorical theory witnessed since the early 1960's has reacquainted teachers with the primary elements of the rhetorical tradition—*ethos*/writer; *pathos*/audience; *logos*/text—and with the way those elements have been played out in the canon of rhetoric. Close attention to the *writer* during this time has resulted in much important work that attempts essentially to answer this twofold question: where do a writer's ideas come from and how are such ideas formulated into writing? Such a question demands a new focus on *invention*, the first canon of rhetoric, and has led in two provocative and profitable directions. The first, represented in the work of Richard Young, Janice Lauer, and Richard Larson (to name only a very few), aims at deriving heuristic procedures or systematic strategies that will aid students in discovering and generating ideas about which they might write. Such strategies may be as simple as asking students about a subject: who, what, when, where, why, and how—the traditional "journalistic formula." Or they can be as complex as the nine-cell matrix presented in Young, Becker, and Pike's *Rhetoric: Discovery and Change*. Essentially, this heuristic asks student writers to look at any subject from different perspectives. For example, a student writing about a campus strike might look at it as a "happening" frozen in time and space, or as the result of a complex set of causes, or as a *cause* of some other effects, or as one tiny part of a larger economic pattern. Looking at the subject in such different ways loosens up mental muscles and jogs writers out of unidimensional or tunnel-vision views of a subject.

We see this interest in procedural heuristics as related theoretically to the work of researchers interested in cognition. Coauthors Linda Flower and John Hayes are best known for their studies of writers' *talk-aloud protocols*, tape-recorded documents that catch a writer's *thoughts* about writing while the writing is actually in progress. In "Interpretive Acts," Flower and Hayes discuss a schema of discourse construction comprising social context, discourse conventions, language purposes and goals, and the activated knowledge of not only the writer but also the reader. Both the writer and the reader balance these elements in order to create and recreate a text.

Stephen Witte has recently built on the work of Flower and Hayes in order to study what he calls a writer's *pretext*, a writer's "trial locution that is produced in the mind, stored in the writer's memory, and sometimes manipulated mentally prior to being transcribed as written text" (397). Other researchers have attempted to map the relationship of affective factors to a writer's invention: John Daly, in terms of writing apprehension, and Mike Rose, in terms of writer's block. All of this research aims to help teachers understand the rich, diverse, complex, and largely *invisible* processes student writers go through in writing.

But a renewed interest in student writers has led in another important direction, notably the work of Ken Macrorie and, more pervasively, of Peter Elbow. Elbow is interested in how writers establish unique voices, in how they realize individual selves in discourse, and his work with students presents dramatic evidence of such activity. In a series of very influential books (*Writing Without Teachers, Writing with Power, Embracing Contraries*), Elbow has focused on how writers come to know themselves, and then to share those selves with others.

The researchers and teachers surveyed here differ in many ways, but their work is all aimed primarily at that point of the rhetorical triangle that focuses on the writer and his or her powers of invention. They want to know what makes writers tick, and how teachers can help writers "tick" most effectively.

In this chapter, *invention* will deal with the development and expansion of three different but closely related elements: the *thesis statement*, which provides a solid declarative sentence that serves as the backbone for an essay; the *subject matter*, which fills out, expands, and amplifies the thesis; and the *argument*, a specialized form of subject matter consisting of persuasive demonstrations of points the writer wishes to prove. Some of the techniques here will work best for one or two of these elements, some for all three. You will see the tendencies of each technique easily, and can then make your own decisions on what you want your students to learn. Before reviewing the techniques of invention, though, you should be aware of a few facts about invention as a whole.

Nearly all of the systems of invention covered in this chapter can be called *heuristic*, or questioning, systems. Janice Lauer, a contemporary rhetorical theorist, describes heuristic procedures in her important study of invention:

> [A] heuristic procedure will be defined as a conscious and non-rigorous search model which explores a creative problem for seminal elements of a solution. The exploratory function of the procedure includes generative and evaluative powers: the model generously proposes solutions but also efficiently evaluates these solutions so that a decision can be made. Heuristic procedures must be distinguished from trial-and-error methods which are non-systematic and, hence, inefficient, and from rule-governed procedures which are rigorous and exhaustive processes involving a finite number of steps which infallibly produce the right solution. (*Invention* 4)

Although the systems described here differ widely in their approaches, with few exceptions they fit Lauer's definition.

To help judge the heuristic procedures that this chapter contains, you can run each one through the set of questions Lauer has developed to test heuristics. The three characteristics possessed by the best heuristic procedures, she says, are *transcendency, flexible order*, and *generative capacity*. Put into simpler question form, the test of a heuristic model looks like this:

1. Can writers transfer this model's questions or operations from one subject to another?
2. Does this model offer writers a direction of movement which is flexible and sensitive to the rhetorical situation?
3. Does this model engage writers in diverse kinds of heuristic procedures? ("Toward" 269)

Before you choose a system, you might try applying this test to it.

The seven systems in this chapter are all discrete; you can choose one and ignore the others, or you can try several concurrently or at different times. Since invention is a central skill in composition, you will want to introduce some system near the beginning of the course, otherwise you may not have a coherent framework on which to hang the other elements you teach. Your students can practice some of these methods (pre-writing, freewriting, brainstorming) with you during class time. They can use the other methods at home, after you have introduced your students to them through in-class exercises.

Ideally, your students will gradually assimilate these systems of invention into their subconscious, recalling them when needed.

The goal is, then, to make these artificial systems of discovery so much a part of the way our students think about problems that they become second nature for students as they have for most teachers. Truly efficient writing is almost always done intuitively and then checked against models for completeness and correctness at the revision stage. We cannot expect that this process of subconscious assimilation will be completed in ten or fifteen weeks, but if a system of invention is conscientiously taught and practiced for that period of time, it will at least become a useful tool for students to fall back upon for help in other classes, and eventually it may become part of their thought processes.

Classical Invention

The tradition of classical rhetoric, as it developed from Aristotle to Cicero and then was codified by Quintilian, is the only "complete" system that we will deal with in this book, and it still remains one of the most definitive methodologies ever evolved by the Western mind. The rhetoric of the Renaissance was largely informed by it; even the "epistemological" rhetoric of the eighteenth century is far less coherent as a system than is classical rhetoric in its finished form. In contrast to classical rhetoric, the "New Rhetoric" of the twentieth century is still in its infancy, with many workable techniques but no informing paradigmatic structure. Many books have been devoted to analyzing and explaining the structure and usefulness of the classical rhetorical tradition, but for our purposes only a few elements of classical theory will be useful.

The two classical techniques that we will concentrate upon as aids to invention are the determination of the *topics,* or seats of argument, and that of *status* or *stasis,* which involves a formula for determining the point at issue in any controversy. Both techniques can be used to conceptualize and formulate the single-sentence declarative thesis that usually constitutes the backbone of a freshman essay, and the topical system can also be used to invent subject matter and arguments. It will be useful to remember that all classical techniques were originally devoted to the creation of persuasive discourse and that classical invention works most naturally in an argumentative mode. It should not be expected to work as well for nonexpository prose.

Status

The concept of *status*, which is not to be confused with the modern sense of the word meaning "place in the social order," has its origin in the legal system of ancient Rome, where it became necessary to be able to determine the point at issue in a court trial. The following formula was developed to assist in identifying the kind of issue upon which the trial hinged; it consisted of three questions that were asked about the subject:

An sit (Whether a thing is)—a question of fact
Quid sit (What a thing is)—a question of definition
Quale sit (Of what quality it is)—a question of quality

The best way to use status as an aid to invention is to consider the given subject in the light of the *types* of questions that can be asked about them. Since a thesis statement is always the answer to a tacit question, if we can find a fruitful question to ask, a thesis will follow. Let us take the Monroe Doctrine and subliminal advertising as examples; we could ask the following questions about these subjects:

The Monroe Doctrine

An sit—questions of fact
  Did Monroe originate the Monroe Doctrine?
  Did the Monroe Doctrine exist in 1812?
  Does the Monroe Doctrine exist today?

Quid sit—questions of definition
  What is the Monroe Doctrine?
  What does it state?
  Is it a formal part of U.S. policy?
  Has it actually been invoked? When and how?
  Does it have historical precedents?

Quale sit—questions of quality or nature
  Has the Monroe Doctrine been good for the U.S.?
  Is it a moral or an immoral policy?
  Has it been useful in dealing with world communism?
  Has it been useful in dealing with the Third World?
  Should it be used in Cuba?
  Should it be invoked in the future?
  Is it an inherently imperialistic policy?

Subliminal Advertising

An sit—questions of fact
Does subliminal advertising exist?
Does Blortschmimitz Vodka use subliminal advertising?
Is subliminal advertising used on television? Does it work?

Quid sit—questions of definition
What is subliminal advertising?
How does subliminal advertising work
Which audiences are most affected by subliminal advertising?
What products use subliminal advertising most often?
Who produces most subliminal advertising campaigns?

Quale sit—questions of quality or nature
Is subliminal advertising an immoral technique?
Is bypassing conscious will unique to subliminal advertising?
Is some subliminal advertising harmful?
What does subliminal advertising show about firms that use it?

These are obviously only some of the many questions that can be raised by using the concept of status; all a writer needs is one intriguing question and he or she has a workable thesis. Obviously the use of *status* is an invention technique of limited applicability, since it cannot generate subject matter very effectively. Within the confines of what it can do, though—create questions that lead to thesis statements—*status* is an effective technique.

The Topics

Aristotle is responsible for our first introduction to the *topics* or "seats of argument," but his doctrine was continued and amplified by the other classical rhetoricians. The topics were conceived of as actual mental "places" (the term itself comes from geography) to which the rhetorician could go to find arguments.

The system of topics described here is a modern arrangement of classical topical invention, adapted from the work of Edward P.J. Corbett, of Richard P. Hughes and P. Albert Duhamel, and of a group of teachers at the University of Chicago (Corbett 45; Hughes and Duhamel; Bilsky et al. 210–16). These topics are not so much places to go for ready-made arguments as they are ways of probing one's subject in order to find the means to develop that subject. The four common topics that are most useful to students are *definition, analogy, consequence,* and *testimony.*

Definition The topic of definition involves the creation of a thesis by taking a fact or idea and expanding on it by the use of precise identification of its nature. The subject can be referred to its class or *genus* and the argument made that whatever is true of the genus is true of the species: "The expansion of the national debt is an inflationary policy"—and should therefore be classed with other inflationary policies. A far less powerful and less sophisticated form of definition is "the argument from the word," the use of dictionary or etymological meanings to define things or ideas. For many beginning writers, the dictionary definition is the easiest place to start.

Analogy The topic of analogy is concerned with discovering resemblances or differences between two or more things, proceeding from known to unknown. It should always be kept in mind that no analogy is perfect and that all deal in probabilities, but analogy is a useful tool for investigating comparisons and contrasts: "The first week of college is like the first week of boot camp." Another type of analogical reasoning is the argument from contraries, or *negative analogy:* "The marijuana laws are unlike Prohibition." Although analogy is often thought of merely as a figure of speech, it is an important demonstrative tool as well.

Consequence The topic of consequence investigates phenomena in a cause-to-effect or effect-to-cause pattern. The best use of consequence is in the prediction of probabilities from patterns that have previously occurred: "Appropriation of all usable agricultural land led to the downfall of the Somoza regime in Nicaragua." The topic of consequence is prone to two fallacies: one is the fallacy of *post hoc ergo propter hoc*—"after, therefore caused by," a logical error to guard against. Just because one element precedes another in time does not mean that the former is a cause. An extreme example of this fallacy might be, "The crossing of the Atlantic in a balloon led to the downfall of the Somoza regime in Nicaragua." The other fallacy, *a priori,* claims but does not demonstrate a cause-and-effect relationship between two phenomena.

Testimony The topic of testimony relies on appeals to an authority, some external source of argumentation. The authority could be an expert opinion, statistics, the law, etc. This topic is not as useful today as it once may have been; not only has our controversial age produced so many conflicting authorities that all too often they cancel one another out, but often celebrities give paid testimony, called advertising. Still, testimony can be a good starting place for an argument, especially when student writers have a familiarity with and an understanding of the source of testimony.

Let us look first at teaching the use of status and the topics in general and then at familiarizing students with the use of the topics in generating theses, subject matter and arguments.

Classroom Use of Classical Invention

Classical invention takes just a short time to teach: Teaching status as a device for arriving at thesis statements can be done in only a day, as can the initial introduction of the topics. Students are often impressed when they are told the background of the technique—at last a high-level classical skill!—and use it with enthusiasm after they learn to apply the different terms.

Start teaching status by putting a subject on the blackboard. You can use one of the two used in the section on status, but only write down the one-or-two-word subject itself at this point. Ask students to try to come up with questions concerning the subject, questions whose answers might be turned into thesis statements. (This exercise, of course, presupposes that you have explained what a thesis statement is.) They will come up with several questions, which you should group on the board into the three categories of *an sit, quid sit*, and *quale sit*. When you have exhausted all of the questions that the students can think of, ask them to try to figure out why you grouped their questions as you did. This can lead to a discussion of what sorts of questions create good thesis statements; out of that discussion you can introduce the concept of status and finally explain the Latin terms under which you have grouped questions: *An sit*—questions of fact, *Quid sit*—questions of definition, *Quale sit*—questions of quality or nature.

Hand out examples showing questions grouped around a subject in the way that was illustrated earlier in this section; after a discussion of what sorts of question fall into which categories, your students can try to use status themselves. Point out first to them the general patterns that opening questions group themselves into the "did, does, is" for *an sit*, the "who, what, which, how," for *quid sit*, and the "could, should, has, is," for *quale sit*. After they have seen these examples, assign subjects and ask students to use status to try to arrive at questions whose answers could become thesis statements. Give time for in-class writing of questions and then ask students to volunteer their questions orally. You can begin with carefully selected "rich" subjects such as "Tuition," moving to more difficult and less concrete subjects as students gain confidence.

Once students have arrived at the questions, the next step is turning the questions into usable theses. Very often the answer to a question generated by status will be a usable thesis, but the best theses are created by mixing together the answers to several questions arrived at under a given category of status. For instance, out of the four model questions listed under "Subliminal Advertising" in the earlier example of *quale sit*, the answers can be combined into a single usable thesis that can be well developed: "Firms which use the harmful and immoral technique of subliminal advertising show that they wish to bypass the conscious will of the consumer to force him to buy their products." Admittedly, this is stretching it a bit, but it does illustrate how theses are developed from status questions. This should probably be done on the blackboard and then by the students in class before you again ask for volunteers to read the theses they have created.

The acid test, of course, is whether students can formulate actual theses. The last step in teaching status is the assignment of several difficult subjects—on current events, for example—with the demand that each student come up with five probable theses for each subject. If your students can do this, they have mastered status, and the only other test you may want to run is that of asking them for theses on a subject that they choose themselves. While not as complex and thorough as some of the other inventive techniques (most of which generate subject matter as well as theses), status is a useful tool that students can memorize and apply easily.

Ultimately, a powerful argument must say something intelligible about the real world. In teaching the topics, this means using examples. Good examples are to be had by applying each topic to a definite subject and coming up with several thesis statements by the use of that topic. You may want to pass out sheets of these examples to the class so that the students have the examples in front of them when they begin to create their own theses. You won't find that drawing theses from the topic is difficult for you. Here are the Battle of Gettysburg and unit-pricing laws run through the topical-thesis mechanism:

Definition Definition always answers the question, "What is it (or, What was it)?" asked in a variety of different contexts. The subject can be defined in its immediate context, or a larger context, in different stipulative settings, in space or in time or in a moral continuum. Here are some examples:

The Battle of Gettysburg was the longest battle of the Civil War.

The Battle of Gettysburg was a damaging defeat for the South.

The Battle of Gettysburg was a tragedy of errors in command on both sides.

The Battle of Gettysburg was a turning point for the Union.

Unit-pricing laws are consumer-protection legislation.

Unit-pricing laws are damaging restraint of free trade.

Unit-pricing laws are opposed by store owners.

Unit-pricing laws are growing more and more popular.

Analogy   Analogy always asks the question, "What is it like or unlike?" and the topic of analogy usually answers the question by explaining a lesser-known element in the context of a better-known element. Because of its explanatory nature, at least one side of the analogical topic statement is often historical or general, as in these examples:

Gettysburg was a Pyrrhic victory for the Union.

The Battle of Gettysburg was for Lee what Waterloo was for Napoleon.

The Battle of Gettysburg was completely unlike the Battle of Shiloh in tactics. (negative analogy)

Pickett's Charge was the American version of the Charge of the Light Brigade at Balaclava.

Cemetery Ridge was the Bunker Hill of the Civil War.

UPLs are for grocers what odometer-tampering laws are for used-car dealers.

UPLs are like the silly seatbelt-interlock laws of 1974 that had to be repealed.

UPLs are fog lights in the thick mists of obscure grocery pricing policy.

UPLs are not at all similar to freedom-of-information laws. (negative analogy)

Consequence   Consequence always answers the question, "What caused/causes/will cause it? or What did it cause/is it causing/will it cause?" It is a topic not to be taken lightly because even in a thesis statement it demands that the creator trace out the chains of consequence leading to ends. Consequence can be either explanatory or predictive.

The Battle of Gettysburg lost the Civil War for the South.

Superior industrial capability allowed the Union to win the Battle of Gettysburg.

If Lee had won at Gettysburg, the South would have taken Washington and won the Civil War.

If Ewell had taken Cemetery Ridge, Lee would have won the Battle of Gettysburg.

The loss of life in Pickett's Charge caused the South to lose the Civil War.

If UPLs are enacted in this state, most small grocers will go out of business.

If UPLs are enacted here, poor people will get better food and more food for their money.

The demand for UPLs arose when manufacturers began to produce nonstandard sizes for their products.

UPLs are the result of creeping socialism.

Testimony Testimony always answers the question, "What does authority say about it?" The authorities can range from experts, to statistics, to eyewitnesses, to accepted wisdom.

Lincoln considered the Battle of Gettysburg to have been the most important battle of the Civil War.

The loss of over 20,000 men from each army crippled the South more than the North. (reliance on statistics)

Bruce Catton, the noted historian, called Gettysburg a black day for both sides.

Pickett's Charge was insanity, for it is only common sense not to charge up a fortified hill without a heavy advance bombardment.

President Reagan says that UPLs are unnecessary in a nation of intelligent people.

In states with UPLs, purchasing of "house brands" has gone up 25%.

Everyone agrees that UPLs are impossible to enforce in a time of rapid inflation. (common-sense testimony)

Ralph Nader has written that "unit-pricing is a right of all Americans."

These are just a few of the possible theses available under each of the topical heads. Using the topics to create theses demands a more immediate knowledge of the subject than does the use of status for two reasons: (1) topical theses are answers, not questions; and (2) the topical breakdown of inquiry is more specific in nature. Although topical theses are not so easy to generate as questions from status, students will derive theses that are more specific. You can also see that some topics will be more fruitful than others in dealing with certain kinds of subjects. The topics of definition, analogy, and consequence are the most useful for thesis creation, while the topic of testimony is most naturally suited to the buttressing of already created theses.

The topics are not magical formulae that can make something out of nothing, but they are useful in organizing unformed masses of information into thesis statements. You need not have more than a lay person's knowledge of the Battle of Gettysburg or of unit pricing to come up with the thesis statements above, but after having created the theses you will know more clearly what you do know. You will also have a much better idea where you need to go to look up information that you do not immediately have.

Work through each topic in class in a way similar to the manner in which you introduced status. Again, you may want to pass out a dittoed sheet with the examples of the topics in action on a particular subject. Spend enough time on each of the first three topics (testimony is a more specialized issue) to allow your students to digest the examples you have provided and to see the process by which you arrive at the statements under each topic. This process takes only a couple of days.

After you have explained the examples and shown how they are derived from the topics, give your students exercises in the form of assigned subjects upon which you ask them to use the topical system. The assignment is to come up with at least three theses under the heading of each topic. After this assignment has been written, either in class or as homework, ask the students to volunteer theses verbally in class. If they have been successful at that assignment, the next step is to ask them to come up with an idea for an essay from one of the other classes they are currently enrolled in and apply topical thesis invention to that subject. They should be comfortable enough with the system at this point—perhaps even openly pleased by it—to be able to reel off theses for other subjects without much trouble.

Using the topics to generate supporting subject matter follows thesis production readily. Once students have chosen their thesis out of the myriad possible ones the topical system offers, they are left with many other statements that are at least indicators of other informational lodes and where they may be found. Very often, after choosing a thesis, students can structure their essays around other possible thesis statements that they change slightly to make subordinate to the main purpose of their essays. If you have the time in class, ask your students to put together a rough "topic outline" of a projected essay by arranging as many of the theses they have generated as possible (remind them that often they may have to change the direction of the theses slightly to subordinate them to the main thesis) in an order that could be used to structure an essay. Here is an example of such a rough list-outline using some of the theses generated under "unit-pricing laws":

> *Main thesis:* Unit-pricing laws are unnecessary and should not be enacted in this state.
>> *Subordinate thesis* 1: UPLs are a damaging restraint of free trade.
>> *Subordinate thesis* 2: If UPLs are enacted, many small grocery stores will go out of business.
>>> *Minor thesis:* UPLs are opposed by store owners.
>> *Subordinate thesis* 3: UPLs are impossible to enforce in inflationary times.
>>> *Minor thesis:* UPLs are like the seatbelt-interlock law of 1974.
>> *Subordinate thesis* 4: UPLs are the result of creeping government interference [note the change in wording] in the lives of individuals.
>>> *Minor thesis:* Ralph Nader likes them.
>>> *Minor thesis:* President Reagan does not.

This is a more structured list than those that many students will come up with, but it exemplifies how such a topic list can be constructed.

Described here is a deductive use of the topics, in which the thesis statement is decided upon and then subject mater is arranged according to the perceived needs of the thesis. The topics can, of course, also be used inductively, to explore the subject and gather a mass of potential material, with the student creating a thesis only after the subject material has been grouped. To teach this sort of inductive use of the topics, it is necessary to leave the whole area of thesis creation until after the topical system has been used by students to gather subject matter. You will find that they often cannot wait to begin to arrange the matter under a thesis and greet the stage of thesis creation with enthusiasm.

Thus far we have discussed fairly simple uses of the topics; using the topical system to support argumentation is a somewhat more complicated task. The best description of classroom use of topical argumentation is found in the article, "Looking for an Argument," by Manuel Bilsky and a group of rhetoricians at the University of Chicago. The method that follows is adapted from the system they describe (Bilsky 215–16).

Before you begin to teach argument, your students should be comfortable with the idea of topics and be able to manipulate them fairly well. To introduce Bilsky's topical arguments, it will be necessary to give the students examples of their use. You can usually find several good examples of arguments from definition, analogy, etc., in any of the widely used freshman readers. Classify the passages by topic and hand them out to your students so that they can see the new angle from which they will have to view the use of the topics. When you have gone over the handouts, try the following exercise.

Choose three propositions that are simple, fairly clear, and controversial, at least to some degree. These can most often be chosen from current news events and can involve political opinions. Ask your students to use the topics to write short supporting statements— no more than one or two sentences—for each proposition as homework, and during the next class convene writing groups or have students exchange papers with their classmates and try to identify the use of specific topics in each other's work.

The next steps are optional. After simple manipulation of topical arguments, expose your students to writings that make use of complex and combined argument. Try the classic persuasive pieces, such as "Federalist #10," "Civil Disobedience," "A Modest Proposal," or more contemporary pieces, such as "I Have A Dream," "College is a Waste of Time and Money," "Motherhood: Who Needs It?" or "Letter from Birmingham Jail." Only after students have been exposed to topical argumentation in its most developed form should they be given the long persuasive assignments that are the final goal of topical argumentation.

Classical invention in its simplified form can be very satisfying to teach. You are aware as you teach it of a tradition of education that is as old as any in Western culture. Students are often impressed by the classical cachet as well. Classical invention is not difficult to impart, and it is easy enough for students to memorize, so that they can carry it with them for use in other classes. It is neither the simplest nor the most complex heuristic system, but it has both a charm and a comprehensiveness that make it one of the most attractive.

Kenneth Burke and the Pentad

In his long life Kenneth Burke has been a poet, short-story writer, music critic, book reviewer, translator, novelist, literary critic, professor, magazine editor, social commentator, essayist, researcher, teacher at at least fourteen different colleges and universities, and foremost of all, rhetorician. He is the author of numerous books of all sorts and is one of those rare people whose analytic and synthetic work is equally brilliant.

Beginning in the early 1950s, Burke's ideas penetrated departments of Communication (or Speech departments, as they were called then), for his analysis of literature had meaning for the study of rhetoric. Gradually, his influence and reputation spread to practitioners of rhetoric and composition in English Departments, where Burke had previously been known only as a brilliant but somewhat obscure literary critic. For some years now, Burke's analytical invention, the *Pentad*, has been used by specialists in the teaching of writing.

Burke calls his central method of analysis "dramatism." The Pentad is sometimes called "the dramatistic Pentad" because "it invites one to consider the matter of motives in a perspective that, being developed from the analysis of drama, treats language and thought primarily as modes of action" (*Grammar* xvi). The idea of "language as symbolic action" runs throughout Burke's critical and rhetorical work, leading to a method of literary analysis that concentrates on what a work does to its audience and to a rhetorical outlook that is far from idealistic or rarified—Burke refers to social communicative situations as "The Human Barnyard," full of action.

Burke's rhetoric is like Aristotle's in many ways, particularly in its insistence on awareness of the nature and needs of the audience. Burke has said that "wherever there is persuasion, there is rhetoric. And whenever there is 'meaning' there is 'persuasion'" (*Rhetoric* 172). If this seems to enlarge the field of rhetoric to include all human actions, that is exactly what Burke means it to do; his investigation of linguistic phenomena ranges from Shakespeare's "Venus and Adonis," to Hitler's *Mein Kampf*, to advertising jingles and to the Ten Commandments, all of which he considers rhetoric: "the use of language in such a way as to produce a desired impression on the reader or hearer" (*Counter–Statement* 165).

Kenneth Burke's contributions to rhetorical metatheory are many, but his primary—although indirect and unintended—contribution to invention is his Pentad. Burke first introduced the Pentad in *A Grammar of Motives* as a device for the analysis of literature. Simply put, it is a list of five terms that can be used as principles on invention. They are as follows:

Act
Scene

Agent

Agency

Purpose

Burke explains the genesis of these terms in the Introduction to *A Grammar of Motives:*

> In any statement about motives, you must have some work that names the act (names what took place, in thought or deed), and another that names the scene (the background of the act, the situation in which it occurred); also you must indicate what person or kind of instruments he used (agency) and the purpose (*Grammar* x).

As William Rueckert has suggested, Burke feels that the stress on act characterizes the realists; the stress on scene, the materialists; the stress on agent, the idealists; the stress on agency, the pragmatists; and the stress on purpose, the mystics—with whom Burke identifies (Rueckert 93–96).

The most immediately obvious quality of the Pentad is its resemblance to the journalistic formula of "What, Where, Who, How, Why?" It has, however, become accepted wisdom that the Pentad differs from the journalistic formula because of a further development of Burke's, the "ratios" between elements in the Pentad. "Simple as it appears," says Richard Young, "Burke's procedure is capable of far more complex analyses. The terms and their references can be combined in various ratios (e.g., act-scene, act-purpose, act-agency), ten ratios in all being possible. The relationships revealed in analyses using the ratios often provide original and important insights into behavior (Young, "Invention," 13).

Not intended as a heuristic that aids discovery or invention, Burke's Pentad nonetheless supplies writers and readers with a method for establishing the focus of a written (or spoken, for that matter) text. His theory of dramatism, focusing as it does on the ratios between the elements in the Pentad, calls attention to the ways these representative terms link up. Dramatism is a theory of action that breaths life into a text, humanizing the action. And the key term of Burke's Pentad is "act," for it is the starting point for text analysis. When a person's acts are to be interpreted in terms of the circumstances, that is, the scene in which action takes place (as in *Robinson Crusoe, Lord of the Flies,* or *Riddley Walker,* for example), behavior would fall under the heading of a "scene-act ratio." in *Lord of the Flies,* both Ralph and Jack, leaders of opposing factions, act in reaction to the *scene:* They are stranded on a desert island without the traditional protection of society. Yet within the *scene-act* ratio would fall a range of behavior that must again be evaluated according to the *agent-act* ratio—the correspondence between a person's character and action. Well-adjusted, optimistic, and athletic, Ralph "naturally" acts out the desire for civilization, while Jack, the cruel and ugly bully, acts out the feral desire for mastery by intimidation and violence. Once students begin to understand the concept of "dramatism," they can analyze Romeo's *act* in response to the *scene* of his apparently dead Juliet or James Worthy's *act* in response to his *scene,* the seventh game of the NBA finals. An awareness of this ratio can help students develop actions in their own texts: what *actions* are taken in response to *apartheid,* for example, or sports violence or dormitory life.

Texts such as *Madame Bovary, Anna Karenina,* and *Portrait of a Lady* reflect a prominent *agency-act* ratio, the texts reflecting correspondence between each character and the character of behavior. Or if students consider the agency-act ratio of *Huck Finn,* for instance, they begin to understand the effect of Emmeline Grangerford's maudlin character on her poetry or the Widow Douglas's high-mindedness on her treatment of Huck. Student writers can then apply their understanding to their own subjects, such as their own reasons for commuting to school or their parent's philosophy of upbringing. And other dynamic relationships, other ratios, disclose still other features of human relations, behavior, and motives.

Classroom Use of Burke's Pentad

Not intended to be used as an isolated heuristic technique, the Pentad can be useful in the writing classroom, for it is one of the easiest heuristics to teach, and students easily remember it. The Pentad can form the basis for several different sorts of invention activities, each of which must be carefully described to students. However, until students are taught how to manipulate it, the Pentad is nothing more than a collection of terms.

For a relatively limited sort of invention that is best used in classes discussing works of literature, W. Ross Winterowd has evolved a use of Burke's terms that can be helpful in the analysis of a piece of writing. Here is his adaptation of the terms of the Pentad:

What does it say?	(Act)
Who wrote it?	(Agent)
In what source was it published?	(Agency)
Where and when was it published?	(Scene)
What is its purpose?	(Purpose)

(The Contemporary Writer 82–89)

The most complete adaptation of Burke's terms for use in general invention has been done by William Irmscher, who in his *Holt Guide to English* compiled fifteen questions which were divided into Burke's five categories. Irmscher's use of Burke is not a method of inventing thesis statements or single declarative statements; what it is best used for, as Irmscher says, is "accumulating a mass of material" on subjects, gathering subject matter in the form of supporting propositions or kernel thoughts (28).

Irmscher's questions run thus:

Action—to generate thought about an action ask:
1. What happened?
2. What is happening?
3. What will happen?
4. What is it?

Actor-Agent—to generate thoughts about an agent ask:
1. Who did it? Who is doing it?
2. What did it?
3. What kind of agent is it?

Scene—to generate thoughts about a scene ask:
1. Where did it happen? Where is it happening?
2. When did it happen?
3. What is the background?

Means-Agency—to generate thoughts about an agency ask:
1. How was it done?
2. What means were used?

Purpose—
1. Why?

You may want to make copies of these questions for your students. Not the only possible approach to the Pentad, Irmscher's is representative of the methods writing teachers use to put the code words of the Pentad into a form that students can use. Unlike other techniques of invention, this one is so simple and schematic that it takes little teaching on your part. Once the students are exposed to the terms and the questions, they can work on their own. You will want to assist your students in distinguishing which of the terms of the Pentad will be most useful when applied to the subject at hand.

If students run a subject through all of the questions suggested by the Pentad, faithfully jotting down an answer to each question, they will generate much information that they can use well in a coherent essay. Our pet subject of subliminal advertising, for instance, can be put into a perspective of any of the five terms, and seen as primarily an action, or in terms of who does it, or where it is done, or the technical means by which it is accomplished, or the purpose behind it. Your task as a teacher of the Pentad will be to assist your students in figuring out how much information they need for an essay and what Pentad questions will most helpfully assist them in mining it.

When you are teaching invention, make sure to use the blackboard so your students can watch the Pentad technique in action. Run a few subjects through the technique for your students before you ask them to try manipulating it themselves. You may find that students can use the Pentad well to provide subject-based questions and material, but that other important elements of rhetorical purpose, such as considerations of audience and arrangement of material, are not natural parts of the inventive system of the Pentad. Your students will probably need your help to determine the purpose of their own essays and to arrange the gathered material into coherent form.

Prewriting

The term *prewriting* applies to all forms of activity that precede actually putting pen to paper to begin the first draft. *Prewriting* is a theory of invention and teaching developed at Michigan State University in the early Sixties by D. Gordon Rohman and Albert O. Wlecke and modified by them and other teachers over the next ten years.

Prewriting as a theory seeks to promote the process of self-actualization in the student. In "Pre-Writing: The Stage of Discovery in the Writing Process," Rohman defines "good writing" as "the discovery by a responsible person of his uniqueness within his subject"; his definition of a responsible person is "one who stands at the center of his thoughts and feelings with the sense that they begin in him. He is concerned to make things happen . . . he seeks to dominate his circumstances with words or actions" (106).

Prewriting claims that writing in general consists of two contexts: the *subject context* and the *personal context*. The subject context is made up of objective material that can be discovered through research, the sort of factual material found in encyclopedias that is inert and manipulable by a writer. The personal context, on the other hand, has to do with the writer's personality; it is within the personal context, says Rohman, that a writer finds "that combination of words that make an essay his" (108). The prewriting theorists were convinced that much student writing was dull because students were fearful of tapping their personal contexts, so prewriting techniques were designed to allow them to do just that. As a result, prewriting diverges in some important ways from other heuristic techniques: not only can it be used to generate material, but it prompts students to respond personally to that material as well.

Rohman tested his theories and techniques in a sophomore-level writing course and found that prewriting classes produced writing that "showed a statistically significant superiority to essays produced in control sections" (112). It is an open question, though, whether techniques of self-actualization and process-thought that worked for elective sophomore classes in the 1960s can work for required freshman classes in the 1980s and 1990s. Prewriting assumes an interest in written self-expression on the part of the students that is often hard to find in freshman composition classes, but its techniques have much of value to offer a teacher willing to experiment with them. Our task as writing teachers is to encourage that middle ground between self-indulgent personalizing and an unimaginative commitment to rules and product.

Classroom Use of Prewriting Techniques

Let's look critically for a moment at the philosophical position prewriting theories occupy in order to understand the nature and tendencies of their classroom-based techniques. Prewriting theorists take an existential approach to composition. They seek an image of an individual within the problem-solving process. This focus on the existential self as an important part of the writing act leads to emphases on the process of thought and on personal writing. These emphases are useful: They point out the sterility of any rules-based system that concentrates only on the product of writing and that ignores the composing process so vital to the writer. However, prewriting concentrates on personal writing to such a degree that it often ignores the needs of the audience. Prewriting can easily be used to produce informal essays, but it must be adapted to the assigned, subject-based discourse demanded by college and the professions.

Because of its emphasis on personal experience, prewriting runs the risk of shortchanging the subject context. Composition teachers today must turn out students who can both write on assigned subjects and engage personally with a topic. As Dixie Goswami and Lee Odell's study shows, actual writing in the professional world is, indeed, done in response to assignments rather than out of free choice. Nevertheless, prewriting techniques can be adapted in many ways and can be extremely helpful in teaching invention.

The Journal Over the last twenty years, journal writing has become an intrinsic part of many English classes. Teachers and students genuinely *like* using journals as a repository of material and concepts that can lead into more formal essays; journal-writing does not impose systematic techniques of invention, and thus can have a salutary effect on students' feelings about writing.

For students to get the most from journal-writing, however, it is necessary to introduce them to the "art" of keeping a journal. First, acquaint your students with a definition of a journal: it is a record of reactions, not of actions. If you fail to be specific about this, students may end up writing diary entries—"Got up at 7:30, went to Commons for breakfast, saw Diane." A journal is not a diary, nor a record of events. Students need to be shown, and then convinced, that a journal is a record of a mind and its thoughts rather than of a body and its movements. One good way of demonstrating this is by the use of excerpts from the journals of established writers like Thoreau, Pepys, Woolf, Hawthorne, and Nin, or from student writing submitted-for-show in previous classes. Compared to journal-keeping, keeping a diary will soon seem a lame activity to most of your students.

Along with familiarizing students with good examples of journal-writing, you may want to provide them with a list like that shown in Example 5–1. Provide just enough prompts that students will occasionally have to grope for a sense of their own will to write something; too many questions and suggestions can be a crutch. Encourage your students to move beyond each prompt to more self-directing writing.

One journal-writing problem for first-year students can be their tendency to rely on ready-made opinions, pre-manufactured wisdom, cliché concepts. Because some students have not yet begun to question their parents' norms, they will repeat the most appalling prejudices as if they had invented them. A ready-made challenge to such secondhand thought is the requirement that students be as concrete in their actual entries as possible. Discourage generalizing and "opinionizing" unless the opinion can be tied to some actual experience in their lives. (This is, after all, just good argumentation—no assertions without concrete support.)

The question of whether to grade or evaluate journals is simple to answer: Don't. Instead, count the number of pages students turn in;

Example 5–1

Ideas for Journal Entries

Any idea you wish to grapple with is suitable, whether it's from a text you're reading or from a conversation you've had with friends or with yourself. If you're stuck for something to write about, try one of these suggestions:

1. Does the way you dress affect your mood?
2. Children often suffer injustice at the hands of adults.
3. What's a hero?
4. What's a heroine?
5. How does your life differ from that of your parents or of your siblings?
6. What Americans do you admire? Explain.
7. What Americans don't you admire? Explain.
8. Are you interested in American politics? Why or why not?
9. Do you know anything about the concerns of nations other than America? Do those concerns interest you? Why or why not?
10. What judgments do we make about people based on the appearance of something they own (cars, clothes, pets, houses)?
11. Why do you think it's often said that you spend your second year in college getting rid of the friends you made your first year?
12. What courses would you never take while in college?
13. Many students are smarter than their grades indicate.
14. Whom do you dislike? Why? Is it jealousy, resentment, hurt, outrage, or disapproval?
15. What's the most interesting thing in your hometown?
16. How do you go about writing a paper? Do you watch television? Stand on your head? Cry? Spend an hour looking for your favorite pen? Describe everything you do and how you feel during the writing process.

---

four pages a week for ten weeks might earn an A; thirty-five total, a B, and so on. Students are expected to write sincerely, presumably for themselves, yet they know that the instructor will see everything in the journal (everything, that is, except those parts labeled "Please Don't Read"). While some teachers put no marks of any kind in journals except for a date after the last entry, others start a written conversation with the students, while still others write on sheets of paper they insert into the journal. At times you will find an entry directed to you—an invitation to reply.

Journals, then, shouldn't be judged by the standards you might bring to a student essay. However, the fact that student journals do have an audience—namely the teacher—means that they "do not speak privately," as Ken Macrorie puts it (130). Macrorie insists that journals:

> Can be read with profit by other persons than the writer. They may be personal or even intimate, but if the writer wants an entry to be seen by others, it will be such that they can understand, enjoy, be moved by. (131)

In *Telling Writing*, Macrorie suggests that students write journal entries on the same topic over a period of time, from "different and developing viewpoints" (137). Such writing opportunities give students the distance they need to reflect upon, deepen, and enrich their perceptions, which will make their stories more moving and effective. But most importantly, Macrorie tells us, journals are the best starting place and the best storehouse for ideas: "A journal is a place for confusion and certainty, for the half-formed and the completed" (141).

Peter Elbow, too, would have students keep a journal, what he calls a "freewriting diary." He warns that it is "*not* a complete account of your day; just a brief mind sample from each day" (*Teachers* 9). Like Macrorie, Elbow sees the "freewriting diary" as the motherlode of ideas for essays. Elbow writes that "freewriting helps you to think of topics to write about. Just keep writing," he tells his readers, "follow threads where they lead and you will get the ideas, experiences, feelings, or people that are just asking to be written about" (*Power* 15).

Most students enjoy keeping and learning from a journal and continue writing in journals after the course is over. You, too, should join your students in their journal-keeping practice by recording your own classroom experiences your responses to your students' journals and essays. Nancy Comley, director of freshman writing at Queens College (CUNY), encourages her teaching assistants to keep their own journals. Comley writes that:

> [t]hrough the journal one comes to know oneself better as a teacher, and in the discipline of keeping a journal the teacher can experience what students experience when they are told to write and do not really feel like it. As part of the journal, I suggest that each teacher keep a folder of the progress (or lack of it) of two of his or her students, noting the students' interaction with the class

and the teacher as well as evaluating their written work. Such data can form the basis for a seminar paper presenting these case histories, augmenting journal observations with student conferences and with research done into special problems or strengths the students had as writers (55–56).

That teachers and students alike should keep journals underpins Comley's sage pedagogical advice: Never give an assignment you have not tried yourself.

Brainstorming Brainstorming is the method used by most professional and academic writers. It is not in the canon of official prewriting techniques (if there is one), but it fits most naturally in this area of invention theory.

The technique of brainstorming is simple. The brainstormer decides on a subject, sits down in a quiet place with pen and paper, and writes down everything that comes to mind about the subject. Alex Osborne codified the main rules of brainstorming in the late 1950s:

1. Don't criticize or evaluate any ideas during the session. Simply write down every idea that emerges. Save the criticism and evaluation until later.
2. Use your imagination for "free wheeling." The wilder the idea the better, because it might lead to some valuable insights later.
3. Strive for quantity. The more ideas, the better chance for a winner to emerge.
4. Combine and improve ideas as you proceed (84).

The brainstormer writes down ideas until the motherlode is exhausted. (Invariably, the lode is not really mined out, and new aspects, arguments, or ideas pop up throughout the writing.)

At this point, the writer either tries to structure the list in some way—by recopying it in a different order, or by numbering the items, crossing some out, adding to others—or finds the list suggestive enough as it stands and begins to work.

Brainstorming is extremely simple—and effective. The most widely used inventive technique, brainstorming moves in naturally to fill the void if no structured method is ever taught. Research suggests that if an inventive system is not internalized by around age 20, brainstorming is adopted, probably because it represents the natural way the mind grapples with information storage and retrieval. Most professional and academic writers were never taught systematic invention and therefore turned to brainstorming.

Sometimes, young, self-conscious writers who have little specialized education experience are initially stymied by brainstorming, for their stores of knowledge and general intellectual resources aren't as developed as those of experienced writers. Hence, they can go dry when confronted with the task of listing ideas about an abstract topic. You may want to walk them through the brainstorming system by doing a sample exercise on the board before you turn them loose with their own ideas.

Mapping or Clustering In *Writing the Natural Way*, Gabriele Lusser Rico offers *clustering*, a prewriting technique similar to *mapping* (developed by Tony Buzan). Based on theories of the brain's hemispheric specialization, Rico's creative-search process taps the right hemisphere of the brain, the hemisphere sensitive "to wholeness, image, and the unforced rhythms of language" (12). Usually, Rico tells us, beginning writers rely solely on the left hemisphere, the hemisphere of reason, linearity, logic. By clustering, they can learn to tap the other hemisphere as well and produce writings that demonstrate:

> a coherence, unity, and sense of wholeness; a recurrence of words and phrases, ideas, or images that [reflect] a pattern sensitivity; an awareness of the nuances of language rhythms; a significant and natural use of images and metaphors; and a powerful "creative tension." Another by-product of clustering seem[s] to be a significant drop in errors of punctuation, awkward phrasing, even spelling. (11)

Clustering is an easy-to-use prewriting activity because there is no right or wrong way to cluster. And Rico guarantees that the words will come and that writing eventually takes over and writes itself. You may want to try clustering with your students, ending up with a cluster like the one in Example 5–2 using "risk" as its nucleus, as its storm center of meaning. The following are Rico's simple directions:

1. Write the word AFRAID in the upper third of the page, leaving the lower two-thirds of the page for writing, and circle it. We'll start with this word because even the most hesitant of us will discover many associations triggered by it.
2. Now get comfortable with the process of clustering by letting your playful, creative . . . mind make connections. Keep the childlike attitude of newness and wonder and spill whatever associations come to you onto paper. What comes to mind when you think of the word? Avoid judging or choosing. Simply let go and write. Let the words or phrases radiate outward from the nucleus word, and draw a circle around each of

them. Connect those associations that seem related with lines. Add arrows to indicate direction, if you wish, but don't think too long or analyze. There is an "unthinking" quality to this process that suspends time.

3. Continue jotting down associations and ideas triggered by the word "afraid" for a minute or two, immersing yourself in the process. Since there is no *one* way to let the cluster spill onto the page, let yourself be guided by the patterning . . . [abilities of your] mind, connecting each association as you see fit without worrying about it. Let clustering happen naturally. It will, if you don't inhibit it with objections from your censoring . . . mind. If you reach a plateau where nothing spills out, "doodle" a bit by putting arrows on your existing cluster.

4. You will know when to stop clustering through a sudden, strong urge to write, usually after one or two minutes, when you feel a shift that says "Aha! I think I know what I want to say." If it doesn't happen suddenly, this awareness of a direction will creep up on you more gradually, as though someone were slowly unveiling a sculpture. . . . [J]ust know you will experience a mental shift characterized by the certain, satisfying feeling that you have something to write about.

5. You're ready to write. Scan [your] clustered perceptions and insights. . . . Something therein will suggest your first sentence to you, and you're off. Students rarely, if ever, report difficulty writing that first sentence; on the contrary, they report it as being effortless. Should you feel stuck, however, write about anything from the cluster to get you started. The next thing and the next thing after that will come because your [right hemisphere] has already perceived a pattern of meaning. Trust it. (36–37)

Even if prewriting seems idealistic or naive to you, the techniques can be used fruitfully to help students find something to say. And perhaps if we can imitate the attitudes of Rohman and his disciples, the originators of prewriting, we might see a type of student whose goal is to be self-actualizing, who feels that her creativity is repressed by convention, who is waiting for us to free her to explore her own humanity through writing.

Tagmemic Invention

For years, composition scholars hoped that the sophisticated, complex work in linguistics would yield a new approach to the teaching

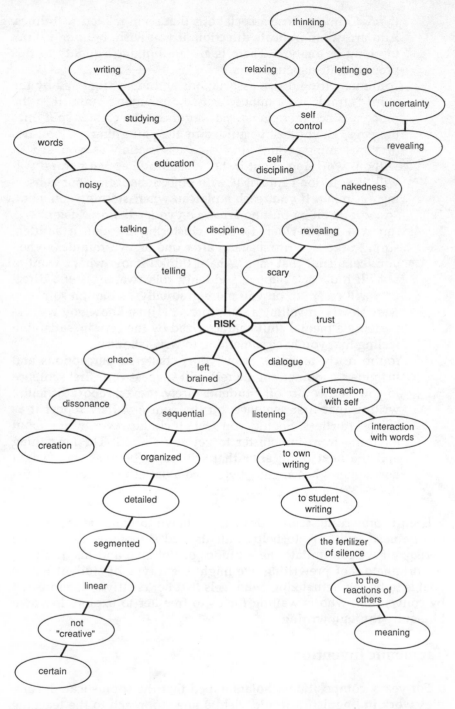

Example 5–2

of writing. But the fields had little successful crossover until Kenneth L. Pike, University of Michigan, began applying terms from his theory of *tagmemic linguistics* to composition.

The ultimate goal of contemporary linguistic theory is essentially explanatory, not prescriptive. Noam Chomsky's transformational-generative (TG) theory of language, for example, is not "practical" or pedagogically oriented. But Pike's theory of tagmemic linguistics is not a general language theory like TG grammar. Pike's theory is a "field theory," developed for use when linguists were translating the Bible into languages that were until then unknown to translation. Tagmemics developed as a theory of discovery, then, as a "slot theory" that aided translators in understanding the *use*—not the nature—of any unknown language.

According to Pike, "a repeatable, relevant pattern of purposive activity is made up of a sequence of functional classes-in-slots. . . . this combination of slot-plus-class is called a tagmeme" (85). The essential nature of the *tagmeme* established it as the basic tool for translating unknown languages.

The "slots" that Pike mentions can be filled in by alternative units within "classes." A simple example in linguistic terms would be the sentence:

Mary *hit* Bill.

The slot between the subject, "Mary," and the object, "Bill," is filled by a class. In this case, the class is composed of verbs of a certain kind. Replace the word "hit" with another word in the class—say, "kissed"—and the slot is filled:

Mary *kissed* Bill.

At the same time, the slot after the verb-slot—the object of the sentence—is also fillable by a class, this time by nouns or pronouns:

Mary hit the *ball.*
Mary hit *him.*

The slot plus the class of alternative files is what Pike calls a tagmeme, and the tagmeme is the basis of his discovery-oriented theory of language. Tagmemics is a method of finding things out, of conceptualizing reality, and it is this method of conceptualization, rather than the tagmeme as an all-purpose tool, that Pike has brought to composition.

Tagmemic invention treats knowledge in terms of repeatable *units* and is concerned with the precise definition of these units. Sloppy rhetoric, according to Pike, is the result of sloppy methods of thought and inquiry; careful phrasing and definition are part of the answer. In *Rhetoric: Discovery and Change*, Young, Becker, and Pike argue that communication is a response to perceived misunderstanding or division. The authors articulate six maxims for resolving such misunderstandings that can help writers understand their own interpretations of the world, develop them, and present them to others. First of all, "people conceive of the world in terms of repeatable units" (26), and those units are part of a larger system, for "units of experience are hierarchically structured systems" (29). At any level of focus, a unit "can be adequately understood only if three aspects of the unit are known: (1) its contrastive features, (2) its range of variation, and (3) its distribution in larger contexts" (56); hence a unit of experience can be viewed "as particle, or as a wave, or as a field" (122). And "change between units can occur only over a bridge of shared features, the prerequisites for interaction and change" (172). Finally, however, all communication boils down to linguistic choices which are made in "relation to a universe of discourse" (301), either consciously or unconsciously, a universe that constrains our linguistic choices. These maxims contain nearly all of the aspects of that elegant inquiry machine, "the tagmemic heuristic," the final product of tagmemic theory.

Tagmemic Aspects of Definition

As Bruce Edwards, Jr., suggests, tagmemicists believe that "the composing *process* should be the focus of composition teaching and that, indeed, it is something which to some degree *can* be taught." Invention for tagmemicists is "essentially a problem-solving activity." If one can make this activity sharable, then one can "isolate and identify its features," and if this process is learned empirically, "then it may form the basis for a new rhetorical procedure which can be taught to the student (15). Tagmemic invention sees problem-solving as beginning with the careful definition of units, a good place to begin.

Contrastive Features   The first mode of inquiry, an investigation of the *contrastive features* of a subject, starts by asking: What features does a unit have that make it different from other similar things? This is the simplest tagmemic mode to apply. Using the Battle of Gettysburg, we might ask these questions: What features does the Battle of Gettysburg have that make it different from other Civil War battles? Of what sort are they? Do they form a pattern? By identifying contrastive features, this mode brings out the most important definitive features of a subject, those elements that create its unique identity.

Range of Variation The second mode of inquiry concerns the subject's possible *range of variations*; it asks how the subject can be variously defined and still remain itself. This mode works best for concrete physical items and for absolute abstracts. The classic examples used in the literature are "divan" and "democracy," both of which have an obvious range of variations (Can a love seat still be a divan? Can a divan have no arms? Can democracy exist without press freedom? Can democracy have a hereditary leader? etc.). It can, though, be applied to any subject.

About the Monroe Doctrine, for example, we might ask: Was all of Monroe's foreign policy part of the Doctrine? Or was it a single statement only? Was it a tradition of policy that Monroe codified, or was it a proclamation in a class by itself? Was Teddy Roosevelt's foreign policy the Monroe Doctrine in action? Was John Kennedy's?

The range-or-variations inquiry can be extremely flexible and useful in the hands of an imaginative questioner, but is often less fruitful than it might be. The key idea for this mode of inquiry is the idea of *change over time while maintaining identity*—like the changes over time each of us makes as we age. It is all very well to invent questions about physical variations of a divan or abstract variations of democracy, but in the uproar of real subject inquiry most important variations are chronological. Is the Monroe Doctrine of Andrew Jackson's time the same policy as that behind the Bay of Pigs invasion? Chronological variations can be real in a way that physical or abstract questions are not.

Distribution in Larger Contexts The last mode of inquiry in Pike's original system is made up of questions about the subject's *distribution* within larger systems. This mode is very directly related to the definition of tagmeme as slot-plus-class; it asks: What place or slot does the unit occupy in a larger pattern? This mode is extremely useful for nearly all subjects because it can locate them in physical patterns, chronological patterns, historical or abstract patterns—in nearly any context.

To run another of our old subjects, deficit spending, through this mode is possible in a number of different ways. What part in current fiscal policy does deficit spending play? When was deficit spending initiated and why? What relation does deficit spending have to stock prices? Is deficit spending a valid government practice historically? How is deficit spending related to the balance of trade? What is the role of deficit spending in inflation? The list is almost endless.

The whole range of questions implied by these three modes is an inventive method in itself, one which can produce a wide range of subject matter. Questions from each mode can be rephrased in several different ways in order to get the most out of that mode, and in using all of the modes a writer can generate a great deal of material. Useful though this method is, however, tagmemic theory has gone farther.

Further Development of Tagmemic Theory

Pike's rhetorical work first appeared in the mid-1960s and continued to be developed through the rest of that decade. Particularly valuable contributions were made by Pike's colleagues at the University of Michigan, Alton L. Becker, Richard E. Young, and Hubert M. English, Jr., who was largely responsible for the first testing of the "three-aspect" method discussed above. The theory was refined and finally, in 1970, Young, Becker, and Pike produced their textbook *Rhetoric: Discovery and Change*, which codified the work done on tagmemic invention in a form that they hoped composition teachers could use.

Rhetoric: Discovery and Change was widely reviewed, with most reviewers agreeing that the tagmemic approach to invention was both novel and important as well. To many reviewers, however, the style of Young, Becker, and Pike's text seemed too difficult for freshmen, and the methods used to relate information appeared too complex to be grasped by any but the most intelligent students. As a result, *Rhetoric: Discovery and Change* has become known as a "teachers' book," and is not often assigned to classes; another result, unfortunately, is that tagmemic invention is not as well known as it should be.

In their text, Young, Becker, and Pike took the invention technique as it had been used by earlier experimenters—the "three-aspect" method investigated by English—and joined it to Pike's *trimodal perspective* of *particle, wave, and field* (originally called *feature, manifestation, and distribution modes* in Pike's linguistics until he noticed their similarity to physicists' theories about light form and analogized them as particle, wave, and field).

Young, Becker, and Pike made it clear throughout their discussion of these perspectives that they are *not* mutually exclusive. Any unit of experience can be discussed as a particle or wave or field, but they warn that "a unit is not *either* a particle *or* a wave *or* a field, but can rather be viewed as all these (*Rhetoric* 122). The particle perspective views units as essentially static, the wave perspective as essentially dynamic, and the field perspective as essentially a network of relationships or part of a larger network.

Particle Perspective Particle perspective has the following features:

1. It deals with the unit's static nature, ignoring changes in time.
2. It selects from a dynamic whole one "bit," usually the central bit, for presentation (the "snapshot" effect).
3. It arbitrarily specifies boundaries.
4. It isolates the unit from its surroundings.

The particle perspective on the Battle of Gettysburg would deal with the battle in suspension, as having begun at a certain time and place, ended at a certain time and place, containing features, A, B, C, D, etc. It would choose a single perspective on the battle and might present a single historical description of it. Particle perspective sees the subject as immovable, alone, and unrelated to physical or chronological continuums.

Wave Perspective The wave perspective has different features:

1. It recognizes some dynamic function of the unit, noting spatial, chronological, or conceptual movement or flow.
2. It points out the central component of the unit.
3. It emphasizes the fusion, flow, or lack of distinct boundaries between the unit and other units.

The wave perspective on the Battle of Gettysburg would deal with the different sorts of movement that it incorporated. It might discuss the battle as the central component of the troop movements and command decisions of the days preceding or following it, or it might look at the changing attitudes of the soldiers on both sides as the tide of battle changes. It might follow the movements of troops throughout the battle or might focus on Pickett's Charge and on what that troop movement meant to the outcome of the battle. Wave perspective emphasizes change and flow.

Field Perspective A unit viewed from the field perspective has two characteristics:

1. It is seen not as isolated but as occupying a place in a system of some kind.
2. It is seen as a system itself, composed of subsystems.

Field perspective of our battle could deal with it in a number of ways. It could view the Battle of Gettysburg as part of the Civil War and deal with its meaning to the War, or as part of Lee's Pennsylvania campaign and its place in that. It could be placed in the system of battle types or tactics and viewed as part of the continuing evolution of warfare. It could be seen as the reason for the downfall of Longstreet in the system of his military career.

If we view the battle as a system in itself, its subsystems could be detailed in different ways: A perspective could follow the Union artillery through the battle, or trace the movements of the Confederate cavalry under Stuart. It could follow the fortunes of one regiment or company within the battle, or could focus on one specific engagement within the larger battle, like the defense of Cemetery Ridge. The field perspective is concerned mainly with relationships between whole and parts.

Like the three tagmemic aspects, this trimodal perspective can be used alone as an invention heuristic. The best current use of it is in the textbook *Four Worlds of Writing*, 2nd. ed., by Janice M. Lauer *et al.* This text simplifies the perspectives for use by freshmen, calling particle perspective *static view,* wave perspective *dynamic view* and field perspective *relative view* (31ff).

Classroom Use of Tagmemic Invention

There have been several important classroom tests of tagmemic invention, notably those of Hubert English, Richard Young, and Frank Koen, and Lee Odell. Nearly unanimously these tests have reported mixed results.[2] Composition teachers have also voiced serious criticisms of tagmemics. James Kinney, for instance, accused tagmemicists of inflated claims, blasted tagmemics in general as being based on an outmoded linguistic theory, and contended that the heuristic was not really much different from the classical topics or other inventive procedures (141–43). How should teachers respond to such criticisms? Should we be discouraged from attempting to use tagmemic invention as a pedagogical tool?

No. As Lee Odell points out in his response to Kinney, systematic inquiry as represented by the tagmemic heuristic is important for our students. As long as there exists an "apparent gap between systematic inquiry and the art of writing," says Odell, our students will be able to use heuristics ("Another" 148). And contemporary rhetoricians have paid attention to criticisms of tagmemics, and worked to make the tagmemic heuristic more helpful in the classroom. A notable example of the revised tagmemic heuristic comes from Charles Kneupper, shown in Example 5–3.

Whether you choose to use Kneupper's system or the original tagmemic heuristic, take note of some items concerning this highly struc-

---

2   See English 136–40; Odell, "Measuring" 235–37; Young and Koen.

tured system. First, students using tagmemic invention sometimes become absorbed in the elegance and sophistication of the system itself, sacrificing ends to means, and concentrate on merely reeling off the information the system provides without any attempt to arrange it in a coherent essay. This fascination with means is to some degree a problem with any heuristic system, but tagmemics invites it particularly because the tagmemic system is complex and novel—and fun. Students who learn to manipulate it can be so exhilarated by the informational possibilities tagmemics gives them that they are loath to come back down to the linearity of arrangement. In your first explanation of the tagmemic system, you will want to stress that the invented material must ultimately be arranged coherently, that a mere pile-up or listing of material does not guarantee successful arrangement.

To offset potential problems, some teachers stress the creation of a thesis *before* the system is tapped for subject matter. Try doing this by asking students to create the list of questions first, using either the modes, the perspectives, or a heuristic. When the questions have been generated, ask them to choose several of the questions, the ones they feel most drawn to, and answer them in one-sentence statements. Then ask them to choose their favorite statement; this statement becomes a possible working thesis for the essay on the given subject, and the students then use the other generated questions to provide supporting information for the thesis.

Second, the method seems to work best when the teacher initially presents students with subjects and problems to run through the heuristic; otherwise, the students may choose "easy ones" to run, problems about which they already knew a good deal. More importantly, the heuristic needs to be used again and again, applied to many different kinds of subjects until its use becomes almost unconscious. Once the use of the heuristic is established and the students are familiar with what it can and cannot do, they can apply it to their own problems. Repetition and a movement from assigned to self-created subjects are the keys to successfully teaching all inventive heuristics, and are particularly necessary for students learning to use tagmemic invention.[3]

The actual classroom use of the tagmemic system proceeds in a manner similar to that advocated for the other invention systems in this chapter. The teacher must first familiarize students with the terms and structure of the technique, usually through the use of handouts and work on the blackboard, and then the students must be

3   See Young and Koen.

Example 5–3

THE REVISED TAGMEMIC HEURISTIC

Unit in Contrast	*Unit as a System*	*Unit in a System*

STATIC

Unit in Contrast	*Unit as a System*	*Unit in a System*
View the unit wholistically as an undifferentiated, isolated entity.	View the unit as composed of separable component parts.	View the unit as part in a larger system.
What feature(s) serve to differentiate the unit from other similar things?	What are the components of the unit?	What are the other components in the larger system?
	How are the components organized in relation to each other?	How are these components organized - in relation to each other?
	What is the structure of the system?	What is the structure of the system?
(1)	(3)	(7,9)

* *

DYNAMIC

Unit in Contrast	*Unit as a System*	*Unit in a System*
View the unit as a dynamic process, object, or event.	View the unit as composed of dynamic separable component parts.	View the unit as dynamic part of a larger dynamic system.
What process of change occurred to create the unit?	How were the parts formed?	How was the larger system created?
How is it changing currently?	What will happen to each in the future?	How is it currently changing?
What will happen to it in the future?	Do different parts change at different rates?	What will happen to it in the future?
What feature(s) serve to differentiate the unit from similar processes, objects, or events?	What does change in a particular part do to the overall system?	How does change in the larger system affect the unit?
	How is the structure of the system changing?	How does change in the unit affect the larger system?
		How is the structure changing?
(2,5)	(4,6)	(8) [165]

asked to manipulate the technique, at first in discrete pieces, and later as a whole. Handouts with examples of the original three-element method and handouts with the entire heuristic work well, but only when you take the time to explain thoroughly how the examples were derived. More than most techniques, tagmemic takes time and repetition in order to allow students to grasp its use. Do not become discouraged when your students still have trouble with the heuristic after a week's work on it. If you keep on with it, eventually the dawn will break.

The subjects that you assign for practice with the tagmemic system should be carefully chosen. You might begin with relatively simply physical items; "your room" works well, as do "the pen" or "the divan." Slowly work up through general abstracts—like The South or socialism, to what might be called "specific abstracts," like the Battle of Gettysburg and unit-pricing laws, that make up so much of the world of writing assignments. Throughout this practice, you can ask for lists of questions or lists of answers to questions, and at any point a list of answers can be developed into the germ of a regular class essay. If you contrive to concentrate in class on the use of the system each class day, both orally and in writing, it will begin to become an automatic response after about three weeks. Eventually you should be able to ask "Variation?" and hear from the back of the room, "Is prostitution a victimless crime?" or another question of the sort. Intuition of the system will come, but only given enough time and work.

Example 5–4 is one student's rendition of "your room." First, the student took her subject, which she changed to "my office," through the tagmemic grid of questioning. Then, after reading over her piled-up information, she organized it into a coherent, sustained piece of discourse.

After the student read through her information, she thought about what information would best lend itself to an accurate description of her office. Her draft is shown in Example 5–5.

Example 5–4

My Office

P A R T I C L E

STATIC   1

My office is pretty big, yet cozy—a hideabed, two walls of windows with bookshelves underneath. It's different from the other rooms because this is the messiest room in the house—papers and books piled high, postanotes stuck to the bookshelves. The shelves are especially nice because my husband built them. He thinks they're rough; I think they're perfect. When I finished them, "to polyurethane" became a verb. It's different from my school office because it's not cold; I can wear T-shirt and shorts. My daughter often sits down on the sofa and reads while I study at my desk. I can see out (not like my windowless office at school) the beautiful Scott's Seed Company lawn across the street.

4

Home offices are pretty much the same, except that someone actually *works* in this home office. They seem to be a yuppie-1980s concept, with a wet bar & built-in TV cabinet. But my office is a place to work. That's why we call it an office. It's still an office if we're all in there talking, yet it would not be an office if we watched TV or had lots of fun in there. It's a working office. It's hard for me to get things done in my school office. Lots of students might like to have an office like mine, a quiet place to work, a place to leave a mess.

7

The office is part of our downstairs, part of our house. It's at the front of the house. When we walk in the front door, we turn left immediately to get to the office. It's easy for ESL students to come here and study. In fact, they always like to come here. Its conceptual context is a place to work, much like our functional kitchen, which is two rooms away. Our living room and dining room are places to socialize, I guess. The dining room is directly opposite the office, also at the front of the house on the other side of the living room.

Example 5– (continued

W
A
V
E

DYNAMIC 2

The dynamism of
this office is the
work that is ac-
complished here.
The energy field
must be tremendous.
Latin verbs are
learned, thirty
hours a week of
Latin homework and
studying are done
here. Statements of
(mis)understanding,
journals, freewrit-
ing are all done at
my desk. I'm not al-
ways sure what's
happening at the
other energy
fields: Sometimes,
Anna sits on the
sofa and does her
too-heavy load of
homework; some-
times, Dave sits at
his desk and
polishes up reports
or works on that
endless mess of
stuff called income
taxes. Late at
night, after I've
spent a long time
at my desk, I sit
on the couch and
reread Shakespeare
plays. The room is
electric with work
being done, reading
being devoured, mas-
ticated, and spat
out on paper. I am
a literary bulimic.

5

The office is chang-
ing in that Anna is
working less in
here. Although some-
times I used to
think that she con-
taminated my per-
sonal space, I
never said anything
to her. Now, I miss
her. It's also
changing in that my
work schedule seems
cyclical: I build
up steam for each
paper, & the room
attracts more
materials. After
I've handed in a
paper, I tidy up
and wipe off the
bookcase tops. Then
my office looks
just like any other
suburban office.
But it continues
to evolve into an
even more alive
place—books and
papers breed on the
shelves and in the
drawers. The
telephone is often
shut off when the
computer is turned
on. I wonder how
what used to be a
tidy study will
look like after
years of being a
work place.

8

The borders between
the living room and
the bathroom are
clear cut, when the
doors are closed.
But when they're
not, the same car-
pet rolls from the
study to the living
room to the dining
room & seeps into
the den/TV room,
and the room draws
people in. The
kitchen and the
bath both have
beige flooring, so
the downstairs is
one big ocean of
being—maybe it's
more like the Gobi
Desert. But when
the doors are shut
and the phone is
"off," the lines of
demarcation are
clear. Don't bother
to bother me; I'm
busy.

Example 5–4 (continued)

MULTI-DIMENSIONAL
SYSTEM   3

F
I
E
L
D

The parts of this office are the books and paper, the desks, the lights, the computer, and the telephone. From the books and papers, I get information that I need to deal with. At the desk, I deal with the information: I memorize, I analyze, I try to understand. The lights, of course, make my studying possible. At the computer, I transmit my ideas into legibility. Over the phone, I reach out for more information, keen insights, for solace. The books litter the space, as the fragments of information litter my brain. People invariably ask, "Have you read all those books?" Well, when you live 40 minutes from school, you need a library. You need research materials. You need resources. The dimension obviously lacking in my office is TIME. I need some time to think, to gain intellectual calories. Right now, I seem to be burning them off too fast.

6

Sometimes, the computer bombinates way into the night, stops for a bit of rest, then resumes its hum at the early hours of the morning. The lights, in winter, come on as early as 5 P.M.; now, they're not lit until 8 or so. The neighbors often comment that they see me sitting at my desk late at night or that when they arise in the morning—just to dash to the bathroom—they see the light in the office. Often, they ask me what I'm going to do with all my education. I tell 'em, "I'm going to take it with me." After sitting at the desk for hours, my butt gets tired. I think of and try to do some work I can do while sitting on the couch. In the winter, I always sink down in the afghan Granny made. She made us an afghan for every room!

9

The office fits into a larger system—that of my life as a student & as a teacher. I suppose everyone manages to adapt to his/her environment. I know I need a place to spread out. I need surfaces to pile high with my organized "stacks." But, most of all, I need to be alone to help balance out the craziness of the rest of my life—the daily commutes, the parking, the dashing between the English department and the Latin Center, the stress of weekly Latin exams and weekly papers, of childcare. The stress and noise of life are assuaged by the undervalued-by-most-people solitude of life in my office.

Example 5-5

My Office

The Yuppyish, 1980s concept of home office, complete with wet bar and built-in stereo, seems to deem all home offices as of one type; but our home office is different—it's alive. It's the work accomplished in here that electrifies the room with an energy field that must be tremendous. Latin verbs are conjugated and memorized in here; thirty precious hours per week are sacrificed on the altar, which does double-duty as my desk, to the Roman god of grades—good ones. Statements of understanding, freewriting, journals come to fruition at my desk. I'm not always sure of the magnetic fields elsewhere in the room: occasionally, Anna works in here, scaling her mountain of homework; once in a while, Dave polishes up reports and works on that endless mess of stuff called income taxes, the symptom of capitalism (Marx's Revenge?). After sitting at my desk for hours, my rear gets tired. Each night, I try to set aside some work to do while I sink into the couch in here, swathed in one of my Granny's afghans. Tonight, I'll slouch down and reread Shakespeare plays, preparation for this weekend's trip to Stratford (Ontario). This place lives off spent energy from work being done, reading being devoured, hardly masticated, and then spat out on paper. I am an academic bulimic.

The pieces of this office are more interesting than all the pieces together, like the expected disappointment when the last piece is put in the jigsaw puzzle. As a whole, it's a sunny, book-lined, littered sort of office, which fills my needs for a place to spread out, for surfaces to pile high with my organized "stacks." As I build up steam for each paper, for each exam, the room's magnetic field sucks in more and more materials—like a Black Hole. The gobs and globs of information vanish into the darkness the day after I've handed in a paper. I tidy up and wipe off the tops of the bookcases. It looks like a Yuppie office, for a while.

But this office, as though it has a life of its own, continues to evolve into a more dynamic place: books and papers, in tangled masses, fornicate on the shelves and in the drawers, giving multiple births to ideas. The telephone is often shut off so that the computer can be turned on. But, most of all, the place fills my need for solitude. I need the solitude of my office to counterbalance the stress and noise of the rest of my life—the daily commutes, the parking, the dashing from the English Department to the Latin Center, the stress of weekly Latin exams and of weekly papers for my English courses, childcare, family life. The noisy stress of daily life is assuaged by the solitude and focus of life in my office.

Sometimes, the computer clicks late into the night, stops for a bit of rest, then resumes its hum in the early morning hours. The neighbors tell me that they see me sitting at my desk late at night; and that sometimes, when they stumble to the bathroom in the middle of the night, they see my light. They asked me what I was going to do with all my education. I told them, "I'm going to take it with me."

Tagmemic invention is the Ferrari of inventive techniques: sleek, elegant, fast when well-tuned. And like a Ferrari, it can break down, that is, if the teacher doesn't understand how to keep it going. For that reason, some teachers claim that tagmemics should be reserved for upper-level students, yet others have used it with great success in the first year. Most teachers agree, however, that if taught well, tagmemics can yield more information and information presented more interestingly than any other system. Hence, you will want to master its intricacies, and practice the technique before you start explaining tagmemic invention to your students.

Freewriting

Freewriting, the technique central to this section, has some striking differences from the other techniques discussed in this chapter. Unlike the other heuristic-type techniques, it is not a device through which experience can be consciously processed, but rather a ritual that can be used to bring out possible subjects for writing to which the conscious mind may not have easy access. Freewriting exercises in their pure form do not provide theses, arguments, or subject matter, mined for all these things. What freewriting does best is loosen the inhibitions of inexperienced writers.

Freewriting exercises have been developed by a number of writers over the past fifty years as methods of getting used to the idea of writing. Perhaps the first mention of freewriting-type exercises is in Dorothea Brande's 1934 advice-to-novelists book *Becoming a Writer*, in which she suggested freewriting as a way for young writers to get in touch with their subconscious selves. Brande advocated writing "when the unconscious is in the ascendent":

> The best way to do this is to rise half an hour, or a full hour, earlier than you customarily rise. Just as soon as you can—and without talking, without reading—begin to write. Write anything that comes to your head . . . Write any sort of early morning revery, rapidly and uncritically. The excellence or ultimate worth of what you write is of no importance yet . . . Forget that you have any critical faculty at all. (50–51)

Brande's technique, the ancestor of freewriting, was largely ignored by teachers of expository writing until the 1950s, when Ken Macrorie, who had read *Becoming a Writer*, began to use an updated version of it in his composition classes. He modified Brande's directions for use in general composition and told his students to "Go home and write anything that comes to your mind. Don't stop. Write for ten minutes or till you've filled a full page." This exercise produced writing that was often incoherent, but was also often striking in its transcendence of the dullness and clichéd thought we all too often come to expect in English papers (*Uptaught* 20).

It was Macrorie who popularized the technique of freewriting with his books *Uptaught* and *Telling Writing,* but it was Peter Elbow who developed and refined freewriting, making it a well-known tool. In *Writing Without Teachers*— a book every writing teacher should read for Elbow's opinions on how to teach and learn writing—Elbow presented the most carefully wrought freewriting plan thus far advanced.

Freewriting is a kind of structured brainstorming, a method of exploring a topic by writing about it—or whatever else it brings to mind—for a certain number of minutes *without stopping.* It consists of a series of exercises, conducted either in class or at home, during which the students start with a blank piece of paper, think about their topic, and then simply let their minds wander while they write. For as long as their time limit, they write down everything that occurs to them (in complete sentences as much as possible). They must not stop for anything; if they can't think what to write next, they can write "I can't think of what to write next" over and over until something else occurs to them. Then, they can stop and look at what they've written. Oh, they may find much that is unusable, irrelevant, or nonsensical. But they may also find important insights and ideas that they didn't even know they had—freewriting has a way of jogging loose ideas. As soon as a word or idea appears on paper, it will often trigger others.

The point of freewriting is to concentrate on writing only, leaving no time for worrying about what other people might think of the writing. Because the writers struggle to keep the words—any words—flowing, they're overloading their "academic superego," which usually worries about content, criticism, spelling, grammar, or any of the other formal or content-based "correctnesses" that so easily turn into writing blocks. In other words, they are writing—for five, ten, or fifteen minutes in each class.

Here are Elbow's directions on freewriting:

Don't stop for anything. Go quickly without rushing. Never stop to look back, to cross something out, to wonder how to spell something, to wonder what word or thought to use, to think about what you are doing. If you can't think of a word or a spelling, just use a squiggle or else write, "I can't think of it." Just put down something. The easiest thing is just to put down whatever is in your mind. If you get stuck, it's fine to write, "I can't think what to say" as many times as you want, or repeat the last word you wrote over and over again, or anything else. The only requirement is that you never stop.(Teachers 3)

This requirement that the pen never be lifted off the paper and that the writing continue even if nothing but gibberish is produced differentiates freewriting from brainstorming and other prewriting exercises. Prewriting exercises are meant to tap certain unconscious processes, as is freewriting, but they do not produce the deliberate overload of the editing mechanism that freewriting does.

The requirement that the student never stop writing matched by an equally powerful commandment to the teacher: Never grade or evaluate freewriting exercises in any way. You can collect and read these freewritings—they are often fascinating illustrations of the working of the mind—but they must not be judged. To do so would obviate the purpose of such exercises; these are *free*-writings, not to be held accountable in the same way as other, more structured kinds of writing. The value of freewriting lies in its ability to let students slip the often self-imposed halter of societal expectations and roam without guilt in the pastures of their own minds. If you grade or judge such productions, your message will be that there is no such thing as "free" writing.[4]

Classroom Use of Freewriting

Most teachers who use pure freewriting use it at the opening of each class, every day for at least four or five weeks of the term. A session or two of freewriting, though interesting, are insufficient. For long-term gains, students must freewrite *constantly and regularly*. Only then will the act of writing stop being the unnatural act it seems to some students and start to be just a part of the function arsenal of a writer. Regular freewriting in class has two particularly worthwhile effects, says William Irmscher: "It creates the expectation that writing

---

4   Although freewriting is a powerful technique for releasing younger writers from writing anxiety, its lack of structure is not so useful for teaching directed, assignment-based invention. In response to this problem, Peter Elbow developed a technique of directed freewriting that can be used for invention assignments, the "loop writing process." Loop writing, according to Elbow, offers the beginning writer "the best of both worlds; both control and creativity" (*Power* 59). For a discussion of the thirteen procedures comprised by loop writing, see *Writing with Power*.

classes are places where people come to write, and it makes writing habitual" (*Teaching* 82–83).

Students can also freewrite at home. You can assign freewriting as homework, grading it according to whether it is done. One nice feature of freewriting is that it is grossly quantitative; therefore, students cannot pretend to substitute quality for quantity.

As students become more used to being pushed by a time-constraint, you will find that their freewritings become more coherent—the "superego" learns to work under pressure, although not with the deadly efficiency it once had. At this point, you can intersperse directed writing assignments with freewritings. You may also want to consider phasing out pure freewriting.

Combined with brainstorming, freewriting can be used as an aid to writing longer pieces. But you won't want to try this combination until students are comfortable with both techniques. And this combination is most fruitful for students if done at home, since most class periods are too short. Give the students a subject to write on and then suggest the following new pattern: (1) first brainstorm the subject for ten minutes; (2) write down a list; (3) then set the alarm clock for an hour and sit down and write for the whole hour—don't stop; use nothing but the brainstorm list.

Yes, they will be tired. Yes, they will throw out much of what they've written. But this piece of writing, or maybe the very next one, will be the first draft of an editable paper, a paper you can grade. This technique works best when you give out the subjects a week or so before the assignment, subjects like "The Meaning of the Funny Papers" or "Women's Liberation."

Another possibility is for students to keep a journal composed of nothing but freewriting done at home. This sort of journal is efficient because, once again, it can be evaluated in quantitative terms. The entries will improve over the course of a term in both quality and coherence, often because the entries in a freewriting journal will be more personal than those in a conventional journal.

Pure freewriting does not provide the neatness of heuristic systems nor even the coherent processes of prewriting techniques. What, then, is its use? The answer is bound up with the nature of first-year students and their level of exposure to the writing process. Freewriting, so long as you explain its purpose and make certain that students don't see it as busywork, can do two things for students. First, it can make beginning writers familiar with the physical act of writing. Mina Shaughnessy suggests that it is hard for some teachers to understand exactly how little experience many first-year students have had in writing (14–15). Their penmanship seems immature, and their command of sentence structure suffers because they literally cannot put words on paper with enough continuity to match brain with pen; as a result, their sentences are often incoherent. Freewriting forces them to produce, without the conscious editorial mechanism making things even harder than they are. A full five or six weeks of this directed freewriting and prewriting can make a difference.

Second, freewriting demystifies the writing process. After simply pouring out and writing down in a freewriting exercise, students can no longer view the ability to write as a divine gift denied them. They soon come to realize the difference between writing and editing, a difference crucial to their willingness and ability to write. Freewriting "primes the pump" for more structured writing by demonstrating that no writer can produce a perfectly finished essay on the first try, that the process has many steps, and that the most seemingly un-promising piece of gibberish can yield valuable material.

Modern Topical Questions

Although the heuristics and techniques of the preceding sections are the most widely known and used inventive systems, Richard Larson's system of Modern Topical Questions also offers classroom benefits. The major benefit of Larson's work is its realistic considera-tion of the classroom situation, with the necessary simplifications and difficult variables. In his article "Discovery Through Questioning: A Plan for Teaching Rhetorical Invention," Larson states that students should come to a "thorough knowledge of their experiences, con-cepts, and propositions through a process of systematic questioning—questioning which students engage in mostly by themselves" (126). Larson has created the following seven groups of questions that can be applied to almost any subject.

    I. Topics that Invite Comment
        A. Writing about Single Items (in present existence)
            What are its precise physical characteristics (shape dimensions, composition, etc.)?
            How does it differ from things that resemble it?
            What is its "range of variation" (how much can we change it and still identify it as the thing we started with?)
            Does it call to mind other objects we have observed ear-lier in our lives? Why? In what respects?
            From what points of view can it be examined?
            What sort of structure does it have?

How do the parts of it work together?
How are the parts put together?
How are the parts proportional in relation to each other?
To what structure (class or sequence of items) does it belong?
Who or what produced it in this form? Why?
Who needs it?
Who uses it? For what?
What purposes might it serve?
How can it be evaluated, for these purposes?

B. Writing about Single Completed Events, or Parts of an Ongoing Process (These questions can apply to scenes and pictures, as well as to works of fiction and drama.

Exactly what happened? Tell the precise sequence: Who? What? How? Why? Who did what to whom? Why? What did what to what? How?

What were the circumstances in which the event occurred? What did they contribute to its happening?

How was the event like or unlike similar events?

What were its causes?

What were its consequences?

What does its occurrence imply? What action (if any) is called for?

What was affected (indirectly) by it?

What, if anything, does it reveal or emphasize about some general condition?

To what group or class might it be assigned?

Is it (in general) good or bad? By what standard? How do we arrive at the standard?

How do we know about it? What is the "authority" for our information? How reliable is the authority? How do we know it to be reliable? (or unreliable?)

How might the event have been changed or avoided?

To what other events was it connected? How?

C. Writing about Abstract Concepts (e.g., "religion," "socialism")

To what specific items, groups of items, events or groups of events, does the word or words connect, in your experience or imagination?

What characteristics must an item or event have before the name of the concept can apply to it?

How do the referents of that concept differ from the

things we name with similar concepts (e.g. "democracy" and "socialism")?

How has the term been used by writers whom you have read? How have they implicitly defined it?

Does the word have "persuasive" value? Does the use of it in connection with another concept seem to praise or condemn the other concept? Why or why not?

Are you favorable disposed to all things included in the concept? Why or why not?

D. Writing about Collections of Items (in present existence) These questions are in addition to the questions about single items, which can presumably be asked of each item in the group.

What exactly do the items have in common?

If they have features in common, how do they differ?

How are the items related to each other, if not by common characteristics? What is revealed about them by the possibility of grouping them in this way?

How may the group be divided? What bases for division can be found?

What correlations, if any, may be found among the various possible subgroups? Is anything disclosed by the student of these correlations?

Into what class, if any, can the group as a whole be put?

E. Writing about Groups of Completed Events, including Processes. (These questions also apply to literary works, principally fiction and drama.)

What have the events in common?

If they have features in common, how do they differ?

How are the events related to each other (if they are not part of a chronological sequence)? What is revealed by the possibility of grouping them in this way (these ways)?

What is revealed by the events when taken as a group?

How can the group be divided? On what basis?

What possible correlations can be found among the several subgroups?

Into what class, if any, can the events taken as a group fit?

Does the group belong to any other structures than simply a larger group of similar events? (Is it part of a more inclusive chronological sequence? One more piece of evidence that may point toward a conclusion about history? And so on.)

To what antecedents does the group of events look back? Where can they be found?

What implications, if any, does the group of events have? Does the group point to a need for some sort of action?

II. Topics with "Comments" Already Attached
  A. Writing about Propositions (statements set forth to be proved or disproved)

What must be established for the reader before he will believe it?

Into what sub-propositions, if any, can it be broken down? (What smaller assertions does it contain?)

What are the meanings of key words in it?

To what line of reasoning is it apparently a conclusion?

How can we contrast it with other, similar, propositions? (How can we change it, if at all, and still have roughly the same proposition?)

To what class (or classes) of propositions does it belong?

How inclusive (or how limited) is it?

What is at issue, if one tries to prove the proposition?

How can it be illustrated?

How can it be proven (by what kinds of evidence)?

What will or can be said in opposition to it?

Is it true or false? How do we know? (direct observation, authority, deduction, statistics, other sources)

Why might someone disbelieve it?

What does it assume? (What other propositions does it take for granted?)

What does it imply? (What follows from it?) Does it follow from the proposition that action must be taken?

What does it reveal (signify, if true)?

If it is a prediction, how probable is it? On what observations of past experience is it based?

If it is a call to action, what are the possibilities that action can be taken? (Is what is called for feasible?) What are the probabilities that the action, if taken, will do what it is supposed to do? (Will the action call for work?)

  B. Writing About Questions (interrogative sentences)

Does the question refer to past, present, or future items?

What does the question assume (take for granted)?
In what data might answers be sought?
Why does the question arise?
What, fundamentally, is in doubt? How can it be tested?
  evaluated?
What propositions might be advanced in answer to it? Is
  each proposition true? If it is true:
What will happen in the future? What follows from it?
Which of these predictions are possible? probable?
What action should be taken (avoided) in consequence?
  (Most of the other questions listed under "Proposi-
  tions" also apply) (130–34)

Classroom Use of Modern Topical Questions

Using this system is very straightforward. Given a subject, students choose one of the seven groups of questions and apply the questions in the group to the subject. The questions—many of which will seem familiar to you by now—are drawn, Larson says, from the work of logicians, rhetoricians, and language theorists. According to its creator, the best way to teach this system is to hand out lists of the questions and discuss in class what subjects fit into which groups of questions and why. Extensive classroom practice will allow the students eventually to decide for themselves the question groups that best address discrete subjects.

The subjects themselves will provide subject matter, but no theses; to do so, says Larson, writers must take the mass of discovered material and run it through another group of questions:

1. What is the subject like? What can it be compared to and why should it be? How can we generalize about the comparison?
2. Do I like it or not like it? Is it good? Bad? Dangerous? What proves or supports my feelings?
3. Is there any conflict, inconsistency, or inexplicability within this material? Is there a problem in it that interests me? Does anything puzzle me, lead me to want to investigate more? (129–30)

These last three question-sets can inform a thesis, tying up most of the generated material, which might otherwise not appear to fit together. Once your students can choose their own question-group, generate their own material, and then pull a thesis out of the material inductively, you will have succeeded in getting them to use this system well.

Your students will not instantly commit these topical systems to memory. Eventually, however, they will begin to grasp the principles and structures of inquiry that lie behind all invention, especially if you provide them with explanatory charts, suggested topics, and provocative questions. With time and practice, the conscious use of the inventive techniques you introduce will become the unconscious set of tools with which experienced writers approach their subjects. Students will see quickly that different procedures prove fruitful for different topics, and as they gain confidence in their ability to make choices, they will come to rely on those procedures that work best for them. Your responsibility is to offer your students a variety of techniques, coaching in the practice of those techniques, and yourself as a supportive audience for individual results.

Works Cited *Chapter 5*

Bilsky, Manuel, McCrae Hazlitt, Robert E. Streeter, and Richard M. Weaver. "Looking for an Argument." *CE* 14 (1953): 210–16.

Brande, Dorothea. *Becoming a Writer.* New York: Harcourt, 1970.

Burke, Kenneth. *Counter-Statement.* Los Altos, CA: Hermes, 1953.

—. *A Grammar of Motives.* Englewood Cliffs, NJ: Prentice-Hall, 1952.

—. *A Rhetoric of Motives.* Englewood Cliffs, NJ: Prentice-Hall, 1950.

Comley, Nancy R. "The Teaching Seminar: Writing Isn't Just Rhetoric." *Training the New Teacher of College Composition.* Ed. Charles W. Bridges. Urbana, IL: NCTE, 1986. 47–58.

Corbett, Edward P.J. *Classical Rhetoric for the Modern Student.* 2nd ed. New York: Oxford UP, 1971.

—. "Toward a Methodology of Heuristic Procedures." *CCC* 30 (1979): 268–69.

Daly, John. "The Effects of Writing Apprehension on Message Encoding." *Journalism Quarterly* 54 (1977): 566–72.

—. "Writing Apprehension and Writing Competency." *Journal of Educational Research* 72 (1978): 10–14.

Edwards, Bruce, Jr. *The Tagmemic Contribution to Composition Theory.* Manhattan, KS: Kansas State U., 1979.

Elbow, Peter. *Embracing Contraries.* New York: Oxford UP, 1986.

—. *Writing with Power.* New York: Oxford UP, 1981.

—. *Writing Without Teachers.* New York: Oxford UP, 1973.

English, Hubert M., Jr. "Linguistic Theory as an Aid to Invention." *CCC* 15 (1964): 136–40.

Flower, Linda, and John Hayes. "Interpretive Acts: Cognition and the Construction of Discourse." *Poetics* 16 (1987).

—"Uncovering Cognitive Processes in Writing: An Introduction to Protocol Analysis." *Research on Writing*. Ed. P. Mosenthal, S. Walmsley, and L. Tamor. London: Longmans, 1982. 207–20.

Goswani, Dixie, and Lee Odell. "Naturalistic Studies of Nonacademic Writing." Paper delivered at CCCC Convention, Washington, DC, 1980.

Harrington, Elbert W. *Rhetoric and the Scientific Method of Inquiry: A Study of Invention*. Boulder: U. of Colorado P, 1948.

Hughes, Richard P., and P. Albert Duhamel. *Rhetoric: Principles and Usage*. Englewood Cliffs, NJ: Prentice-Hall, 1967.

Irmscher, William F. *The Holt Guide to English*. New York: Holt, 1972.

—*Teaching Expository Writing*. New York: Holt, 1979

Kinney, James. "Tagmemic Rhetoric: A Reconsideration." *CCC29* (1978): 141–45.

Kneupper, Charles W. "Revising the Tagmemics Heuristic: Theoretical and Pedagogical Consideration." *CCC* 31 (1980): 161–67.

Larson, Richard L. "Discovery Through Questioning: A Plan for Teaching Rhetorical Invention." *CE* 30 (1968): 126–34

Lauer, Janice. "Heuristics and Composition." *CCC* 21 (1970): 396–404.

—. "Invention in Contemporary Rhetoric: Heuristic Procedures." Diss. U. of Michigan, 1970.

—. "Toward a Methodology of Heuristic Procedures." *CCC* 30 (1979): 268–69.

—. Janet Emig, and Andrea A. Lunsford. *Four Worlds of Writing*. 2nd ed. New York: Harper, 1985.

Macrorie, Ken. *Telling Writing*. Rochelle Park, NJ: Hayden, 1970

—. *Uptaught*. Rochelle Park, NJ: Hayden, 1970.

Odell, Lee. "Another Look at Tagmemic Theory: A Response to James Kinney." *CCC* 29 (1978): 146–52.

—. "Measuring the Effect of Instruction in Pre-Writing." *Research in the Teaching of English* 9(1974): 228–40.

Osborne, Alex F. *Applied Imagination*. New York: Scribner, 1957.

Pike, Kenneth. L. "A Linguistic Contribution to Composition." *CCC* 15 (1964) 82–88.

Rico, Gabriele Lusser. *Writing the Natural Way*. Los Angeles: Tarcher, 1983.

Rohman, D. Gordon. "Pre-Writing: The Stage of Discovery in the Writing Process." *CCC* 16 (1965): 106–12.

Rose, Mike. *Writer's Block: The Cognitive Dimension*. Carbondale, IL: Southern Illinois UP, 1984.

Rueckert, William. "The Rhetoric of Rebirth: A Study of the Literary

Theory and Critical Practice of Kenneth Burke." Diss., U. of Michigan, 1956.

Winterowd, W. Ross. *The Contemporary Writer,* New York: Harcourt, 1975.

Witte, Stephen. "Pre-Text and Composing." *CCC* 38 (1987): 397–425.

Young, Richard E. "Invention: A Topographical Survey." *Teaching Composition: Ten Bibliographic Essays.* Ed. Gary Tate. Fort Worth: Texas Christian UP, 1976. 1–44.

—, and Alton L. Becker. "Toward a Modern Theory of Rhetoric: A Tagmemic Contribution." *Harvard Education Review* 35 (1965): 50–68.

—, Alton L. Becker, and Kenneth L. Pike. *Rhetoric: Discovery and Change.* New York: Harcourt, 1970.

—, and Frank Koen. *The Tagmemic Discovery Procedure: An Evaluation of Its Uses in the Teaching of Rhetoric.* Ann Arbor: U. of Michigan Dept. of Humanities, 1973.

Chapter 6

Teaching Arrangement

One of the continuing criticisms of classical rhetoric concerns its seemingly arbitrary division into the canons of rhetoric. Is there any essential reason for assuming that the process of generating discourse should be divided into the restrictive classifications of invention, arrangement, style, delivery, and memory? And if these are arbitrary divisions, with no real connection to the composing process, why not put them behind us?

Controversial though they may be, the divisions of rhetoric are useful conventions. Were we to try to describe the composing process as the seamless interaction of form and content it apparently is, our discussion of it would have to be considerably deeper and more theoretical than space allows here. Separating invention and arrangement is a convenient tool for discussing certain features of the composing process, even though the two operations are not carried out separately, one after the other, by practiced writers.

Invention, arrangement, and style are inextricably intertwined in the practice of experienced writers; no approach to one can ever ignore the others. Largely because of this intimate relationship between form and content, "form in complete essays has not been the subject of much theoretical investigation," writes Richard Larson ("Structure" 45). Invention, with its many open-ended systems, has received much more recent attention than has arrangement, perhaps because of the expressive and romantic biases of our age, many of which militate against formal requirements in general and prefer to dwell upon self-ordered expression. Still, the demands of arrangement remain an integral part of rhetoric.

Some teachers argue that preconceived arrangement is artificial, that all organization should grow naturally out of the writer's purpose; others see readily identifiable organization and form as the first step toward successful communication. Each teacher must gradually develop his or her own concept of forms, and strike a balance between form and content. This chapter can only suggest the various alternatives available, which have been used throughout the history of the teaching of rhetoric.

Forms and arrangements are sometimes assigned and used artificially; therefore, when we discuss form with our students, we must remind them (and ourselves) of the relationships between structure and content: that purpose, the needs of the audience, and the subject should dictate arrangement—not vice versa. We cannot, then, merely offer our students one or two arrangements as all-purpose lifesavers. Instead, we must regularly ask students to recognize the interconnections between form and content, and help students in the subtle task of creating forms that fit their ideas and emphases.

Whatever forms or methods of arrangement you choose to teach, you will want your students to realize that you are teaching them *conventions*, to be adapted and changed as the writer specifies the needs of a particular subject and a particular audience. Methods of arrangement can provide a rough framework upon which an essay can be built, but they should neither limit the development of an essay nor demand sections that are clearly unnecessary.

The prescriptive arrangements in this chapter, then, should be thought of and taught only as stepping-stones—not as ends in themselves. You will want to teach your students to transcend them as well as to use them. Kenneth Burke tells us that "form is an arousing and fulfillment of desires, . . . correct in so far as it gratifies the needs which it creates" (124). If the prescriptive forms we give our students can help them to realize this primary purpose of arrangement, then we can offer the forms with the certainty that they will provide support only until the students can kick them away and walk on their own.

General Patterns of Arrangement

The arrangement of material in an essay grows out of a complex blend of the author's purpose, his or her knowledge of the subject, and the formal expectations of the audience. In the course of ten or thirteen weeks, though, few teachers can present and even fewer students can grasp all of the actual intricacies in the marriage of form and content, nor all of the techniques and intuitions of experienced writers. Students can, however, begin to appreciate these intricacies if you ask them to examine the patterns of arrangement in articles and essays written in their major field of study, and to deduce the conventional formats wherever possible. Teachers can also introduce students to general conventional forms for arrangement, ranging from simple and short formats that can be adapted to nearly any subject matter, to longer and more complex ones specifically used in argumentation. You can demonstrate and assign to your students one, two, or all of these patterns of arrangement. But you and your students will want to remember that these patterns are not absolutes, should not be taught as absolutes, and must be seen as convenient teaching devices, not as rigid structures.

The elements discussed as parts of each method of arrangement have *no necessary correlation* with paragraphs (see Chapter 8). Some students are tempted to conceive of a "six-part" essay as a six-paragraph essay, but except for some minor forms such as the "five-paragraph theme," you can stress to your students that each element in a discourse scheme consists of a single paragraph *as a minimum.* Thus, a "four-part" essay might consist of a single paragraph for the Introduction, three paragraphs for the Statement of Fact, four paragraphs for the Argument, and a single paragraph for the Conclusion. Each element of arrangement can theoretically control an unlimited number of paragraphs, and you should beware of letting your students fall into the habit of perceiving a single element as a single paragraph.

Classically Descended Arrangements

Aristotle may have been responding to the complicated, "improved" methods of arrangement retailed by his sophistic competition when he wrote, "A speech has two parts. You must state your case, and you must prove it. . . . The current division is absurd" (*Rhetoric* 1414b). We will not discuss the two-part discourse here, for Aristotle relented, in his next paragraph, allowing for four parts to a discourse, a pattern that we will cover.

With the exception of the three-part essay, which has been generalized and modernized, all classical arrangements descend from Aristotle and all are essentially argumentative in nature—like classical rhetoric itself. These arrangements, organized formally rather than according to content, rarely suit narrative or descriptive writing and can confuse students who try to use them for nonargumentative purposes. In *Classical Rhetoric for the Modern Student,* Edward P.J. Corbett points out that instead of being topically organized, classical arrangements are "determined by the functions of the various parts of a discourse" (303).

Three-Part Arrangement

"A whole," says Aristotle in his *Poetics,* "is that which has a beginning, a middle, and an end" (24). Aristotle's observation—original, true, and now obvious—is the starting place for the most widely accepted method of rhetorical arrangement, the three-part arrangement. Like the dramatic works Aristotle was describing, a complete discourse, such as a successful essay, has three parts: an introduction, a body of some length, and a conclusion. From the simplest single-paragraph exercise to a forty-page research paper, every writing assignment looks for these three parts: introduction, body, and conclusion.

The simplicity of this arrangement has both positive and negative aspects. On the one hand, it is easy to teach, easy to exemplify, not overstructured, and the one truly universal pattern of arrangement, workable for exposition and argumentation alike. On the other hand, it gives students little actual guidance in structuring their essays, especially if the assignment calls for a response longer than five hundred words. Beyond that length, the student often finds that although he is able to write and place his introduction and conclusion, the body of the essay is still amorphous. The three-part essay provides nothing in the way of interior structures that help guide beginning writers in constructing the body of their essays, nearly always the longest part. The three-part arrangement, then, is suitable and most helpful for shorter assignments, under five hundred words. Each part can be taught separately.

Introduction "The Introduction," writes Aristotle, is the beginning of a speech, . . . paving the way . . . for what is to follow. . . . [T]he writer should . . . begin with what best takes his fancy, and then strike up his theme and lead into it . . . " (*Rhetoric* 1414b). In the three-part essay, the introduction has two main tasks. First, it must catch and hold the reader's attention with an opening "hook"—an introductory section which does not announce the thesis of the essay, but instead begins to relate the as yet unannounced thesis in some brief, attention-catching way. The introduction can open with an anecdote, an aphorism, an argumentative observation, a quotation. Donald Hall calls such an opening strategy a "quiet zinger,"—"something exciting or intriguing and at the same time relevant to the material that follows." (38).

Second, the introduction must quickly focus the attention of the reader on the thesis itself. The thesis or central informing principle of the essay is determined by the writer's purpose, subject, and audience. It is usually found in the form of a single-sentence declarative *thesis statement* near the end of the introduction. This thesis statement represents the essay-length equivalent of the topic sentence of a paragraph; it is general enough to announce what the following essay plans to do, yet specific enough to suggest what the essay will not do.

Body of the Essay   The body of the essay is, according to Aristotle, a middle which follows something as some other thing follows it. In truth, little more can be said in terms of the theory of the three-part essay, but in practice, writers can choose from many organizational plans. Some teachers trail off into generalities when they discuss the body of the essay, talking about "shaping purpose," "order of development," and "correct use of transitions"—necessary considerations but of little help to students adrift between their first and last paragraphs. The body of the three-part essay can take many shapes; writers can develop their essays spatially, chronologically, logically, by illustrating points, by defining terms, by dividing and classifying, by comparing and contrasting, by analyzing causes and effects, by considering problems and solutions. Whatever organizational plan writers choose, they will want to be sure that the main points of the body relate not only to the thesis but to one another.

Conclusion   Like introductions, conclusions present special challenges to a writer, for a conclusion should indicate that a full discussion has taken place. Often a conclusion will begin with a restatement of the thesis and then end with more general statements that grow out of it; this pattern reverses the common general-to-specific pattern of the introduction. This restatement is usually somewhat more complex than was the original thesis statement, since now the writer assumes that the reader can marshal all of the facts of the situation as they have been presented in the body of the essay. A typical if obvious example of the opening of a conclusion might be: "Thus, as we have seen . . . " followed by the reworded thesis.

The second task of the conclusion is to end the essay on a graceful or memorable rhetorical note. Writers can draw on a number of ways to conclude effectively and give their text a sense of ending: a provocative question, a quotation, a vivid image, a call for action, or a warning. Sheridan Baker writes that the successful conclusion satisfies the reader because it "conveys a sense of assurance and repose, of business completed" (22). Yet William Zinsser insists:

> The perfect ending should take the reader slightly by surprise and yet seem exactly right to him. He didn't expect the [piece] to end so soon, or so abruptly, or to say what it said. But he knows it when he sees it" (78–79).

Zinsser goes on to tell nonfiction writers that when they are ready to stop, they should stop: "If you have presented all the facts and made the point that you want to make, look for the nearest exit" (79).

Classroom Use of the Three-Part Arrangement

Although it is applicable to many modes of discourse, the classical three-part arrangement simply does not provide enough internal structure for students putting together a middle section for their essay. The three-part form *is* useful as an introduction to the conventions of introductions and conclusions. The easiest way to approach the body section of an essay is to teach these patterns of development.

After you introduce the basic three-part structure, you can move on to teaching the importance of introductions and conclusions. Try to choose examples that put special emphasis on the structure of beginnings and endings. Ask students for their responses to your examples. You might assign a series of short in-class essays on a series of topics chosen by your students. Because you want your students to concentrate on recognizable introductions and conclusions, you might want to allow them to dispense with the actual writing of the body of each essay, and have them substitute a rough outline or list of components that might make up the body of the essay.

This exercise is more useful when the students break into their writing groups. On the class day after each short essay is written, convene the groups, and ask students to read over and evaluate the success of the introductions and conclusions of each other's essays. They might answer specific questions, such as:

What does the opening of this essay accomplish?

How does it "hook" the reader"

Can you help the author improve the opening?

Does the essay end in a memorable way? Or does it seem to trail off into vagueness or to end abruptly?

If you like the conclusion, explain why.

Can you help the author improve the conclusion?

You may want to put the most effective introduction and conclusion on the blackboard so that the entire class can share them. After the students have conferred and improved one another's work, and after the introductions and conclusions have been hammered into a final form, allow those students who have become intrigued by the ideas they've been working with to complete the essay for a grade. Several days of this kind of practice can give students a solid competence in beginning and ending essays.

Four-Part Arrangement

After blasting hair-splitting pedagogues of his day and declaring that oration had only two parts, Aristotle relented and admitted that as speakers actually practiced rhetoric, a discourse generally had four parts: The *proem* or *introduction,* the *statement of fact,* the *confirmation* or *argument,* and the *epilogue* or *conclusion* (*Rhetoric* 200). Specifically an argumentative form, this four-part arrangement does not adapt well to narrative or description.

Introduction. Called by Aristotle the *proem* (from the Greek word *proemium,* meaning "before the song") and by the author of the Roman handbook *Rhetorica ad Herrenium* the *exordium* (from the Latin weaving term for "beginning a web"), the introduction to the four-part essay has two functions, one major and one minor. The major task is to inform the audience of the purpose or object of the essay, and the minor task is to create a rapport or relationship of trust between the writer and the audience.

"The most essential function and distinctive property of the introduction," writes Aristotle," [is] to show what the aim of the speech is" (*Rhetoric* 202). Edward P.J. Corbett tells us that the introduction serves two important audience-centered functions: first, it orients the audience within the subject, but second, and even more important, it seeks to convince the audience that what is being introduced is worthy of their attention (304). In a fashion similar to the "quiet zinger" that opens the three-part essay, the four-part essay can catch the attention of the reader by using different devices. Richard Whately lists a number of different types of introductions that can arouse reader interest in a subject (189–92). The usefulness of these types of introductions is, of course, not limited to the four-part essay, although they do complement argumentative subject matter:

> *Introduction Inquisitive*—shows that the subject in question is "important, curious, or otherwise interesting."
>
> *Introduction Paradoxical*—dwells on characteristics of the subject which, though they seem improbable, are none the less real. This form of introduction searches for strange and curious perspectives on the subject.
>
> *Introduction Corrective*—shows that the subject has been "neglected, misunderstood, or misrepresented by others." As Whately says, this immediately removes the danger that the subject will be thought trite or hackneyed.
>
> *Introduction Preparatory*—explains peculiarities in the way the subject will be handled, warns against misconceptions about the subject, or apologizes for some deficiency in the presentations.

Introduction Narrative—leads into the subject by narrating a story or anecdote.

These various introductions can accomplish the major task of acquainting the audience with the subject, and they often also accomplish the minor task of rendering the reader attentive and well-disposed toward the writer and her cause. In rendering an audience benevolent, writers must be aware of certain elements concerning the rhetorical situation in which they find themselves. Corbett offers five questions writers must ask themselves regarding their rhetorical situation before they can be certain of the conditions for their discourse:

1. What do I have to say?
2. To or before whom is it being said?
3. Under what circumstances?
4. What are the predispositions of the audience?
5. How much time or space do I have?
   (311)

The introduction is the best place to establish "bridges" with the reader by pointing up shared beliefs and attitudes—that is, creating what Kenneth Burke calls *identification* between the writer and her audience.

The introduction to the four-part essay, then, performs functions similar to that of the three-part essay. It draws readers into the discourse with the promise of interesting information and informs them of the main purpose of the discourse while rendering them well-disposed toward the writer and the subject.

Statement of Fact The Romans called this section of a discourse the *narratio*, and it is sometimes today referred to as the *narration* or *background*. But Corbett's term *statement of fact* works well, especially since we now use the term *narration* to signify dramatized activities; also, this section presents more than just background information. The statement of fact is a non-argumentative, expository presentation of the objective facts concerning the situation or problem—the subject—under discussion.

The statement of fact may contain circumstances, details, summaries, even narrative in the modern sense. It sets forth the background of the problem and very often explains the central point as well. The best general advice, perhaps, remains Quintilian's, who, in 50 A.D., recommended that the statement of fact be *lucid, brief*, and *plausible*. Writers can order their statement of fact in a number of different ways: by use of chronological order, by moving from general situation to specific details, by moving from specific to general, or by proceeding according to topics. The tone of the statement of fact should be neutral, calm, and matter-of-fact, free of overt stylistic mannerisms and obvious bias. Writers are best served by understatement, for the audience will readily trust a writer they deem as striving for fairness.

Confirmation Also called the *argument*, this section is central to the four-part essay, is often the longest section. Corbett tells us that the confirmation is easily used in expository as well as argumentative prose; historically, it was used mainly in argumentation. Simply put, the confirmation section is used to prove the writer's case. With the audience rendered attentive by the introduction and informed by the statement of fact, the writer is ready in the confirmation to show the reasons why his position concerning the facts should be accepted and believed. Most of the argumentative material discovered in the invention process is used in this section.

Of the three kinds of persuasive discourse—deliberative, forensic, and epideictic—the first two were truly argumentative. Aristotle theorized that argumentative discourse dealt with two different sorts of questions: deliberative or political oratory was always concerned about the future, and forensic or judicial oratory, about the past. (Epideictic or ceremonial oratory was concerned with the present.) If the question is about events in the past, the confirmation will try to prove:

1. Whether an act was committed
2. Whether an act committed did harm
3. Whether the harm of the act is less or more than alleged
4. Whether a harmful act was justified

Similarly, if the question is about a course for the future, the confirmation will try to prove that:

1. A certain thing can or cannot be done; if it can be done, then the confirmation tries to prove that
2. It is just or unjust
3. It will do harm or good
4. It has not the importance the opposition attaches to it

After the writer has decided on a question and a position, he or she can move into the argument, choosing from definitions, cause-effect demonstrations, analogical reasoning, authoritative testimony, maxims, personal experiences—evidence of all sorts in order to prove his or her point in the confirmation.

Writers can build their arguments in different ways, but classical rhetoricians offer a rough plan. If there are, for instance, three specific lines of argument available to the writer, one strong, one moderately convincing, and one weak, they should be grouped thus: the moderate argument first, the weak argument second, and the strongest argument last. This arrangement both begins and ends the confirmation on notes of relative strength and prevents the writer's position from appearing initially weak or finally anticlimactic.

Conclusion   Called the *epilogue* by the Greeks and the *peroration* by the Romans (from *per-oratio*—a finishing-off of the oration), the conclusion, according to Aristotle, has four possible tasks:

1. It renders the audience once again well disposed to the writer and ill-disposed toward his opponent.
2. It magnifies the writer's points and minimizes those of the opposition.
3. It puts the audience in the proper mood.
4. It refreshes the memory of the audience by summarizing the main points of the argument. (*Rhetoric*)

Most conclusions do recapitulate the main points, or at least the central thesis, of the discourse. The other three possible tasks are less concrete. Although the conclusion tends to be the most obviously emotional of all the sections, the use of *pathos* (emotional appeal) in written assignments is a dangerous technique for beginners, in whose hands it can all too easily degenerate into *bathos* (laughable emotional appeal). The best conclusions restate or expand their main points and then sign off gracefully with a stylistic flourish that signals the end of the discourse.

Classroom Use of Four-Part Arrangement

Although the four-part pattern of arrangement gives more direction to an essay than does the three-part pattern, it is not so adaptable to different sorts of discourse. The four-part pattern generally demands subject-directed, nonpersonal writing that can support an argumentative thesis, so that students usually need several days to conceptualize and investigate their subjects. Students will also need to apply techniques of invention or do research on their subjects before writing their first drafts. Some teachers prefer to provide the subjects on which the students write, at least in the beginning, for the four-part arrangement works best when applied to rigidly defined questions.

You may want to assign subjects that need little or no research, and can support several different argumentative theses. You can decide whether you wish to begin with a question involving actions in the past (a *forensic* question) or with a question of future policy (a *deliberative* question). Some possible forensic topics might be:

Major Reno's conduct at Little Big Horn

John Kennedy's role in the Bay of Pigs Invasion

The fairness of the campus parking policy

Cotton Mather's responsibility for the Salem Witch-Trials

Paul Robeson—traitor or patriot?

And deliberative topics might include:

Should there be a moratorium on nuclear power plants?

Is a "bottle bill" good for this state?

Should the foreign-language requirement be reinstated?

Should the drinking age be changed in this state?

Obviously, deliberative topics change as the issues of the day change. Current campus controversies make excellent topics.

While students can certainly master the forms in a week, that short amount of time does not permit complete research of a topic. You may want to overlook the generalizations and abstract, vague arguments your students make while they learn to apply the four parts of the arrangement. You can also give them some tools to work with.

After your students have finished their first drafts of the four-part assignment, ask them to break into their writing groups and read each other's drafts. Have them ask the following questions about each section of the essay.

Introduction
> Do the first four sentences attract my interest?
> Is the subject clearly defined in the introduction?
> Is the introduction too long?
> Does the introduction seem to be aimed at a specific audience? What is it?
> Do I want to know more, to keep reading? Why?

Statement of Fact
> Does this section clearly explain the nature of the problem or situation?
> Is there anything not told that I need to know?

Does the problem or situation continue to interest me?
Confirmation
Is the argumentation convincing and believable?
Does the order of presentation seem reasonable?
Has any obvious argument been left out?
Has the opposing position been competently refuted?
Conclusion
Has the case been summarized well?
Do I feel well disposed toward the writer? Why?
Does the ending seem graceful?

After the groups discuss these questions and evaluate one another's drafts, ask for a typed copy of the assignment. Many teachers like to drift among the writing groups and remind the students that any form must be adapted to its content. To best help each student adapt form to content, you may want to talk to each student separately during the group meetings. You may want to distribute copies of student papers (excluding the author's names) and review with the class the strengths and weaknesses of each argument. Often, students will volunteer a draft of their paper when they know they can remain anonymous and receive the help and attention of the entire class. The more students know about what is successful in argument and about the formal qualities of the arrangement form, the easier it will be for them to write their next papers.

Two More Detailed Arrangements

The classical oration form used by Cicero and Quintilian was a four-part form, but the Latin rhetoricians went on to divide the third part, the confirmation, into two separate parts, *confirmatio* and *reprehensio*. Cicero said that "the aim of confirmation is to prove our own case and that of refutation (*reprehensio*) is to refute the case of our opponents" (337). Thus, the classical oration was composed of five parts:

the *exordium* or introduction
the *narratio* or statement of facts
the *confirmatio* or proof of the case
the *reprehensio* or refutation of opposing arguments
the *peroratio* or conclusion

Splitting off the refutation section is not a really meaningful change from the four-part arrangement, since the confirmation section of the four-part essay could also be refutative. Still, a separate section of refutation makes the task of dealing with opposing arguments mandatory; hence, it can provide more structure for a discourse. Although the refutation does not always present the writer's own positive arguments, it usually does—that is, unless the opposing arguments are so powerful or so generally accepted that the audience would not listen to an opposing confirmation without first being prepared by the refutation.

Corbett tells us that refutation is based on *appeal to reason*, on *emotional appeals*, on the *ethical or personal appeal* of the writer, or on *wit*. Refutation can usually be accomplished in one of two ways: (1) the writer denies the truth of one of the premises on which the opposing argument is built; or (2) the writer objects to the inferences drawn by the opposition from premises which cannot be broken down.

The most detailed of the classically descended arrangements is the six-part arrangement recommended by Hugh Blair in his extremely influential *Lectures on Rhetoric and Belles-Lettres* of 1783. Blair's conception of arrangement was largely influenced by the classical theorists, but he was also a practitioner of pulpit oratory. Hence, his arrangement shows both classical and sermonic elements. Blair's model of a discourse was composed of these elements:

the exordium or introduction
the statement and division of the subject
the narration or explication
the reasoning or arguments
the pathetic or emotional part
the conclusion
(341)

In this breakdown, the introduction captures the attention of the audience, renders the reader benevolent, and so on. Like some of the classical theorists, Blair distinguishes two sorts of introductions: the *principium*, a direct opening addressed to well-disposed audiences, and the *insinuatio*, a less direct, subtler method that prepares a hostile audience for arguments counter to their opinions. The *insinuatio* generally opens by first admitting the most powerful points made by the opposition, by showing how the writer holds the same views as the audience on general philosophical questions, or by dealing with ingrained audience prejudices. The *principium*, on the other hand, can proceed with the knowledge that the audience is sympathetic and can go directly to the task of rendering them attentive.

Blair's first large departure from the four-part essay is in the second of his divisions, the "statement and division of the subject." In this arrangement, as in the three-part arrangement, the thesis is clearly stated at the end of the introduction, but here the thesis is immediately followed by the "division" or announcement of the plan of the essay. Both the proposition and the division should be short and succinct. According to Blair, the division should avoid "unnecessary multiplication of heads." In other words, it should contain as simple an outline as possible, presented in a natural, nonmechanistic fashion.

The next two sections, "narration" and "reasoning," correspond to the statement of fact and confirmation sections in the four-part essay. However, Blair then proposes that a new division of arrangement, termed "the pathetic part," follow the argumentation section. The word *pathetic* in this case refers to the *pathetic appeal* of classical rhetoric. Thus, after presenting his or her argument, Blair's writer would appeal to the audience's feelings; in addition, he or she would begin to draw the discourse to a close.

Using a formula remarkably similar to T.S. Eliot's "objective correlative," for arousing the emotions of the audience: the writer must connect the audience's emotions with a specific instance, object, or person. A writer arguing against nuclear power, for instance, might close her arguments with specific examples of nuclear harm—factory workers rendered sterile by isotope poisoning, or workers killed in grisly fashion in nuclear accidents, for example. A writer arguing for nuclear generation of electricity might paint a dreadful picture of poor people freezing to death because the cost of heating without nuclear power was too great for them to bear. In the pathetic part, the writer should conclude his or her argumentation with a powerful emotional appeal, an appeal that will bring together the arguments for the readers, causing them to act on their feelings. The pathetic appeal at the end of the arguments can be very effective.

The pathetic part should also be short, Blair says, and must *not* rely on any stylistic or oratorical flourishes; the language of the pathetic part should be bold, ardent, and simple. And finally, Blair warns, writers should not attempt to create a pathetic effect if they themselves are not moved, for the result of such attempts will not only be ineffective and artificial, but hypocritical as well.

Following the pathetic part of this six-part form is the conclusion, similar to the conclusion presented for less detailed arrangements.

Classroom Use of the More Detailed Arrangements

For the advanced or honors student, the more detailed forms are profitable. Based on the four-part essay, these forms are best taught as mere extensions of it. Teachers who provide their students a more complex arrangement structure often find that they are unwilling to go back to the less detailed structure and its larger burden of decision. Often, teachers present both forms, spending time on the four-part structure and then progressing from the less structured to the more detailed. Each successive structure subsumes those that precede it.

Because your students will probably need more time to think through and develop their argument essay than any other type of discourse, your choice of assignment is of paramount importance. Even when they understand argumentative arrangement, students cannot assemble their argumentative essays overnight. The forensic and deliberative topics mentioned earlier can be profitably applied to these arrangements. But by the time you have reached the stage of teaching these forms, it is often close to the end of the term, and students will be able to choose their own argumentation topic. Having been led through the four-part form, they know which topics can be well argued and which will present problems. Sometimes, however, the class will need to work together, coming up with and developing topics for stumped classmates.

Both the five- and the six-part forms provide specific sorts of practice, the five-part form in refutation, the six-part form in emotional appeals of a certain sort. Students using the five-part form should be able to list at least two arguments their opposition would be likely to use before they begin to write; otherwise their refutation sections could be too general, or indistinguishable from their confirmations. Students using the six-part form must keep in mind the difference between pathos (emotional appeal) and bathos (laughable emotional appeal) to avoid some genuinely embarrassing attempts to "sway the emotions." The six-part form is best used by honors or upper-level students whose emotional perceptions are likely to be informed by the rational and calculating judgment necessary for effective pathetic appeal.

To familiarize your students with the soon-to-be-assigned form, you may want to introduce a model of that form, in a handout. You will want to exemplify as well as introduce each element in a new argument. Some teachers elicit an argumentative subject from the class and then, with the class, outline the course of that argument on the board. Students often have strong ideas of how one specific form of arrangement best suits a particular argument. Working together this way is the best practice you can give your class.

During each stage of teaching these prescriptive arrangements, you'll want to illustrate to your students that the demands made by these forms are *flexible*. The more complex the pattern of arrangement, the greater the chance that one or more of the sections will be extraneous or actually harmful to the discourse. Students must learn to use common sense in deciding whether or to what degree the method of arrangement fits the real needs of the writer and his or her audience.

NONCLASSICAL ARRANGEMENT

Richard Larson's Problem-Solving Form

"Problem-solving," says Larson, is "the process by which one moves from identifying the need to accomplish a particular task (and discovering that the task is difficult) to finding a satisfactory means for accomplishing that task" ("Problem-Solving" 629). What this emphasis on action-based task definition means, of course, is that the problem-solving form is both exploratory and argumentative. It deals more successfully with situations in which a change needs to be accomplished than with narrative or purely expository writing. Defining a problem leads, as in the classical deliberative oration, to arguing for one specific answer. The novel and valuable aspect of Larson's method is that it uses the very process of arriving at an arguable position as the pattern of arrangement for the essay.

In his article, "Problem-Solving, Composing, and Liberal Education" (631–33), Larson identifies eight steps that must be accomplished in order to complete the process of identifying and solving a problem, steps that can be used as a pattern of arrangement.

1. *Definition of the problem* After a short introduction, this section provides "a clear statement of exactly what is to be decided." This statement usually involves a choice between possible courses of action or the identification of an undesirable condition needing correction.
2. *Determination of why the problem is indeed a problem—a source of difficulty for the decision-maker* If a course of action is clear, as Larson points out, there can be no problem. This section clarifies the need for a decision on policy or an explanation of what is undesirable about the current situation. This explanation may demand a causal analysis of the present situation.
3. *An enumeration of the goals that must be served by whatever action is taken* Sometimes the determination of the goals to be striven for is in itself a problem-solving situation, but most possible subjects for student essays present readily identifiable

"goods" as goals—continued world peace, equitable distribution of wealth, the best quality education, and so on.

4. *Determination of the goals which have highest priority* This step can be difficult. Usually there are several goals in any realistic problem-solution, and if possible goals include mutually exclusive goods such as "free trade" and "fair trade" (for instance), some decision must be made on priority. This assigning of priorities may need to be argued for in itself, depending upon the audience projected for the essay.

5. *"Invention" of procedures that might attain the stated goals* If the question is one of choosing between several possible courses of action, no invention will be necessary unless some sort of compromise is proposed. If the problem-solver must discover how to improve an undesirable situation, though, invention of possible methods will be necessary. For example, the problem of poor urban transit could be solved by creating more bus stops, or by buying more buses, or by instituting peak-hour special runs. If choices are not immediately apparent, they must be created.

6. *Prediction of the results that will follow the taking of each possible action* This is the most difficult step, requiring careful study of evidence about conditions, precedents, laws of nature, history, past cause-and-effect sequences, and so on. This entire section must be based on intelligent appraisals of probability. Each possible action must be weighed against the good it would accomplish, how much it would cost, and any unavoidable evil attached to it.

7. *Weighing of the predictions* This part of the essay compares the possible actions and their projected outcomes, trying to gauge which action will be most likely to attain the chosen goals with the fewest unwanted side effects.

8. *Final evaluation of the choice that seems superior* This section closes the essay by determining whether the chosen alternative does indeed solve the problem. It may include some modification of the chosen action to minimize the bad effects or to maximize the good. (631–33)

Larson posits this method as both a pattern of arrangement and a system of invention. As mentioned in the Introduction, one canon implies the other; both canons of rhetoric—arrangement and invention—are inherent in problem-solving. All patterns of arrangement contain aspects of invention within them.

Classroom Use of Problem-Solving Form

The problem-solving technique has many uses for students outside of English classes; thus, it can be one of the most practical forms to teach. It is, for example, the primary report form used in technical and professional writing of all sorts, a tool that many students will be able to use throughout their professional careers. It also provides a method of thinking situations through that may help remedy the easy assertions and cut-corner thought processes that plague introductory English classes.

It is important to guard against making Larson's eight-step method into a sterile formula—a problem which is central to all systems of arrangement. Once you have introduced your students to the eight steps of the problem-solving process, you may find that they tend to stick slavishly to them, no matter how often you caution flexibility. More than most arrangements, problem-solving form is a duplication of actual conceptual steps, so even if students' essays are formulaic to some degree, they will not generally be sterile. As students discover the real demands of problems they face, their dependence on the form should decrease.

To introduce your students to the problem-solving pattern of arrangement, hand out sheets that detail the eight steps involved. The example of the use of this arrangement mentioned by Larson is Swift's "A Modest Proposal," which can be found in many readers. If you wish to expose your students to a more modern example, you might look through technical writing texts for models of the feasibility study, which is usually an important technical-writing assignment. You might also ask a colleague who teaches technical writing if he has any copies of student essays using the form that you can borrow and reproduce. The simpler the example, the better; try to stay away from too much technical detail, which can discourage first-year students.

After you have explained and demonstrated the steps of the process, and when you feel your students are comfortable with and able to identify the steps, ask them for a simple problem-solving outline—just two or three sentences under each heading—on a campus topic: "Should the school newspaper be free or should it be sold for a nominal sum?"; "Should the library go to a closed-stack system?" The best problem-solving topics are deliberative, having to do with future policy. Students usually need several days to come up with this outline. On the day it is due, convene the writing groups and ask the students to evaluate one another's work, examining each step of the outline for strengths and weaknesses. At this stage, they need to examine the logical structure of the outline, making certain that no important goal or prediction has been ignored or underplayed.

Students are now usually ready for a longer assignment. You can ask them to expand the outlines they have been constructing into full-length essays, or you may go directly to a full-length deliberative question and assign a problem-solving essay based on it. Any of the deliberative topics mentioned in connection with the classical forms will work here; others, on current political and cultural questions, will probably suggest themselves to you. It is a good idea to discuss the outline of this paper with your students before they commit themselves to a first draft or ask them to review one another's outline in their groups.

Larson's is not, of course, the only problem-solving technique available; it merely happens to be a good problem-solving heuristic that is adaptable as a method of arrangement and offers service as an invention technique. Larson's technique is useful as an arrangement mainly because it is one of the most schematic of problem-solving heuristics.[1] Problem-solving offers the student writer a model for planning rigorous arguments on complex issues, and it is also a technique by which students can investigate systems and draw intelligent, defensible conclusions. If you expose your students to this system, you will be providing them not only with a rhetorical tool, but also with a method of analysis that will leave them better able to handle the complex demands made on educated people by contemporary culture.

Editing and Planning Techniques in Arrangement

Thus far we have been discussing methods of arrangement that are "transcendent"; they prefigure the essays patterned on them. Some rhetoricians call these arrangements "generative." Although some of the prescriptive arrangements we have seen are more flexible than others, many teachers distrust the idea of prescriptive or transcendent arrangements. Rather than using pre-exisiting arrangements, these teachers subscribe to the organic model of composition, one in which invention, arrangement, and style are all informed by the writer's perceptions of his or her subject, purpose, and audience. Most mature writers do compose organically. But teachers continue to offer stu-

---

1 For further discussion of problem-solving methods in Composition theory, see Flower and Hayes, *"Problem-Solving Strategies."*

dents section-by-section prescriptive arrangements; otherwise, teachers may feel they have little more to offer than vague maxims: "Organize your points clearly," "Strive for unity, order, and coherence," "Don't ramble or digress."

Teachers can offer students sound advice without being prescriptive; they can offer some of the following techniques of editing and section-rearrangement that are very useful to student writers.

The Outline

The outline can be successfully used as an editorial technique. For the last hundred years, however, it has often been advanced as *the* primary arrangement-generative tool available to students. Many teachers still hold to the sentiments of John F. Genung, whose 1893 textbook *Outlines of Rhetoric* reads, "It is strongly advisable, perhaps we had better say necessary, to draw up a careful plan of what you are going to write. . . . Even if a writer gets by experience the ability to make and follow a plan mentally, he must ordinarily have acquired that ability by planning much on paper" (239).

The "careful plan," of course, was an outline of topics the essay would treat. Like a skeleton (a frequent analogical comparison), it would give structure to the body of the essay. In composition courses, the idea of the outline became very complex, with expectations of Roman and Arabic numerals, large and small letters—a full blueprint, in fact, of every topic, sub-topic, and sub-sub-topic in the proposed essay. The idea of outlining before writing became accepted practice in high schools and continues to be taught there and in many colleges.

But outlining before writing can be terrribly inefficient. The full outline, with all of its sets and subsets, is not a method that accurately reflects the mental processes by which writing is actually accomplished. Often, outlining before writing can be frustrating and discouraging for writers, who often don't know what they are going to write about until they write.

Many students need to see a context of previous expression before they can decide where their essays should go next. As we are gradually learning, the writing itself is an epistemological tool. Composition researchers are proving that, indeed, writing *is* a way of knowing. As the famous E.M. Forster quote goes, "How can I know what I think until I see what I say?" When using a subset outline, the student must generate both form and content simultaneously in an abstract context. To see just how difficult this process can be, try writing a full-blown subset outline before you write *your* own next essay.

Many successful writers draw up an ordered list of topics before they write, but the list is related more closely to prewriting notetaking than to a baroque outline. Full-scale outlines, written before writing, have very little generative capacity. Hence, teachers are turning to ordering lists or brainstorming lists for the generative part of the composing process; such lists are invaluable in helping to keep the general flow of ideas going, while the subset outline is interruptive and confining when used as an generative tool. What many teachers have discovered about the full-scale outline is that its use can be much more helpful to students in the *editing* stage of composition, after the first draft has been written. To understand this use of outlining, let us look more closely at outlines themselves.

The two most common sorts of outlines that have been proposed for use in composition are the *topic outline* and its more complex sibling the *topic-sentence outline*. The topic outline, as its title suggests, is a listing of the sections of the proposed essay, its topics and their subtopics, with a key word or a short clause attached to each letter or number as a designation of content. The topic-sentence outline asks that the writer create a topic sentence for each paragraph in the proposed essay and order these topic sentences as the topics and subtopics of the essay; thus the major and minor ideas of the essay can be ranked according to their importance or the writer's purpose. This sort of outline is, as you may imagine, extremely difficult to create beforehand.

Both of these types of outlines can be turned around by students and written *after* the first draft of the essay has been written, and what were devices for creating frustration can become easily usable and illuminating editing tools. Here is the way it works.

When your students have completed their first drafts of papers, either using one of the forms of arrangement already covered or proceeding intuitively, ask them to draw up an outline of the paragraphs in their drafts as they currently exist. Do not insist on sets and subsets at this point; merely suggest a numbered list. Each number will represent a paragraph; after each number the student should write a short sentence summarizing that paragraph.

After each paragraph has been thus represented and charted, each student will have what is in essence a map of where the argument of the essay is going. At this point, have the students meet in workshop groups or merely exchange lists with one another and discuss them for ten minutes or so. Questions to be asked about each list include:

1. Are there any paragraphs or topics that don't seem to relate well to the development of the subject?
2. Is there anything that should be cut?

3. Might one or several paragraphs work better in another position in the essay?
4. Is there any important part of the essay that seems to be missing?

After writing and discussing their post-facto outlines, students will have a much clearer idea of what changes need to be made in the paragraph arrangement of a rough draft before it is finalized. Generally, adding a few paragraphs, cutting a few, or rearranging a few will be the result, yielding a much more consciously organized final draft. The practice in paragraph-level transitions that the students will get is an extra bonus.

The same sort of after-the-fact outlining can also be done using the simpler topic outline, but the sentence outline produces clearer realizations for the students about what it is they are saying as their arguments proceed.

W. Ross Winterowd's "Grammar of Coherence" Technique

In his 1970 article "The Grammar of Coherence," W. Ross Winterowd argues that beyond the sentence level—that is, at the level of paragraphs and essay-units (what Willis Pitkin calls "discourse blocs")—*transitions* control coherence (830). Form and coherence, says Winterowd, are synonymous at the paragraph and discourse-bloc level, and we perceive coherence as consistent relationships among transitions. To be aware of and able to control these transitional relationships is a very important skill for students, and the editorial technique that can promote this awareness is implicit in Winterowd's discussion.

Winterowd has identified seven transitional relationships between parts in an essay, and the application of knowledge of these seven relationships can help students order the parts of their essay. The seven relationships are:

Coordination—expressed by the terms *and, furthermore, too, in addition, also, again*

Obversativity—expressed by *but, yet, however, on the other hand*

Causativity—expressed by *for, because, as a result*

Conclusativity—expressed by *so, therefore, thus, for this reason*

Alternativity—expressed by *or*

Inclusativity—expressed by a colon

Sequentiality—expressed by *first . . . second . . . third, earlier . . . later,* etc.

Winterowd suggests that this list of transitional relationships can be used for many generative and analytic purposes, but here, we can use it for maintaining coherence among the parts of an essay. To use this list, first introduce your students to the transitional concepts, using illustrative handouts. Winterowd suggests that these concepts are much more easily illustrated than defined or explained, especially to beginning writers. A look through any of the common anthologies of essays will usually provide good material for these examples. Choose blocs of two or three paragraphs—the shorter the better—to reproduce. After talking about the transitional relationships in the example paragraphs for a few minutes, ask the students to do a short imitation exercise as homework, copying the transitional form of several of the examples while substituting their own content. The next step is to go directly to the reader and work orally on the transitional links between paragraphs that are picked out of random essays. By this time, students should be able to manipulate the terms fairly confidently. This practice helps students obtain a working understanding of the transitional relationships.

After this imitation exercise and class work, ask students to bring into class one of the essays they have already written and had evaluated. Then, ask them to go over this essay, marking each paragraph *as it relates to the previous one.* Each paragraph will be marked "Alternativity," "Causativity," etc. After the imitation practice, this task is not so hard as it sounds; most students are able to see most transitional relationships fairly easily. There will, of course, be the occasional mystery paragraph, which they can discuss with a friend or save to discuss with the entire class. This exercise gives students an immediate method of analyzing their own papers for coherence and of learning to strike or regroup paragraphs that have no observable relation to those around them.

After having practiced it on finished papers, your students should be ready to use this analytical method on rough drafts of in-progress papers. Winterowd's system, not for generating arrangements, works well for checking arrangements already generated. You may want to ask your students to break into their writing groups and check one another's papers for transitional relationships between the paragraphs. Although papers with clear transitions between paragraphs and discourse blocs may have other problems, they will generally be coherent. Continually using this method in class will help to ingrain transitional relationships in the students' minds, and

ultimately an intuitive grasp of transitions that will benefit them
throughout the drafting process.

Works Cited *Chapter 6*

Aristotle. *Poetics.* Trans. S.H. Butcher. *Criticism: The Major Texts.* Ed.
    W.J. Bate. New York: Harcourt, 1970.
—.*Rhetoric.* Trans. Rhys Roberts. New York: Modern Library, 1954.
Baker, Sheridan. *The Practical Stylist.* 3rd ed. New York: Crowell, 1969.
Blair, Hugh. *Lectures on Rhetoric and Belles Lettres.* 1783. Philadelphia:
    Zell, 1866.
Burke, Kenneth. *Counter-Statement.* Los Altos, CA: Hermes, 1953.
Cicero. *De Partitione Oratoria.* Trans. H. Rackham. London:
    Heinemann, 1960.
Corbett, Edward P.J. *Classical Rhetoric for the Modern Student.* 2nd ed.
    New York: Oxford UP, 1971.
Flower, Linda, and John Hayes. "Problem-Solving Strategies and the
    Writing Process." *CE* 39 (1977): 449–61.
Genung, John F. *Outlines of Rhetoric.* Boston: Ginn, 1893.
Hall, Donald. *Writing Well.* 2nd ed. Boston: Little, 1976.
Larson, Richard L. "Problem-Solving, Composing, and Liberal Educa-
    tion." *CE* 33 (1972): 628–35.
—."Structure and Form in Non-Fiction Prose." *Teaching Composition:
    Twelve Bibliographic Essays.* 2nd ed. Ed Garytate. Fort Worth: Texas
    Christian UP, 1987.
Whately, Richard. *Elements of Rhetoric.* 6th ed. London: Fellowes, 1841.
Winterowd, W. Ross. "The Grammar of Coherence." *CE* 31 (1970):
    828–35.
Zinsser, William. *On Writing Well.* 3rd ed. New York: Harper, 1985.

Chapter 7

Teaching Style

Once considered little more than the study of schemes, tropes, and rhetorical flourishes, style is now the most important canon of rhetoric today—at least, Corbett tells us, if success is measured by the sheer number of works published ("Approaches" 73). Besides Corbett's classic work on stylistic analysis, other scholars have taken the study of style into the realms of personal and business writing, have considered the socio-economic ramifications of style and revision, and have deepened our understanding of the connections among style, substance, and meaning along a historical as well as contemporary continuum.

All composition teachers benefit from a stylistics background, and one of the easiest ways to obtain such a background is to borrow the duality W. Ross Winterowd created in his *Contemporary Rhetoric*. Winterowd divides the study of style into two areas: (1) *theoretical stylistics*, concerned primarily with the nature and existence of style, the application of stylistic criteria to literary studies, and the linguistic attributes of different styles; and (2) *pedagogical stylistics*, which deals with the problem of teaching students to recognize and develop styles in their own writing (252). This chapter deals almost completely with the teachings of works on pedagogical stylistics, far fewer in number than works in the fascinating but not always classroom-practical field of theoretical stylistics.

Perhaps the central theoretical problem presented by the study of style is the question of whether "style" as an entity really exists. Is it, as some claim "the totality of impressions which a literary work produces," or is it merely "sundry and ornamental linguistic devices" tacked onto a given content-meaning? (Chatman and Levin 337–38). There is no agreement at all on this question among the foremost stylisticians of our time, yet it is a question that must be answered by every writing teacher before he or she can decide on a teaching method. Three distinct views on this question of the nature of style have emerged, says eminent stylistician Louis T. Milic, who identifies and describes these three views in his articles "Theories of Style and their Implications for the Teaching of Composition" (126).

The first of Milic's theories to be discussed here is the one to which he gives the daunting name *Crocean aesthetic monism*, because it is based on the critical theories of Benedetto Croce. Milic writes that

Crocean aesthetic monism, the most modern theory of style, "is an organic view which denies the possibility of any separation between content and form. Any discussion of style in Croce's view is useless and irrelevant, for the work or art (the composition) is a unified whole, with no seam between meaning and style" ("Theories" 67). For instance, to the Croceans, the sentences "John gave me the book" and "The book was given to me by John" have different semantic meanings as well as different syntactic forms.

The second theory is what Milic calls *individualist or psychological monism* and is best summed up by the famous aphorism of the French naturalist Georges Buffon, *"Le style, c'est l'homme même,"* usually translated as "Style is the man." Psychological monism holds that a writer cannot help writing the way he or she does, for that is the dynamic expression of his personality. This theory claims that no writer can truly imitate another's style, for no two life experiences are the same; it further holds that the main formative influences on writers are their education and their reading ("Against" 442). This theory and the Crocean theory are both *monisms* because they perceive style and content as a unity, inseparable from each other, either because different locutions say different things, or because an individual's style is his or her habitual and consistent selection from the expressive resources available in language—not consciously amendable to any great degree.

The third theory of style, and the one most applicable to teaching, is what Milic calls the *theory of ornate form* or *rhetorical dualism*. The assumption behind rhetorical dualism is that "ideas exist wordlessly and can be dressed in a variety of outfits depending on the need or the occasion" ("Theories" 67). As critic Michael Riffaterre puts it, "Style is understood as an emphasis (expressive, affective, or aesthetic) added to the information conveyed by the linguistic structure, without alteration of meaning." In other words, "Language expresses and style stresses" (Riffaterre 413).

Milic points out that the two monisms make the teaching of style a rather hopeless enterprise, since for the Croceans there is no "style," form and content being one; for the individualists, style is an expression of personality, and we cannot expect students to change their personalities. These monisms leave teachers helpless, and all of the resources of rhetoric rendered useless (Milic, "Theories" 69). In order to retain teaching options, then, teachers must be dualists, at least to some degree. Although dualistic theory cannot be proven true empirically, it still seems the only approach we have to improving students' writing style. If we cannot tell a student that the struggle to find the best words in which to express an idea is a real struggle, then we cannot teach style at all.

A confessed individualist himself, Milic is aware that dualism must be adopted at least conditionally if we are to teach style. He tries to resolve the division between his beliefs and the pedagogical options offered by dualism in an important essay called "Rhetorical Choice and Stylistic Option: The Conscious and Unconscious Poles." Milic argues that most of what we call style is actually the production of a huge unconscious element that he calls the "language-generating mechanism." This mechanism, processing subconscious choices and operating at a speed that the conscious mind cannot possibly match, creates most of what we call style. After these decisions have been made, an editing process takes over that can make any stylistic changes the author consciously desires.

Milic distinguishes between *stylistic options*, decisions made unconsciously while the language-generating mechanism is proceeding, and *rhetorical choices*, decisions made consciously while the mechanism is at rest. Rhetorical choices, in other words, are an evaluation of what has been intuitively created by the "language-generating mechanism," an editorial element that can be practiced consciously, and thus something we can teach to our students in an attempt to improve their styles. Of course, certain rhetorical choices can become habits of mind, and thus become stylistic options. This process of adding to the repertoire of the "language-generating mechanism" is what we hope to be able to accomplish. Thus Milic seems to integrate successfully his roles as theorist and as teacher.

This chapter, then, will be a discussion of rhetorical choices, since they are the only elements of style that can be handled consciously. In the realm of pedagogical stylistics, we must keep our discussion at a considerably lower level of abstraction than are most of the works mentioned by Corbett in his bibliographical essay.[1] The possibilities of our changing styles of our students in ten or thirteen weeks are limited, an opinion supported by Milic, who tells us that the process of learning to write takes a dozen years and must be begun much earlier than at eighteen. Style is the hardest canon to teach, linked as it is to reading. Only avid and accomplished readers can generate and perceive style, recognizing it in a contextual continuum. The more models and styles a writer knows and is aware of, the more raw data there are to feed the "language-generating mechanism," and the more informed the choices that can be made both intuitively and consciously.

Let us examine what we *can* accomplish, and some of the things we need to know in order to proceed. An excellent essay by Winston Weathers called "Teaching Style: A Possible Anatomy," mentions

1 See Tate 294–312.

several obligatory tasks for those who would teach style in college. The first task is "making the teaching of style significant and relevant for our students" (144). Many beginning writers view the concept of style with suspicion, as if it were something that only effete snobs should be interested in. It is our task, says Weathers, to justify the study of style on the grounds of better communication and as a proof of individuality. Style can be taught as a gesture of personal freedom, a rebellion against rigid systems of conformist language, rather than as dainty humanism or mere aesthetic luxury. Students convinced that style is, indeed, a gesture of personal freedom will invest maximum effort into stylistic concerns.

The second task Weathers mentions is that of revealing style as a measurable and viable subject matter. Style seems vague and mysterious to many beginning writers because they have mostly been exposed to the metaphysical approach to style, in which arbitrarily chosen adjectives are used to identify different styles—the "abrupt," the "tense," the "fast-moving," the "leisurely," and the ever-popular "flowing" styles. As a result of hearing styles described in these nebulous terms, students cannot see how such an amorphous entity as style might be approached or changed. They need to be exposed to the actual components, the "nuts and bolts," of style—words, phrases, clauses, sentences, paragraphs—and to methods of analyzing them, before they can begin to use them to control their rhetorical options.

We do have important tools for explaining these stylistic features. In "A Primer for Teaching Style," Richard Graves tells us that the following four explanatory methods are primary:

1. We can identify the technical name of a particular stylistic feature or concept.
2. We can give a definition or description of the feature.
3. We can provide a schematic description of the feature.
4. We can provide an example or illustration of the feature.(187)

The goals of these methods are recognition and then gradual mastery of the different stylistic features, and such explanations can be used in both stylistic analyses and exercises in imitation, the central practical activities in this chapter. In addition to discrete skills and practice exercises, though, there are questions about style that must inform every paper a student writes. Style, like the other canons of rhetoric, must be approached philosophically as well as practically.

The study of style needs to be prefaced by a careful discussion of the purpose of each piece of writing a student does, and of a writer's need to be aware of the interrelationships of author, subject, universe, and audience. M.H. Abrams presents a useful diagram of these elements in *The Mirror and the Lamp*(8):

These four elements, based on the rhetorical theory of Aristotle, form a central construct in modern communication theory. Composi-

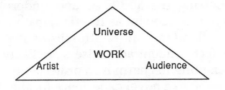

tion teachers use a version of this construct called the "communication triangle" to help students formulate their concepts of the whole rhetorical situation they find themselves in:

Each of these elements suggests a question every writer must face every time he or she sits down to write: a significant factor in these

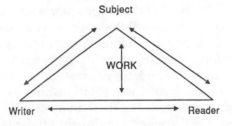

questions must necessarily be style. However, no one factor can predominate in a successful piece of writing, and Wayne Booth's famous essay "The Rhetorical Stance" offers a well-expressed overview of this fact. The "rhetorical stance" he discusses "depends on discovering and maintaining in any writing situation a proper balance among the three elements that are at work in any communicative effort: the available arguments about the subject itself, the interests and peculiarities of the audience, and voice, the implied character of the speaker" (74).

A "corruption" of the rhetorical stance, according to Booth, emphasizes any one of the three elements of the communication triangle of author-audience-subject. Student compositions can be prone to all three sorts of corruptions or imbalances. The first is the *pedant's stance,* which concentrates only on the subject while ignoring the author-audience relationship. This reliance upon nothing but subject-based discourse makes the pedant's stance dry and uninteresting. It makes no concessions to a personal voice or to reader interest. It is the sort of depersonalized prose that students often think their teachers want to hear in English classes. Ken Macrorie's famous term for it is "Engfish," and it is to be found in its purest form at a relatively high academic level: as "dissertation style."

The second sort of imbalance is the *advertiser's stance*, which concentrates on impressing the audience and underplays the subject. This imbalance is not so frequent as the first, mainly because only experienced writers will attempt it. Booth tells us that the "advertiser" overvalues pure effect. Student-advertisers are likely to write directly to the teacher, attempting to charm him or her with candor, humor, or personal attention—often a novel experience for the teacher.

Related to the advertiser's stance is the *entertainer's stance*, which "sacrifices substance to personality and charm." An imbalance in favor of the speaker's ethical appeal, this stance is the rarest corruption of the rhetorical stance found in student essays. Most students are unaware of the methods used by writers to generate ethical appeal; hence, their imbalances are likely to tilt in other directions. Many first-year writers were taught in high school never to use "I" in their writing—the key word of the entertainer's stance.

Booth's question of rhetorical balance is essential to an understanding of the methods available for manipulation of stylistic choices. The question of the relationship between writer and subject is important, but more central to your students' understanding of style will be the question of their relationships as writers to their audience—an audience that, in the final analysis, will usually be composed only of you, their teacher. Obviously, students will attempt to choose a style that will suit their identified readership, but the voice they choose for a letter to a close friend will be very different from the one they choose for the English teacher. The danger of artificiality is all too real.

Teachers and scholars have explored the problem of making the teacher a final audience for students' texts by trying to create other plausible audiences, with the most obvious sorts of such assignments being "letters to the editor" of a local newspaper, "letters to the President" of the United States or the University or the dorm. Some assignments have been created that specified a very complex writing situation, complete with subject and audience; one example might be an assignment that asks students to define and give examples of "conventional diction" to a group of ninth-grade French students who knew basic English but who needed more information about how Americans really used it.

The problem with these plausible or created audiences (not including ethical problems some teachers have with the sophistic, or artificial, aspect of audience creation) grows out of the fact that the students are always aware that behind the "editor" or the "French students" stands the teacher, who ultimately wields the power of the grade. Their awareness makes the assignment even more complex. The student knows that, in reality, she is writing the way the teacher thinks one should write for the editor or for the ninth-graders, not the way one really would actually write to them. In other words, a student must try to write for *another person's* conception of a fictional audience. It is no wonder that students often freeze solidly into take-no-chances dullness in such assignments.

The alternative, to specify no audience at all, leaves the student in a simpler but no less difficult situation. Most freshmen, accustomed to the rich contextual responses of verbal communication, find it difficult to conceptualize that abstract, fictionalized "universal audience" which the Belgian rhetorician Chaim Perelman says is the ultimate audience for written discourse (402). Many first-year writers find it difficult to adjust their styles, which are sharpened and skillful on the oral level, to what seem to them the difficult conventions of non-contextual written discourse. As a result, they tend to write pedantically, on the assumptions that stressing the subject is the safest thing to do, and that they may, as college students, need to sound "grown up." They cannot create a fictional audience easily, so they tend to "write into the void."

The problem of audience is not easily answered, since both over- and under-specification of audience can have unfortunate consequences. Perhaps the best compromise is to admit that the teacher is the audience and to attempt to work accordingly. In *Teaching Expository Writing*, William Irmscher tells us that:

> In the classroom it is difficult to escape the hard fact that the teacher is usually the only reader. The teacher is therefore the audience, and the style will no doubt be accommodated to the teacher. That's not all bad if the teacher is someone whom the student respects, feels comfortable with, and wants to write for. I have on occasion simply said to students in my classes that they should write for me, not so much me in the role of a professor who is going to give a grade, but me in the role of reader/critic or editor, who is going to make a professional judgment about their writing. (133–34)

Although students have a hard time seeing past their teacher as "judge," armed with red pen and gradebook, to a "coach" who is honestly pulling for every student to get an A, this compromise solution is the best we have yet found.

Intimately related to the question of audience is the conception of different levels of style. Cicero mentions the High, Middle, and Low styles of oratory and suggests that each has its place and purpose. In the early days of composition teaching, however, this sort of liberalism was supplanted by prescriptive judgments about the different levels of style. Style was either Right or Wrong, Correct or Incorrect, and in general, only an attempt to write in a high, "literary" style was acceptable to the teacher. Gradually this dichotomy of Good and Bad gave way to the three hierarchical levels of style that many of us were raised on: Formal or Literary Style, Informal or Colloquial Style, and Vulgar or Illiterate Style. Of these three, only the Formal was really proper for writing; the other two styles instead reflected the way we talked, or the style of letters to friends (the Vulgar style was how *they* talked, not how we talked). Toward the middle years of this century this vertical hierarchy was liberalized further, becoming a horizontal continuum from which any stylistic form could be chosen (Marckwardt viii).

Today many teachers accept another extension of this continuum, one developed by language theorist Martin Joos, whose book *The Five Clocks* posits five major levels of style that run along a horizontal continuum. Perhaps the most important feature of Joos's theory is that it makes no judgments about stylistic validity. His most formal style is no more or less valid than his least formal, for Joos views the levels of style as alternatives available to all language users for deployment in different situations. Following is a listing of Joos's five styles, the breadth of each style, and the degree of responsibility each assumes for successful communication in any communicative situation:

Style	Breadth	Responsibility
Frozen	genteel	best
Formal	puristic	better
Consultative	standard	good
Casual	provincial	fair
Intimate	popular	bad

According to Joos, the main element separating these levels of style is that of audience participation, the sender's reliance on the receiver for shared background and participation. Audience participation plays a major role in the Intimate style, while the background and participation of the audience is least expected in the Frozen style. Since the Intimate, Casual, and Consultative styles all rely on a verbal context of signals, most expository writing takes place on the Formal or Frozen levels. Once again, this is not a negative judgment against the other styles:

Good intimate style fuses two personalities. Good causal style integrates disparate personalities into a social group which is greater than the sum of its parts. . . . Good consultative style produces cooperation without the integration, profiting from the lack of it. Good formal style informs the individual separately, so that his future planning may be the more discriminate. Good frozen style, finally, lures him into educating himself. (Joos 111)

There are, in other words, reasons that are not merely arbitrary or conventional for telling your students to write to certain formal standards. If Joos is correct, the nature of writing itself promotes using the Formal or Frozen styles.

The main characteristic of Formal style, according to Joos, is that participation of the audience is lost. Without the immediate context provided by responses, Formal style has a "dominating character" and must be logical and organized. It demands advance planning in order to make all its points without reminders from the audience, and its hallmarks are detachment and cohesion. The Frozen style, even farther removed from an audience, is, according to Joos, a style for print and declamation, a style for the most formal literary tasks and for oratory. This level of style is not useful for most students because it sacrifices much of its humanity through enforced absence of intonation. Joos says that this is a style used between social strangers; thus, it won't be usable in many classroom contexts.

The old Correct-Incorrect duality that teachers have for so long applied to style is not completely wrongheaded. Certain levels of stylistic formality really do correspond to the needs and perceptions of readers of exposition better than do others. Certainly, some content can be expressed using any of Joos's five styles, but other content can be best served by one or another. For this reason, we can teach the formal styles not as more correct but as more useful for writing. Formal style can be seen as a dialect like any other, teachable to those who feel that learning it is important. To demonstrate the nature of the formal styles, you might ask your students to do a simple exercise. First, you will want to discuss and demonstrate Joos's first four styles (Intimate style, essentially private language, can be difficult to exemplify); then, translate a few simple phrases from one style to another. Ask your students to try to translate into Casual or Consultative style this passage by Richard Weaver, which is written in his own curious blend of Formal and Frozen styles.

It will be useful to review here this flight toward periphery, or the centrifugal impulse of our culture. In the Middle Ages, when

there obtained a comparatively clear perception of reality, the professor of highest learning was the philosophic doctor. He stood at the center of things because he had mastered principles. On a level far lower were those who had mastered only facts and skills.
—from *Ideas Have Consequences*

After a student has made the brave beginning, "Now it will be cool to check out here this run toward the edge . . . " and has realized that the sense of the thought is already lost and that he has yet to try to tackle "the centrifugal impulse of our culture," he begins to see the point of the assignment. This exercise works to show your students that some content simply cannot be translated from level to level without seriously undermining its efficiency or meaning. Conversely, of course, there are messages that cannot be well served by Formal or Frozen style, but the preceding exercise shows that these more formal styles are not merely empty conventions enforced by English teachers. Styles grow organically out of the needs and nature of written exposition.

The several sorts of activities that can help students improve their styles are not limited to this chapter. Much of the material in Chapter 8 is also devoted to working with style on the sentence and paragraph levels. Francis Christensen's work on sentences has been found to be a valuable stylistic tool as have the sentence-combining exercises of John Mellon and Frank O'Hare. Tagmemic and generative-rhetoric paragraphing exercises also affect style. Style is ubiquitous, a part of all canons of rhetoric. If invention and arrangement are, indeed, a seamless whole, then style provides the final tonal definition of that whole.

In *Style: An Anti-Textbook,* Richard Lanham condemns the utilitarian prose and the "plain style" most commonly taught in freshman classes, asserting that language as play should be the key concept in composition classes. "Style," says Lanham, "must be taught for and as what it is—a pleasure, a grace, a joy, a delight" (20). Given the limitations under which most writing teachers labor, you may not get that far. Students cannot learn to control style in three or four months, but if you provide them with methods of analysis and good models to imitate, they will become aware of style as a concrete, controllable entity. Winston Weathers's *An Alternate Style: Options in Composition* is perhaps the most accessible text for students interested in expanding their repertoire of stylistic options. Weathers writes that

One of our major tasks as teachers of composition is to identify compositional options and teach students the mastery of the options and the liberating use of them. We must identify options in all areas of vocabulary, usage, sentence forms, dictional levels, paragraph types, ways of organizing material into whole compositions: options in all that we mean by style. Without options, there can be no rhetoric, for there can be no adjustment to the diversity of communication occasions that confront us in our various lives. (5)

Thus, it ultimately rests with teachers to introduce students to their stylistic options. And once students stop viewing their styles as predestined and unchangeable and begin to perceive style as quantitative, manipulable, and plastic, they can begin to seek Lanham's "grace" and "delight" as they learn better and better how to control both their rhetorical choices and their stylistic options.

Style Analyses

Most first-year students declare that they have no writing style—that mysterious "extra" quality that only professional writers have. It is not a wonder our students feel this way: even if they have been introduced to style, it was probably to literary style, that vague quality described by their teacher as "vigorous" or "curt" or "smooth," that quality found only in the writing of Hawthorne or Baldwin or Woolf. Style, nebulous and qualitative, is not to be found in student writing.

Before you can make style understandable to your students and demonstrate to them that they, too, can develop their own styles, you must make style measurable and describable. Teachers have to provide students with the necessary tools for dissecting and examining their own writing styles; the techniques of stylistic analysis can give us such tools.

Many different style analyses can be performed today; they have come a long way from the reliance upon tropes and figures that once characterized stylistic analysis. A trope (or "turn") involves a change or transference of a word's meaning from the literal to the imaginative, in such devices as allegory, metaphor, or irony. The *figures* (or *schemes*) sometimes involve changes in meaning as well, but they are primarily concerned with the shape of physical structure of language, the placing of words in certain syntactical positions, their repetition in varying patterns (to make an analogy with music, tropes exist in a vertical plane, like pitch or harmony; the figures exist in a horizontal plane, like rhythm or other stress devices). For years, tropes and schemes were mechanically multiplied, and students of style found themselves memorizing them all, a practice many upper-level graduate students continue to find useful today.

But today, stylistic analysis means more than simply an analysis of the tropes and schemes: it encompasses many of the elements of diction, usage, sentence construction, and paragraph treatment that writers use unconsciously. And today, stylisticians can rely on the computer to do the bean counting for them, allowing them to concentrate on responding to and analyzing the style. In his bibliographical essay, "Approaches to the Study of Style," Corbett tells us of two such programs: HOMER and The Writer's Workbench, both of which measure and display statistical (raw) data, ready for response. HOMER offers the total number of words in the text, the number of sentences, *to be* verbs, shun words and woolly words; The Writer's Workshop, aimed at helping students analyze their own prose, provides the type and length of sentences, the kinds of sentence openers, and the percentages of abstract words, nominalizations, passive verbs, and *to be* verbs. With the computer, we can glean more information, faster, but unless we understand how to analyze that information, neither we nor the computer can help our students.[2]

Corbett's style analysis is relatively simple and straightforward. It relies on the following teaching method:

1. Teachers introduce students to the terms and techniques of the method of analysis.
2. Students apply the method to simple examples and practice it on familiar pieces of prose.
3. They practice the method by analyzing the style of professional prose and discussing the findings in class.
4. Finally, they use the method to analyze their own prose, and they compare their findings with other sorts of prose.

As Winston Weathers points out, "improvement in student style comes not by osmosis, but through exercises" ("Teaching Style" 146). More than anything else, stylistic analyses reveal to students the understandable base of seemingly subjective labels on style. In addition, these analyses reinforce the notion that no writer, not even a student writer, is the prisoner of her own unchangeable ways of writing.

2 See also Cohen and Lanham; Kiefer and Smith.

Edward P.J. Corbett's Prose Style Analysis

Developed in the early 1960s and refined throughout that decade, Edward P.J. Corbett's method of analyzing style remains a flexible teaching tool, offering up a large number of stylistic features for possible analysis. It should be noted that many features of the aforementioned computer programs for analyzing prose are based on Corbett's own method. Teachers can choose from a few or the full range of features discussed by Corbett and assign them according to their students' abilities.

Counting is at the heart of Corbett's method (just as tabulating is at the heart of the computer programs). "Tedious counting and tabulating" are the necessary first steps, the only way to obtain the raw data concerning the stylistic features of the prose work being examined—a time-consuming but fairly easy task. The next step, more challenging, is relating "what the statistics reveal to the rhetoric of the piece being analyzed" ("Method" 296). Corbett explains the method in "A Method of Analyzing Prose Style with a Demonstration Analysis of Swift's *A Modest Proposal*" and presents the method in a more finished form in his text *Classical Rhetoric for the Modern Student*.

Corbett's method investigates three main areas of style: sentences, paragraphs, and diction. The piece of prose to be analyzed should be at least five to six hundred words in length and no longer than a thousand words. By using and filling in the following charts, students can begin to analyze prose and map out various stylistic elements. Of import is Corbett's definition of a sentence: "a group of words beginning with a capital letter and ending with some mark of end-punctuation" (*Classical* 40).

Stylistic Study—I

(Sentences and Paragraphs)

EVALUATION   Professional Student
A. Total number of words in the piece studied   _____ _____
B. Total number of sentences in the piece
   studied   _____ _____
C. Longest sentence (in no. of words)   _____ _____
D. Shortest sentence (in no. of words)   _____ _____
E. Average sentence (in no. of words)   _____ _____
F. Number of sentences that contain more
   than 10 words over the average sentence   _____ _____

EVALUATION   Professional Student

G. Number of sentences that contain 5 words
   or more below the average   _____ _____
H. Percentage of sentences that contain more
   than 10 words over the average   _____ _____
I. Percentage of sentences that contain 5
   words or more below the average   _____ _____
J. Paragraph length
   longest paragraph (in no. of sentences)   _____ _____
   shortest paragraph (in no. of sentences)   _____ _____
   average paragraph (in no. of sentences)   _____ _____

Stylistic Study—II

(Grammatical Types of Sentence)

A simple sentence is a sentence beginning with a capital letter, containing one independent clause, and ending with terminal punctuation.

A compound sentence is a sentence beginning with a capital letter, containing two or more independent clauses, and ending with terminal punctuation.

A complex sentence is a sentence beginning with a capital letter, containing one independent clause and one or more dependent clauses, and ending with terminal punctuation.

A compound-complex sentence is a sentence beginning with a capital letter, containing two or more independent clauses and one or more dependent clauses, and ending with terminal punctuation.

Title of professional essay _____

Author_____

                                                      Professional Student

A. Total number of sentences in essay   _____ _____
B. Total number of simple sentences   _____ _____
C. Percentage of simple sentences   _____ _____
D. Total number of compound sentences   _____ _____
E. Percentage of compound sentences   _____ _____
F. Total number of complex sentences   _____ _____
G. Percentage of complex sentences   _____ _____

Professional Student

H. Total number of compound-complex
   sentences   _____ _____
I. Percentage of compound-complex sentences _____ _____

Stylistic Study—III

(Sentence Openers)

Title of professional essay _____

Author_____

For this study use only *declarative* sentences. No interrogative or imperative sentences.

Total number of declarative sentences: Professional _____
                                        Student _____

Sentences beginning with:	Professional		Student	
	No.	%	No.	%
A. Subject (e.g., *John broke the window. The* high cost of living will offset. . .)	___	___	___	___
B. Expletive (e.g., *It is plain that . . .*, *There are ten Indians.* Exclamations: *Alas, Oh*)	___	___	___	___
C. Coordinating conjunction (e.g., *And, But, Or, Nor, For, Yet, So*)	___	___	___	___
D. Adverb word (e.g., *First, Thus, Moreover, Nevertheless, Namely*)	___	___	___	___
E. Conjunctive phrase (e.g., *On the other hand, As a consequence*)	___	___	___	___
F. Prepositional phrase (e.g., *After the game, In the morning*)	___	___	___	___
G. Verbal phrase (e.g., participial, gerundive, or infinitive phrase)	___	___	___	___
H. Adjective phrase (e.g., *Tired but happy, we. . .*)	___	___	___	___
I. Absolute phrase (e.g., *The ship having arrived safely, we. . .*)	___	___	___	___
J. Adverb clause (e.g., *When the ship arrived safely, we. . .*)	___	___	___	___

Sentences beginning with:	Professional		Student	
	No.	%	No.	%
K. Front-Shift (e.g., inverted word order: *The expense we could not bear. Gone was the wind. Happy were they to be alive.*)	___	___	___	___

Stylistic Study—IV

(Diction)

Title of professional essay _____

Author _____

For this investigation, confine yourself to this range of paragraphs: paragraphs _____ through _____ . For the investigation of your own prose, confine yourself to a comparable number of paragraphs.

In A, B, and C below, count only substantive words—nouns, pronouns, verbs, verbals, adjectives, and adverbs

	Professional	Student
A. Total number of substantive words in the passage	_____	_____
B. Total number of monosyllabic substantive words	_____	_____
C. Percentage of monosyllabic substantive words	_____	_____
D. Total number of nouns and pronouns in the passage	_____	_____
E. Total number of concrete nouns and pronouns	_____	_____
F. Percentage of concrete nouns and pronouns	_____	_____
G. Total number of finite verbs in all dependent and independent clauses in the passage	_____	_____
H. What percentage does G represent of A?	_____	_____
I. Total number of linking verbs	_____	_____
J. Percentage of linking verbs (using A)	_____	_____
K. Total number of active verbs (do not count linking verbs)	_____	_____
L. Percentage of active verbs (using A)	_____	_____
M. Total number of passive verbs (do not count linking verbs)	_____	_____

	Professional	Student
N. Percentage of passive verbs (using A)	_____	_____
O. Total number of adjectives in the passage (do not count participles or articles)	_____	_____
P. Average number of adjectives per sentence (divide by the total number of sentences in the passage)	_____	_____

(*Classical Rhetoric* 450–58)

Classroom Use of Corbett's Style Analysis

Since Corbett's method was actually developed for use in the classroom, most of our discussion of it will take place in this "practical-use" section. As previously stated, the flexibility of this system allows it to be used profitably for nearly any analytic purpose. To begin this assignment, you need to choose which of the charts you wish your students to use in their analyses. Chart I, dealing with the lengths of sentences and paragraphs, is the simplest of the four and the only chart that requires almost no teaching time to prepare students to use it. Chart II, which deals with the different grammatical types of sentences, requires more preparation on the part of both teacher and student. You will want to tell your students exactly what elements make up a dependent clause. In order for the analysis to succeed, you must make *certain* before you begin that your students can recognize different types of sentences: simple, compound, complex, and compound-complex. Practice in sentence identification is really the only way to do this. For this activity, your reader can serve as a useful tool.

After you have defined simple, compound, complex, and compound-complex sentences and given examples on the board, go through the reader picking out examples, asking for identifications, and discussing the different stylistic effects of sentence length and structure. After this sort of practice, students are usually conversant enough with grammatical classification to use Chart II. Just to be certain, though, Corbett included definitions of the sentence types at the top of Chart II, and it is a good idea to reproduce his definitions along with the chart.

While it does not call for really difficult recognitions, Chart III seems to be the most complex of the charts, the chart first dispensed with by teachers of less-prepared students. A study of sentence openers can be extremely revealing and profitable for a class of juniors or seniors, but most first-year students have trouble using the chart, for they usually have command of only three or four types of openers. If you do decide to use Chart III, you will want to familiarize your students with its terms, just as you did for Chart II above.

Although Chart IV looks complicated, it is really nothing more than an analysis of monosyllables, nouns, verbs, and adjectives. In order to use it, you will have to give a short refresher course in grammatical nomenclature, but the terms are simple enough that this shouldn't take more than a class period. This chart can provide a great deal of interesting material and will well repay the time you spend teaching its terms.

You may want to advance under the assumption that upper-level students can use all four charts, that advanced lower-level students can handily grasp Charts I, II, and sometimes IV, and that Basic Writing students should probably be asked to do no analyses more complicated than those in Chart I. If students are asked to try to analyze stylistic elements that are difficult for them to grasp, the whole exercise becomes both a prolonged and a useless agony. You will find, if you are worried that the use of only a single chart seems unrevealing, that even one chart will provide a great deal of possible material to consider.

The charts are the mechanical element in Corbett's analytical system, which his accompanying method brings to life. With most other methods of style analysis, the results are tabulated and commented upon, and that's the end of it. The prose can be a professional essay or a student theme; the important activity is the analysis itself. Not so with Corbett's system. Though it can certainly be used to dissect discrete pieces of discourse—he used it thus himself in "A Method of Analyzing Prose Style"—the pedagogical use of the more completely evolved method presented in *Classical Rhetoric* is much more productive: an assignment that asks students to analyze both professional prose and a sample of their own writing and then to write an essay that draws conclusions from the comparative analysis (450).

The essay Corbett used as the professional model in his assignment was F.L. Lucas's "What Is Style?", but almost any of the available readers has several essays that can serve as valuable reference points. Obviously, you will want to ask students to compare exposition with exposition or description with description, rather than argumentation with narration, or exposition with description. Some teachers suggest that students choose a central section of around a thousand words from the essay, rather than an opening or concluding section; these extremities often have stylistic peculiarities that make them difficult to use as models. As for the sample of student writing to be used, it should be *at least* five to six hundred words long, and if the students can offer longer pieces of writing, so much the better. You can ask freshmen to use a paper written earlier in the course, but a long paper from their senior year in high school works better; students will approach such an essay with some detachment, which, will make their analyses more objective. This assignment can be especially effective if the students analyze, evaluate, and discuss the style of a professional piece, then wait a few weeks before they approach their own texts.

To complete the project, the student analyzes both writing samples—one at a time—and fills in the appropriate blanks on the assigned charts, a time-consuming task. You will want to devote several homework assignments to this part of the task. Students will want to use a pocket calculator for the quantitative part of the assignment. When the assignments are due, devote a class to making certain that everyone has done the counting correctly by discussing and putting on the board the correct answers for the professional piece. If students have counted or see how to count the professional prose correctly, they will be able to count their own prose correctly. After this is done, you can ask each student to write an essay that draws conclusions about his or her own style based on the comparative analysis of professional and student prose.

When the essays are due—and your students will probably need two weeks for this assignment—ask that the data-filled charts be attached to the ends of the essays so you can refer to them. These essays, even on the first-year level, are often extremely perceptive; Corbett calls them the "best themes" he has seen. By comparing their own writing with professional writing, students come to realizations that months of lecturing or nonpersonal analyses could never produce. For example, a first-semester student wrote this perceptive analysis.

Sentence length is the area of greatest discrepancy between my writing and that of professional Anne Bernays. Bernays's longest sentence in words is 51, and her shortest is 4. This is a range of 47, a range that is quite extensive. On the other hand, my range is only 17 with a low of 11 and a high of 28. This, of course, is an extremely noticeable difference. This range difference shows that my current style of writing is rather "choppy." In other words, the length of sentences throughout the writing remains practically constant, creating a boring style. . . . The main problem in my present style is inexperience. I have not practiced the use of varied sentence openers and sentence structures as much as I should have practiced. A little more variety in a number of aspects of my style should make a visible difference in my writing.

One warning about this assignment: it will make all other stylistic analyses seem anticlimactic to students. As John Fleischauer has suggested, after students have mastered statistical analysis, it quickly becomes a chore; and Corbett's system is complete and illuminating enough if is introduced completely and used carefully to make other systems superfluous (Fleischauer 100).

Imitation

Different imitation techniques, whether they consist of direct copying of passages, composition of passages using models, or controlled mutation of sentence structures, all have one thing in common: they cause students to internalize the structures of the piece being imitated. With those structures internalized, a student is free to engage in the informed processes of choice which are the wellspring of real creativity. William Gruber puts it succinctly when he suggests that imitation does not affect creativity but rather assists in design:

> Standing behind imitation as a teaching method is the simple assumption that an inability to write is an inability to design—an inability to shape effectively the thought of a sentence, a paragraph, or an essay (493–94).

Imitation exercises provide students with practice in that "ability to design" that is the basis of a mature prose style.

Two Different Imitation Techniques

Perhaps more than any other contemporary rhetorician, Edward P.J. Corbett is responsible for the resurgence in the popularity of imitation. His central statement on imitation and a large number of exercises in copying and creative imitation are to be found in his textbook *Classical Rhetoric for the Modern Student. Corbett recommends several different sorts of exercises, the first and simplest of which involves "copying passages, word for word, from admired authors." This task is not quite as simple as it may seem, though; in order to derive benefit from this exercise, the imitator must follow a few rules:*

1. He must not spend more than fifteen or twenty minutes copying at any one time. If he extends this exercise much beyond twenty minutes at any one siting, his attention will begin to wander, and he will find himself merely copying words.

2. He must do this copying with a pencil or pen. Typing is so fast and so mechanical that the student can copy off whole passages without paying any attention to the features of an author's style. Copying by hand, he transcribes the passage at such a pace that he has time to observe the choice and disposition of words, the patterns of sentences, and the length and variety of sentences.

3. He must not spend too much time with any one author. If the student concentrates on a single author's style, he may find himself falling into the "servile imitation" that rhetoricians warned of. The aim of this exercise is not to acquire someone else's style but to lay the groundwork for developing one's own style by getting the "feel" of a variety of styles.

4. He must read the entire passage before starting to copy it so that he can capture the thought and the manner of the passage as a whole. When he is copying, it is advisable to read each sentence through before transcribing it. After the student has finished copying the passage, he should read his transcription so that he once again gets a sense of the passage as a whole.

5. He must copy the passage slowly and accurately. If he is going to dash through this exercise, he might as well not do it at all. A mechanical way of insuring accuracy . . . is to make his handwriting as legible as he can (510).

Corbett provides a number of specimen passages for imitation in *Classical Rhetoric*, covering prose styles ranging from the King James Bible to James Dickey's *Deliverance*.

For students who have spent some time copying passages, Corbett recommends a second kind of imitation exercise, *pattern practice*. In this exercise, the student chooses or is given single sentences to use as patterns after which she is to design sentences of her own. "The aim of this exercise," says Corbett, "is not to achieve a word-for-word correspondence with the model but rather to achieve an awareness of the variety of sentence structure of which the English language is capable." The model sentences need not be followed slavishly, but Corbett suggests that the student observe at least the same *kind, number*, and *order* of phrases and clauses. Here are a few of the model sentences and examples of imitations that Corbett gives:

MODEL SENTENCE: He went through the narrow alley of Temple Bar quickly, muttering to himself that they could all go to hell because he was going to have a good night of it.—James Joyce, "Counterparts"

IMITATION: They stood outside on the wet pavement of the terrace, pretending that they had not heard us when we called to them from the library.

MODEL SENTENCE: To regain the stage in its own character, not as a mere emulation of prose, poetry must find its own poetic way to the mastery the stage demands—the mastery of action.—Archibald MacLeish, "The Poet as Playwright"

IMITATION: To discover our own natures, not the personalities imposed on us by others, we must honestly assess the values we cherish—in short, our "philosophy of life."

MODEL SENTENCE: If one must worship a bully, it is better that he should be a policeman than a gangster.—George Orwell, "Raffles and Miss Blandish"

IMITATION: Since he continued to be belligerent, it was plain that cajoling would prove more effective than scolding. (535)

Another useful imitation technique is *controlled composition*. According to Edmund Miller, controlled composition is "the technique of having students copy a passage as they introduce some systematic change" ("Controlled Composition" 1).[3] The changes that might be introduced can range from putting a third-person narrative into the first person to changing active to passive voice. Students are first given practice in copying the original model, making certain that every element of the copy is correct; they are then asked to rewrite it, making the stipulated changes. Here is an example of one of Miller's controlled composition assignments, from *Exercises in Style*:

Let's Hear It for Mickey Spillane
1. Watching television may be interesting and informative. 2. But reading a trashy novel is even more interesting and informative. 3. Even if you read two blood-and-guts thrillers a week, you can always count on finding them informative. 4. We learn not only from what is well written but also from what is poorly written. 5. Reading an inadequate book improves the reader's critical skills and also his general facility with reading. 6. Watching a mindless television show like "The New Treasure Hunt," "Gilligan's Island," or "Mork and Mindy" is considerably less in-

---

3 Controlled composition is often used successfully in Basic Writing courses. For an exemplary textbook, see Gorrell.

formative. 7. This is because television is passive and aural, engaging the ear but only a small compartment of the mind. 8. Neither mind nor body gets challanged to do its best. 9. Reading, however, is always active and mental. 10. Body and mind help each other make reading even *Kiss Me, Deadly* or *The Erection Set* or *Me, Hood* an experience of an entirely different order from watching "The Mary Tyler Moore Show."
Directions:

I. Add the word *both* to each sentence, being careful to make all changes necessary for the proper use of the word but no other changes.

II. Leaving as much of the *original* sentence structure as possible, add the following *ideas* to the correspondingly numbered phrasing of the additions as necessary for good style:

1. Movie-going may be interesting and informative.
2. Reading a trashy novel gives us pleasure.
3. You can count on finding even some unforgettable Agatha Christie stories read to pass the time on a plane informative.
4. What is written indifferently also teaches.
5. We improve ourselves when we read great literature.
6. "The Dating Game" is a mindless television show.
7. Film too is a medium that requires our passivity.
8. Mind and body are working at less than full strength when we watch T.V.
9. Reading opens up our minds to new ideas.
10. A revival showing of Eisenstein's film classic "Ivan the Terrible, Part I," does not give us the same sort of experience that even a second-rate book does. (5–6)

Corbett's and Miller's exercises can serve to help students understand the context in which they create writing. Without knowledge of what has been done by others, there can be no profound originality. Speaking of his own instruction through the use of imitation, Winston Churchill said, "Thus I got into my bones the essential structure of the ordinary British sentence—which is a noble thing." If we can help our students get the structure of ordinary sentences "into their bones," the time and effort of imitation exercises will have been worthwhile.

Classroom Use of Imitation Exercises

There are many ways to introduce imitation exercises into a freshman class, and you can decide how you wish to approach imitation based on the amount of time you have available. Some kinds of imitation can be done as homework, but others really need the sort of teacher encouragement that only a classroom setting can provide. One important point that applies to all sorts of imitation: if you choose to use imitation, be prepared to work with it throughout the entire term if you want results from it. Like sentence-combining (with which it shares other attributes), imitation has value only insofar as it leaves students with an intuitive sense of good discourse patterns that they can apply to all of their writing assignments.

There are problems in teaching imitation. Students are initially suspicious of the method, seeing it as a block to their originality. They balk at the rigidity of some of the exercises. Higher-level students sometimes resent imitation as babywork, beneath their capacities (and obviously for some students it will be). You will see little improvement unless you work on the exercises regularly and expose your students to as many kinds of distinctive sentences as you can. You will have to keep reminding your students of the two criteria for successful imitation: (1) the "further away" the new content is from the original, the better the imitation will be, and (2) the new content should coincide perfectly with the given rhetorical model.

Press on and you *will* see a change. Imitation can liberate students' personalities by freeing them of enervating design decisions, at least temporarily. Paradoxically, through exercises that connote servitude, you will be promoting freedom.

Works Cited *Chapter 7*

Abrams, M.H. *The Mirror and the Lamp.* New York: Oxford UP, 1953.

Booth, Wayne. "The Rhetorical Stance." Winterowd 71–79.

Chatman, Seymour, and Samuel R. Levin., eds. *Literary Style: A Symposium.* London: Oxford UP, 1971.

—.*Essays on the Language of Literature.* Boston: Houghton, 1967.

Cohen, Michael E., and Charles R. Smith. "HOMER: Teaching Style with a Microcomputer." Wresch 83–90.

Corbett, Edward P.J. "A Method of Analyzing Prose Style with a Demonstration Analysis of Swift's *A Modest Proposal.*" Tate 294–312.

—. "Approaches to the Study of Style." Tate 83–130.

—. *Classical Rhetoric for the Modern Student.* 2nd ed. New York: Oxford UP, 1971.

Fleischauer, John. "Teaching Prose Style Analysis." *Style* 9 (1975): 92–102.

Golden, James L., et al., eds. *The Rhetoric of Western Thought.* 3rd ed.

Gorrell, Donna. *Copy/Write: Basic Writing Through Controlled Composition.* Boston: Little, 1982.

Graves, Richard. "A Primer for Teaching Style." CCC 25 (1974): 186–90.

Gruber, William. "'Servile Copying' and the Teaching of English." CE 39 (1977): 491–97.

Irmscher, William F. *Teaching Expository Writing.* New York: Holt, 1979.

Joos, Martin. *The Five Clocks.* New York: Harcourt, 1961.

Kiefer, Kathleen, and Charles R. Smith. "Improving Students' Revising and Editing: The Writer's Workbench." Wresch 62–82.

Lanham, Richard. *Style: An Anti-Textbook.* New Haven: Yale UP, 1974.

Marckwardt, Albert H. Introduction to *The Five Clocks.* Joos i–x.

Milic, Louis T. "Against the Typology of Styles." Chatman and Levin 442–50.

—. "Rhetorical Choice and Stylistic Option: The Conscious and Unconscious Poles." Chatman 77–88.

—"Theories of Style and Their Implications for the Teaching of Composition." CCC 16 (1965): 66–69, 126.

Miller, Edmund. "Controlled Composition and the Teaching of Style." Paper presented at CCCC 29, Denver, CO, 1978.

—. *Exercises in Style.* Normal: Illinois State U., 1980.

Perelman, Chaim. "The New Rhetoric: A Theory of Practical Reasoning." Golden et al., 403–23.

Riffaterre, Michael. "Criteria for Style Analysis." Chatman and Levin 442–50.

Tate, Gary, ed. *Teaching Composition: Twelve Bibliographic Essays.* 2nd ed. Fort Worth: Texas Christian UP, 1987.

Weathers, Winston. *An Alternate Style: Options in Composition.* Rochelle Park, NJ: Hayden, 1980.

—. "Teaching Style: A Possible Anatomy." CCC 21 (1970): 114–49.

Weaver, Richard. *Ideas Have Consequences.* Chicago: U. of Chicago P., 1948.

Winterowd, Ross, ed. *Contemporary Rhetoric: A Conceptual Background with Readings.* New York: Harcourt, 1975.

Wresch, William, ed. *The Computer in Composition Instruction.* Urbana, IL: NCTE, 1984.

Chapter 8

Teaching the Sentence and the Paragraph

Teaching the Sentence

A number of theories and methods of instruction in writing approach the writing process through practice in syntax: the writing of good sentences. Imitation exercises can be considered a syntactic method because they ask students to practice sentence-writing, but the best known and most completely tested syntactic methods are Francis Christensen's *generative rhetoric of the sentence,* and *sentence-combining* as evolved by John Mellon, Frank O'Hare, and William Strong. Developed to make students aware of the components of a good sentence and to provide practice in writing such sentences, these systems were all influenced to some degree by Noam Chomsky's transformational-generative grammar.[1]

A key word in syntactic theory is "maturity," the ability to compose sentences that compare favorably with those of more experienced writers. Francis Christensen called this goal *syntactic fluency* (1963), but the term *syntactic maturity* was born only after Kellogg Hunt published his study of *Grammatical Structures Written at Three Grade Levels* and found that intra-sentence structures could be quantified according to the age and experience of the writer. Thereafter, sentence-combining theorists announced their goal of increasing students' syntactic maturity.

Syntactic maturity is *not,* of course, the same thing as overall quality of writing, although the two are often confused. Kellogg Hunt, whose research lay behind the concept of syntactic maturity, never claimed that students who are more syntactically mature write better (Morenberg 3). Theoretically at least, syntactic maturity is an evaluation of elements completely separate from overall quality of writing. "Words per clause," "clauses per T-unit," etc., do not and cannot measure tone, voice, organization, content—all qualitative factors that make up good writing. As John Mellon said after his sen-

---

1 See Chomsky, *Reflections on Language; Syntactic Structures.*

tence-combining study, "Syntactic maturity is only a statistical ar-
tifact"(Morenberg 4).

However, important tests of syntactic methods all found that as
syntactic maturity increased in student writing, so did the overall
quality of the writing as perceived by experienced English teachers.
The syntactic methods tested were compared to traditional content-
oriented methods and were found to produce student writing that
teachers judged better on the average. Although they measure two
different things, syntactic maturity and writing quality may seem in
fact to be linked.

This development is a bit confusing, even for supporters of syntactic methods. O'Hare, while carefully avoiding inflated claims for sentence-combining, suggests that style may have a powerful immediate
effect on the reader of an essay:

> This final choice made by every writer is . . . frequently a syn-
> tactic one. . . . The present study's findings strongly suggest
> that style, rather narrowly defined as the final syntactic choices
> habitually made from the writer's practical repertoire of syntactic
> alternatives, is an important dimension of what constitutes writ-
> ing ability. (*Sentence-Combining* 74)

We do not know why syntactic methods can produce overall better
writing, but evidence indicates that they do.[2] Syntactic methods are
particularly valuable because they allow students to work on and
practice many writing skills at once. They can be used to assist students whose sentences frequently contain grammatical errors such as
fragments or run-ons. They are good exercises for students who need
more familiarity with intra-sentence punctuation, especially with
commas. They give students control over the sentence and the options that sentence form offers. They can, in fact, provide an entire
lexicon of "sentence sense" concerning the way elements work
together within a sentence.

Traditional sentence theory, though it may seem outdated by its
more modern relatives, can still be a useful editorial tool for students,
allowing them to check suspect areas of their syntax with a testing
paradigm. It can also help students identify flaws, reconstruct the
purpose of the original sentence, and recast the sentence so that its
form is correct, yet still reflects the situation they began with. Traditional sentence theory can work hand-in-glove with syntactic practice
to produce good sentences that are also correct sentences.

2 See Faigley; Kerck et al.; Morenberg.

Much still lies outside our ken. As advanced as our understanding of syntactic units is, we still pay too little attention to the other levels on which sentences are structured: the semantic, the logical, and the rhythmic.[3] However, sentence theory *can* help students increase their syntactic fluency. Given the interactive relationship that exists between syntax and semantics, the task of helping our students to write syntactically fluent and mature sentences is one that can hardly be overestimated.

Traditional Sentence Theory

Western rhetorical theories about the sentence date back to classical antiquity, and have come to their present form by a long process of accretion. They have their roots in Latin grammar and in the oral rhetorical theories of the classical period. Because of their antique origins, they strike many teachers today as outdated. Certainly, they are dated, yet this is after all the teaching tradition which produced Burke, Madison, Melville, and Lincoln. Though traditional sentence theory must be approached through the critical filters that inform present-day theories, it remains a highly effective way to teach sentence construction. For the purposes of this section, we will discuss the rhetorical components of traditional sentence theory and examine each individually.

Functional Sentence Types   Along with the breakdown of sentences by grammatical types—simple, compound, complex, and compound-complex—the traditional classification of sentences is by function:

A *declarative sentence* is one that makes a statement, that formulates a single, though sometimes complex, proposition:

"In 1945 the United Nations had fifty-one members."

"Despite their physical similarities, the twins had somewhat different personalities, as Ray became a monk while Victor ended up directing Broadway plays."

An *imperative sentence* gives a command or makes a request. Unless it is a short command, the sentence seldom remains purely imperative. A purely imperative sentence might be:

"Please stop talking and open your books."

3 See Kane, "The Shape and Ring of Sentences."

An imperative-declarative (mixing command with proposition) might be:

"Finish your dinner or I'll send you to bed."

An *interrogative sentence* asks a question. It is always terminated by a question mark:

"Which book did you like most?"

"How did you live through last summer's heat?"

An *exclamatory sentence* expresses strong feeling. It is nearly always followed by an exclamation point.

"Say, the study of grammar is fascinating!"

"Victor, that's the most brilliant play I've ever seen!"

Traditional Rhetorical Classifications   From the beginning of classical rhetorical theory the sentence has been an object of study, and although that rhetorical sentence classifications are not taught as often as formerly, they can still be useful. There are several different types of rhetorical classifications, all relating to the traditional conception of a sentence as "a single complete thought," a statement which suggests that, as John Genung puts it, "it is requisite that . . . every part be subservient to one principal affirmation" (176).

The first traditional rhetorical division of sentences is into *short* and *long*. No quantitative definition of long or short sentences is possible, of course; as William Minto says in his *Manual of English Prose Literature*, "It would be absurd to prescribe a definite limit for the length of sentences, or even to say in what proportion long and short should be intermixed" (7). This unwillingness to be precise in numerical prescription is representative of traditional rhetorical theory, but Genung, Minto, and other composition teachers of the past were in agreement that long and short sentences must be intermixed in order to produce a pleasing style. Short sentences were to be used to produce an effect of vigor and emphasis, and long sentences were used for detail and to create cadence and rhythm.

Beyond the injunction to intermix lengths, there is little to be done with the classification of sentences into long and short. Far more important is the traditional rhetorical classification of sentences into *loose, periodic,* and *balanced*. Of these three classes of sentences, by far the most important are the loose and the periodic, for taken together they represent a complete traditional taxonomy of the sentence. The balanced structure can be either loose or periodic, and thus is not an equal or mutually exclusive class.

So far as we know, the division of sentences into loose and periodic is as old as the art of rhetoric itself. Aristotle made a distinction in his *Rhetoric* between "running" and "compact" sentences. "The style necessarily is either running, the whole made one only by a connecting word between part and part . . . or compact, returning upon itself. . . . the compact is the style which is in periods" (202). As rhetoric was developed through the Classical age and into the Medieval era, this conception of loose and periodic styles remained a central doctrine of sentence construction, especially since Latin constructions in the periodic style are much more common than in most other languages.

We take up the story in the second great age of rhetorical innovation, the eighteenth century, with the first truly modern statement of the doctrine, that of George Campbell in his *The Philosophy of Rhetoric* of 1776. Following Classical theory, Campbell claimed that there are two kinds of sentences, periodic and loose. Campbell's description of periods and loose sentences has not been surpassed for clarity and ease of understanding:

> A period is a complex sentence, wherein the meaning remains suspended until the whole is finished. . . . The criterion of. . . loose sentences is as follows: There will always be found in them one place at least before the end, at which, if you make a stop, the construction of the preceding part will render it a complete sentence (424—26)

Campbell provides examples of typical periodic and loose (which we refer to today as *cumulative*) constructions that express the same thought.

> "At last, after much fatigue, through deep roads and bad weather, we came with no small difficulty to our journey's end."

> "We came to our journey's *end* at *last*, with no small *difficulty*, after much *fatigue*, through deep *roads*, and bad *weather*."

Notice that the second, loose (cumulative) sentence could be grammatically concluded after any of the underlined words, while the period sentence must continue to its termination.

Campbell's definitions of loose and periodic sentences were used throughout the nineteenth century with few changes, and the different stylistic natures of the two kinds of sentences were given close attention. Campbell had said of the periodic and loose constructions, "the former savours more of artifice and design, the latter seems more the result of pure nature. The period is nevertheless more susceptible of vivacity and force; and the loose sentence is apt, as it were, to languish and grow tiresome" (426). This conception of the drama of the periodic sentence and the naturalness of the cumulative sentence continued throughout the nineteenth century. Both sorts of sentences, of course, are always found in the practice of real writers, and the predominance of one or the other helps to classify the author's style. In the nineteenth century the writings of De Quincy were said to typify the periodic style and those of Carlyle, the cumulative; in our own day we might point to the writings of Henry James as exemplifying the periodic style and those of Ernest Hemingway, the cumulative.

In the practice of most English writers, the cumulative sentence is far more common than the periodic. The history and nature of the language compel it, and we can even trace the decline of the periodic style in English as the French and native influences won out over the Latinate and Germanic constructions that were common in Old English. For the most part, modern English *demands* a predominance of loose sentences over periods. This is borne out by the problems inherent in the periodic style when it is pushed to extremes. The reader of a sentence in Henry James's later novels, for example, sometimes feels as if the author is working him very hard—*too* hard, in the minds of many. Too much reliance upon periodicity can exhaust the reader.

The cumulative and periodic sentence structures are mutually exclusive, but the final traditional rhetorical classification, the *antithetical* and the *balanced* sentence, can be either cumulative or periodic. The balanced sentence is a later development in rhetorical theory. Though the Greeks used it, it does not appear clearly in classical rhetoric, and then after it does appear, it is confused for a while with antithesis. Campbell discusses antithesis as a sort of periodic sentence, but Richard Whately, in his *Elements of Rhetoric* of 1828, states that "antithesis has been sometimes reckoned as one form of the Period, but it is evident that . . . it has no necessary connexion with it" (356). Gradually over the course of the nineteenth century, antithesis came to be associated with a single type of sentence. Alexander Bain stated in 1866 that "when the different clauses of a compound sentence are made similar in form, they are said to be Balanced" (302). John Genung makes the definition slightly more precise: "When the different elements of a compound sentence are made to answer to each other and set each other off by similarity of form, the sentence is said to be balanced" (191).

The writing of Samuel Johnson, perhaps more than that of any other author, gives examples of balanced sentences; for Johnson, they were habitual. "Contempt is the proper punishment of affectation, and detestation the just consequence of hypocrisy." "He remits his splendour, but retains his magnitude; and pleases more, though he dazzles less" (Campbell 425–26). Balanced sentences can sound pompous and mechanical if overused, and for that reason their use must always be limited. However, they can also present the reader with an "agreeable surprise" and enliven otherwise workaday prose with an element that can be oratorical and even poetic without calling attention to itself. As Genung later suggests, the balanced sentence can be used well for emphasis and for introducing paired concepts, but because of its tendency to become monotonous, writers should use care in determining the frequency of its appearance (191–192).

These three sentence types, then, represent the traditional rhetorical classification: The English-French-descended loose sentence, which makes up seventy to eighty percent of most English prose; the Latin- and German-descended periodic sentence, which makes up the other twenty to thirty percent, and the oratorical-sounding balanced sentence, which can be either loose or periodic. All have specific stylistic effects, and all are subject to corruptions, extremes, and overemphasis if not used carefully.

Classroom Use of Traditional Sentence Theory

The traditional classification is not a panacea for all student writing ills, but it can be used successfully in the classroom. If you decide to teach it, remember that the balance between loose and periodic sentences in modern American prose favors the loose or cumulative sentence. You will want to familiarize students with cumulative and periodic constructions and with the stylistic and organizational differences between them, and you might suggest that the periodic construction not be overused or overextended.

Begin teaching with some simple exercises on the blackboard. Transpose a short sentence from a cumulative to a periodic construction without mentioning the names of the types: "We went shopping to buy some sugar" to "To buy some sugar, we went shopping." Discuss the difference between the two sentences, pointing out that the (unnamed) cumulative sentence can be ended after "shopping" but the (unnamed, proceed inductively) periodic sentence cannot. You may want to pass out sheets of examples and ask students to work with the transposition of simple sentences for a while, both at the board and at their seats. Discuss some of the periodic structures thus created and critique them. You can gradually work into more complex cumulative and periodic structures.

After the concepts of the two different sorts of sentences are established, you can name them and ask students to check the percentages of them in their own work, perhaps in an essay already done. Many, of course, will find no periodic structures at all in their papers. Finally, you may want to suggest that a spread of ten to twenty percent of periodic sentences be in each succeeding essay. None of those periodic sentences should be longer than three clauses. Yes, you may get occasional stylistic monstrosities, but you will also get appealing and thoughtful periodic combinations as a result of students' attempts to widen their options.

As for balanced sentences, we know that our students, no Bacons or Johnsons, have little occasion to write them. But should you decide to teach the balanced sentence, you can use methods similar to those for the cumulative and periodic sentences—since students seldom seem to write them well or naturally.

Francis Christensen's Generative Rhetoric

In a series of essays, Francis Christensen described a new way of viewing sentences and a pedagogical method that could be used to teach students how to write longer, more mature, more varied and interesting sentences. Christensen considered the sentence the most important element in rhetoric because it is "a natural and isolable unit" ("The Course in Advanced Composition" 168). His theory of sentence-composing articulates four principles.

Addition The traditional formula for a good sentence has always been to use a concrete noun and an active verb, but Christensen's theory disputes this recipe. The composition of sentences is instead a process of adding different sorts of modifiers, some consisting of only a word, others consisting of a number of words or a clause.

Direction of Modification Writing moves in linear space: whenever a modifier is added to a sentence, it is added either before or after the word or clause it modifies. If the modifier is added before the noun, verb, or main clause being modified, the direction of modification can be indicated by an arrow pointing forward; if it is added after the unit being modified, by an arrow pointing backward:

"With a rear fender torn loose, the battered *Trans-Am* slowly

limped, squeaking and grinding, to the curb."

You will notice here that there are two kinds of modifiers in this example sentence. There are the *close* or *bound* modifiers of the noun and verb—"battered" and "slowly," And there are the *free* or *sentence modifiers*—"with a rear fender torn loose," "squeaking and grinding," and "to the curb" that modify the *clause* "Trans-Am limped." The difference between the two sorts of modifiers is simple: Bound modifiers are generally fixed in position, and the only choice one has about them is whether to use them at all. Free modifiers, on the other hand, are added to a clause and can be placed in many different positions in order to create different stylistic effects. Bound modifiers are usually said to be *embedded,* while free modifiers are said to be *added.*

Christensen claimed that overuse of bound modifiers is responsible for some of the worst excesses of teaching practice: what he calls the injunction to students to "load the patterns" with bound modifiers. "Pattern practice" thus sets students to writing sentences like this: "The small boy on the red bicycle who lives with his happy parents on our shady street often coasts down the steep street until he comes to the city park." This sort of sentence can result if noun clusters and verb clusters are not kept short. Heavy use of single-word bound modifiers does not necessarily make for good prose.

Bound modifiers, then, have limitations in terms of helping students write varied and interesting sentences. Free modifiers, in contrast, offer a wider range of possibilities. Sentences created through the use of free modifiers are considered by Christensen to be cumulative, the central sentence type used in modern prose. And since the free modifiers sharpen, focus, and define the thought of the main clause of a cumulative sentence, "the mere form of the sentence generates ideas," as Christensen puts it ("A Generative Rhetoric of the Sentence" 156). The careful use of free modifiers compels writers to examine their thoughts and can thus be more than a merely descriptive tool.

Levels of Generality Addition and direction of modification are structural principles, but for Christensen the structure has no meaning until a third principle is introduced, that of *levels of generality* or *levels of abstraction* ("A Generative Rhetoric" 157). In terms of the cumulative sentence, if two clauses or modifiers are at the *same* level of generality, they can be called *coordinate;* if a modifier is at a *lower* level of generality than the clause of modifier adjacent to it, it can be called *subordinate.* Free modifiers are subordinate to the main idea of a sentence, and thus function at a lower level of generality, as in this example: "The man sat silent, staring at his hands and his pipe, unable to still his trembling fingers."

Cumulative sentences can be diagrammed according to their levels of abstraction, with a higher number indicating a lower level of generality (*higher-numbered* levels are more specific than *lower-numbered* levels):

    1 He shook his hands,
        2 a quick shake, (noun cluster)
            3 fingers down, (absolute verb cluster)
                4 like a pianist. (prepositional phrase)
                        ("A Generative Rhetoric" 158)

Texture   This fourth principle provides an evaluative term that can be used when the first three principles are applied to prose. Christensen gives us a succinct definition of texture:

> If a writer adds to few of his nouns or verbs or main clauses, the texture may be said to be thin. The style will be plain or bare. . . . But if he adds frequently or much or both, then the texture may be said to be dense or rich. ("A *Generative* Rhetoric" 157)

The pedagogic end of Christensen's method is to introduce students to methods by which they can increase the density of their sentences and make the texture of their writing richer. Christensen's rhetoric does not follow the traditional canons of rhetoric; instead, it opts for a view that all other skills in language follow syntactic skills naturally. For Christensen, you could probably be a good writer if you could learn to write a good cumulative sentence.[4]

Classroom Use of Christensen's Generative Rhetoric

A good way to introduce Christensen's theory of the cumulative sentence is to discuss free modifiers versus bound modifiers. Put these two sentences on the blackboard:

---

4 Richard Coe has elaborated and extended the work of Christensen. In *Toward a Grammar of Passages*, Coe takes the traditional syntactic relationships between form and function—coordinate, subordinate, and superordinate—and subdivides them further: (1) coordination: contrasting, contradicting, conjoining, and repeating on the same level of generality; (2) subordination: defining, exemplifying, giving reasons, deducing (deductive conclusion), explaining (making plain by restating more specifically), qualifying; and (3) superordination: drawing conclusion, generalizing (making an inductive inference), commenting on a previously stated proposition. Then Coe goes on to develop a system for mapping these relationships. This syntactical system has been tested extensively with student writers, in classes ranging from ESL to technical writing, and from basic writing to advanced composition, with dramatic results. Students learn to "map" their own texts and thereby have a means of deciding whether those texts are coherent and "make sense."

"The old woman with the white hair who picks through the smelly trash in our crowded backyard gestured wildy and shrieked out joyfully."

"White-haired and beady-eyed, the old trashpicker gestured wildy and shrieked out joyfully, her work-gloved hands beating the air, her thin voice rising and cracking, the smelly trash falling around her in our crowded backyard."

Discuss the differences between these two sentences with the class. Ask them which is better, and why. Point out the *base clause* in both sentences, "the old woman gestured and shrieked." Most students will choose the second sentence as better, despite the fact that it contains no more propositional information than the first. Through this discussion, you can gradually come around to the question of bound and free modifiers and how they affect the sentences.

At this point, explanation through example is the easiest course of action. Pass out a sheet of examples of two-level cumulative sentences (you can use examples from books *or* make up sentences yourself). These sheets should not include diagrammed sentences—that will come later. Type the sentences without indicating levels of abstraction. Using this sheet of examples and transferring some sentences to the board, you can introduce the principles of *addition* and *order of movement*. Show how each of the sentences has a base clause and how the free modifiers define or specify the material in the base clause. Use arrows to show the direction of modification.

From this point onward, your students should begin to be able to write and manipulate cumulative sentences. You will need to continue to check their work, since they will have a tendency, especially at these early stages, to degenerate into "loading the patterns" with bound modifiers. Another problem to guard against is a tendency of students to attempt to write a free modifier and instead come up with a dangling modifier. In order to keep an eye out for these problem areas, you might begin to ask four or five students per day to prepare cumulative sentences and put them on the blackboard before class starts. The five minutes your class spends each day critiquing and discussing these sentences can pay large dividends, because this exercise gives students practice both at recognizing and at writing cumulative sentences.

However, the actual instruction in writing cumulative sentences is not yet over. The third principle, that of levels of generality, must still be examined, even while students are studying two-level cumulative sentences on the board. Only after some practice will students be able to grasp this third principle and then be able to manipulate free modifiers in a really "syntactically fluent" way.

To illustrate how levels of generality work, distribute sheets of the same sentences as were on the original example sheets this time diagrammed according to their levels of generality. You will have to go over once again how the base clause is the center of the sentence, how it is diagrammed by marking it 1, how it is identified, and how the free modifiers are identified and all marked 2 because they are a step more specific. Although Christensen recommends that students be able to use the grammatical names of the different kinds of free modifiers, you can choose whether or not you want to teach the grammatical terminology beyond an initial introduction.

One important factor that you will have to take into account when using cumulative-sentence practice in this generative way is the strong element of description and narration implied in the cumulative sentence. Cumulative sentences simply do not work as well for exposition or argumentation as they do for narration and description. What this means for the generation of sentences using the Christensen method is that generation exercises work best when they are based on immediate observation, for this pushes the student to use precise language.

The next stage of instruction is introduction to the multilevel sentence, the cumulative sentence with more than one level of abstraction. This subject gets complicated, and you cannot expect quick results. To introduce the multilevel sentence, pass out examples of such sentences, diagrammed to show their different levels of generality. Point out how some of the modifiers are on the same level and are thus called coordinate, and how some are on lower levels because they modify modifiers rather than the base clause, and are thus called subordinate. Go through the familiarization exercises as with the two-level sentence, first asking students to diagram example sentences and then to generate sentences to fill in given line diagrams. Here are a few of the multilevel sentence exercises Christensen uses in *A New Rhetoric*:

A. Copy these sentences, using indentation and numbering to mark the levels. If your instructor so directs, mark the grammatical character of the levels added to the main clause.
   1. Crane sat up straight, suddenly, smiling shyly, looking pleased, like a child who had just been given a present. /Irwin Shaw
   2. For once, the students filed out silently, making a point, with youthful good manners, of not looking at Crane, bent over at his chair, pulling his books together. /Irwin Shaw

3. She was very old and small and she walked slowly in the dark pine shadows, moving a little from side to side in her steps, with the balanced heaviness and lightness of a pendulum in a grandfather clock. /Eudora Welty
4. As he walked into the club he noticed them, objectively and coldly, the headwaiter beckoning haughtily, head tilted, lips in a rigid arc reserved for those willing to pay the price of recognition and attention, the stiffly genteel crowd, eating their food in small bites, afraid of committing a breach of etiquette.(39)

Work with multilevel sentences completes the introduction to the cumulative sentence; the job from this point on is getting students to *use* cumulative sentences in their writing. After introducing the Christensen method, you must continue to emphasize the cumulative sentence if you want your students to remember and use it. The exercises that students have been putting on the board before each class help them practice cumulative sentences, but further practice is needed to gain results. At this point bring up Christensen's fourth principle, that of texture. Create some examples of thin and of dense prose that have similar content pattern and reproduce them to pass out, juxtaposing the thin with the densely textured passages. Then feel free to give a short soapbox speech about the advantages of dense texture and the usefulness of the cumulative sentence in students' own writing assignments. This lecture will be the end of the beginning of the study of Christensen' sentence theory.

From this point on, at least two hours per week, generally as homework, need to be devoted to the writing of cumulative sentences if anything is to be gained. If the cumulative sentence does not become a writing habit for students, it will have no real value. Practice can be set up in a number of ways: You can supply base clauses and ask students to modify them, or give short observation assignments to be written using cumulative sentences. But you must make certain that students do practice the work every week. Like sentence-combining, cumulative sentence work must be done often if students are to succeed.

The Christensen technique seems less useful for teaching students to write exposiiton than for teaching them description and narration, because cumulative sentences just naturally lend themselves to narrative or descriptive writing. Since the best cumulative sentences are based on observation, students may initially have a hard time moving them to the more abstract modes of argumentation and exposition, even though those modes often do contain elements of narration and description. One way of helping students deal with this problem is to follow Christensen sentence work immediately with Christensen paragraph theory, an introduction to which is included in this chapter. The Christensen paragraph is based on expository paragraphs just as the sentence theory is based on narrative sentences, and the two theories work to balance one another out.

Finally, if you find Christensen's theories congenial, look at his original articles and investigate the entire Christensen rhetoric program as found in the texts *A New Rhetoric* and *Christensen Rhetoric*. This short overview cannot do justice to the delightfulness of his writing style. Few teachers see the answers to all rhetorical problems in Christensen's syntactic work, but his theories remain among the strongest and most respected weapons in our arsenal.

Sentence-Combining

Sentence-combining in its simplest form is the process of joining two or more short, simple sentences to make one longer sentence, using *embedding, deletion, subordination,* and *coordination*. Although its history stretches back to the *grammaticus* of classical Rome, not until recently has sentence-combining been applied with any coherent scientific methodology or recognized as an important technique.

The theoretical base upon which sentence-combining would be founded was established in 1957, when Noam Chomsky revolutionized grammatical theory with his book *Syntactic Structures*.[5] This theoretical base was, of course, Chomskian *transformational generative grammar* (TG grammar), which caused immense excitement in the field of composition. TG grammar, which swept aside both traditional and structural grammar, seemed to present the possibility of a new pedagogy based on the study of linguistic transformations.

In 1963, Donald Bateman and Frank J. Zidonis of The Ohio State University conduced an experiment to determine whether teaching students TG grammar would reduce the incidence of errors in their writing. They found that students taught TG grammar made fewer errors and also developed the ability to write more complex sentence structures. Despite some questionable features in the Bateman and Zidonis study, it did suggest that TG grammar had an effect on student writing.[6]

The Bateman and Zidonis study was published in 1964; in that same year a study was published that was to have far more importance for sentence-combining: Kellogg Hunt's *Grammatical Structures*

---

5 Teachers new to Chomsky may want to look first at *Reflections on Language*.
6 See Bateman and Zidonis, *The Effect of a Study of Transformational Grammar*.

Written at Three Grade Levels. Hunt's work provides the basis for most measurements of *syntactic maturity*, which has come to be seen as an important goal of sentence-combining. Briefly, Hunt wished to find out which elements of writing changed as people matured, and which structures seemed to be representative of mature writing. To this end he studied the writings of average students at 4th-, 8th-, and 12th-grade levels, and expository articles in *Harper's* and *The Atlantic*. Hunt at first studied sentence length, but quickly became aware that the tendency of younger writers to string together many short clauses with "and" meant that sentence length was not a good indicator of maturity in writing ("A Synopsis" 111). He studied clause length, and "became more and more interested in what I will describe as one main clause plus whatever subordinate clauses happen to be attached to or embedded within it"—his most famous concept, the *minimal terminable unit* or *T-unit* ("A Synopsis" 111–12).

Each T-unit, says Hunt, is "minimal in length and each could be terminated grammatically between a capital and a period." He gives the example of a single theme written by a 4th-grader divided up into T-units.

> Here . . . is a simple theme written by a fourth-grader who punctuated it as a single 68–word sentence.

> I like the movie we saw about Moby Dick the white whale the captain said if you can kill the white whale Moby Dick I will give this gold to the one that can do it and it is worth sixteen dollars they tried and tried but while they were trying they killed a whale and used the oil for the lamps they almost caught the white whale.

> That theme, cut into these unnamed units, appears below. A slant line now begins each clause. A period ends each unit, and a capital begins each one.

> 1. I like the movie/we saw about Moby Dick, the white whale.
> 2. The captain said/if you can kill the white whale, Moby Dick, /I will give this gold to the one/that can do it.
> 3. And it is worth sixteen dollars.
> 4. They tried and tried.
> 5. But/while they were trying/they killed a whale and used the oil for the lamps.
> 6. They almost caught the white whale.(112)

The T-unit, Hunt found, was a much more reliable index of stylistic maturity than sentence length. Eventually he determined the best three indices of stylistic maturity: the average number of words per T-unit, the average number of clauses per T-unit, and the average number of words per clause. When they were applied to writing at different grade levels, he found that these numbers increased at a steady rate.

The studies of Bateman and Zidonis and of Hunt used no sentence-combining at all, but they did represent the bases from which modern sentence-combining sprang: the methodological linguistic base of TG grammar, and the empirical evaluative base of Hunt's studies of syntactic maturity. These two were brought together in the first important experiment involving sentence-combining exercises, that of John Mellon. Reported in his *Transformational Sentence-Combining: A Method for Enhancing the Development of Syntactic Fluency in English Composition*, Mellon's was the first study actually to ask students to practice combining kernel sentences rather than merely to learn grammar. "Research," wrote Mellon," . . . clearly shows that memorized principles of grammar, whether conventional or modern, clearly play a negligible role in helping students achieve 'correctness' in their written expression" (*Transformational Sentence-Combining* 2). What *could* help students do this, reasoned Mellon, was instruction in TG grammar *plus* practice exercises in combining short sentences into longer, more complex sentences.

Despite his disclaimer of interest in teaching students to memorize grammar, Mellon actually asked the seventh-graders he used in the experiment to learn a rather complicated set of grammatical rules, including transformational terms like "T: rel, T: gerund." The students were taught these rules and then asked to use them in signaled sentence-combining exercises with complex TG directions. Here is one of Mellon's exercises:

SOMETHING used to anger Grandfather no end. (T:exp)

SOMETHING should be so easy. (T:fact—T:exp)

The children recognized SOMETHING. (T:infin)

SOMETHING was only a preliminary to SOMETHING sometime. (T:wh)

He insisted SOMETHING. (T:gerund)

They had enough peppermints. (T:fact)

He gave them still another handful. (T:gerund)
(*Transformational Sentence-Combining* 129)

Without going thorugh the rules that Mellon asked his students to learn, it is difficult to explain how this exercise is to be done. Essentially, the transformational direction at the end of each kernel sentence showed how that sentence needed to be changed to fit into the combination, and the SOMETHING direction showed where information from other kernels was to be included. The sentence that Mellon's students were to create from this set of kernels goes like this: "It used to anger Grandfather no end that it should be so easy for the children to recognize that his insisting that they had had enough peppermints was only a preliminary to his giving them still another handful."

This sort of sentence-combining exercise may seem difficult, but Mellon's experiment was a success. Using Hunt's data on normal growth in writing maturity, Mellon found that his experimental sentence-combining group showed from 2.1 to 3.5 years' worth of syntactic growth while his control group did not show even a year's growth. Sentence-combining was established as an important tool in helping students write more mature sentences.

Further research on sentence-combining left theoreticians doubtful as to its efficacy in improving student's writing.[7] However, in 1973, Frank O'Hare's *Sentence Combining: Improving Student Writing Without Formal Grammar Instruction* showed beyond a doubt that sentence-combining exercises that did not include grammar instruction helped students achieve syntactic maturity. Again testing seventh-graders, O'Hare used sentence-combining exercises with his experimental group over a period of eight months without ever mentioning any of the formal rules of TG grammar. The amount of time spent on the combining exercises was considerable but not excessive; as O'Hare notes, "The sentence-combining treatment lasted an average of one hour and a quarter per week in class, and the students spent about half an hour per week on related homework assignments" (*Sentence-Combining* 42–3). The control group was not exposed to sentence-combining at all.

The type of sentence-combining exercises used in the O'Hare study was related to Mellon's exercises, but O'Hare wanted to avoid the cumbersome TG nomenclature of the signals in Mellon's exercises. To achieve this goal and yet still give suggestions that would help students work the exercise, O'Hare devised a simpler, nongrammatical signaling system for his study. Here is an example of one of his exercises:

SOMETHING led to SOMETHING.

James Watt discovered SOMETHING. ('S + DISCOVERY)

7 See Miller and Ney.

Steam is a powerful source of energy. (THAT)

Britain established an industrial society. ('S + ING)

(Sentence-Combining 86)

In O'Hare's exercises, Mellon's transformational cues were replaced by easy-to-understand word change and replacement directions, while the SOMETHING directions still indicated where information from other kernels was to be placed. The student is asked to bring the parenthesized term to the front of the sentence it followed and use it to change what is needed to be changed in order to effect the combination. In the example, the first kernel gives the general shape of the sentence to be created. Bringing each direction to the front of the sentence it follows and making the connection implied by the first kernel leads to the combined sentence that is the correct answer: "James Watt's discovery that steam is a powerful source of energy led to Britain's establishing an industrial society."

Some of O'Hare's later exercises did away completely with parenthesized cues and substituted a system of eliminating repeated words and underlining words to be kept:

The alleys <u>were littered with bottles and garbage.</u>
The alleys were <u>between the apartment buildings.</u>
The apartment buildings were <u>dismal.</u>
The bottles were <u>broken.</u>
The garbage was <u>rotting.</u>

This exercise specifies those words that will be needed in the final combined sentences by underlining them. By discarding those parts of the later kernels that are not needed, we get the final combination: "The alleys between the dismal apartment buildings were littered with broken bottles and rotting garbage."

O'Hare's test measured six factors of syntactic maturity and found that significant growth had taken place in all six. His experimental group of seventh-graders, after eight months of sentence-combining, now wrote an average of 15.75 words per T-unit—more than Hunt had reported as the average for twelfth-graders. The other factors were similarly impressive. Just as important, though, were the results of a second hypothesis O'Hare was testing: whether the sentence-combining group would write compositions that would be judged better in overall quality than those of the control group. Eight experienced English teachers rated 240 experimental and control essays written after the eight-month test period; when asked to choose between matched pairs of essays, they chose an experimental-group essay 70 percent of the time. The results suggest that sentence-combining exercises not only improve syntactic maturity but also affect perceived quality of writing in general (Sentence-Combining 67–77).

Further research on sentence-combining has suggested that its positive effects on student writing diminish over time.[8] Scholars continue to debate the issue; such controversy, though intriguing, can be safely ignored by new teachers of writing, who need know only that sentence-combining offers a viable way to help students write cleanly focused, grammatically correct, and thoughtfully worded sentences.

Classroom Use of Sentence-Combining

Two types of sentence-combining exercises, *cued* and *open*, can be used successfully in the classroom. Cued exercises have only one really "correct" answer, and they suggest it by using signals within or at the end of certain of the kernel sentences. Mellon's complex TG grammar signals are no longer used; instead, simple word cues and underlining instruct the combiner, as in this example from Frank O'Hare's *Sentencecraft (81):*

The next letter comes from a viewer.
The viewer doesn't understand something. (WHO)
A polar bear would know something somehow. (HOW)
A polar bear is *living in the arctic region.* (WHERE)
The *sun never sets* in the arctic region. (WHERE)
The bear is *to go to sleep sometime.* (WHEN TO)

The best solution to this example is the following sentence: "The next letter comes from a viewer who doesn't understand how a polar bear living in the arctic region, where the sun never sets, would know when to go to sleep."

Open exercises, on the other hand, merely present a series of kernel exercises and rely on intuition to create a grammatical sentence. Some open exercises are so simple that for all intents and purposes they have only one correct answer, as in this example from William Strong's text *Sentence-Combining: A Composing Book (109):*

The trout were blanketed.

---

8 See Combs; Daiker et al., "Sentence-Combining and Syntactic Maturity; Kerek et al., "Sentence-Combining and College Composition"; Morenberg et al., Sentence-Combining at the College Level"; Ney.

The trout were called rainbows.
The blanketing was with ferns.
The ferns were green.
The ferns were sweet smelling.

The best solution to this exercise is: "The rainbow trout were blanketed with green, sweet-smelling ferns." Other open exercises can be more complex and admit of a number of answers, as in this example from Daiker, Kerek, and Morenberg's *The Writer's Options* (138):

The vampire's existence may not appeal to many people.
The appeal is conscious.
But the all important promise of life after death strikes a chord.

The chord is deep in our unconscious.
The chord is the powerful will to live.
This is despite the cost.

Although there is no one "right" answer to the open exercises, the range of acceptable answers is limited, as you will see if you try to combine these kernels. They can be rewritten, "The vampire's existence may not appeal consciously to many people, but the all-important promise of life after death strikes a chord deep in our unconscious: the powerful will to live, despite the cost." Another possibility is, "The vampire's existence may not have conscious appeal to many people, but the all-important promise of life after death strikes a chord of the powerful will to live, despite the cost, that is deep in our unconscious." Other possibilities exist.

Both cued and open exercises are needed for most classes. Open exercises work well for students who have already acquired some degree of syntactic maturity, while cued exercises are helpful to students whose syntactic skills are still fairly undeveloped. Open problems keep up the interest of students who want some element of creativity in their exercises, while cued problems push students to learn and practice particular structures in a given full-sentence configuration.

Once you have decided on an exercise format and on the book or books you wish to use, the question still remains of how to teach sentence-combining.[9] You might want to begin with cued exercises. After

---

9 Teachers interested in using a sentence-combining text in the classroom should consider the most recent editions of Daiker et al., *The Writer's Options* (3rd ed., 1986); Memering and O'Hare, *The Writer's Work* (2nd ed., 1984); Strong, *Sentence Combining: A Composing Book* (2nd ed., 1983). See also O'Hare, *Sentencecraft*; Strong, *Sentence-Combining and Paragraph Building*.

explaining the sentence-combining process and how the cues work, assign six or eight problems per night as homework, using class time the following day to go over the answers. Ask students to read their answers or put them on the blackboard. From this sort of practice you can gauge students' progress in cued combination; if they seem comfortable with signaled exercises you can go on to open exercises. You will want to hold class discussions of the different combinations possible for open problems; if you have access to an opaque projector you can use projections to compare different student combinations of the same kernels and discuss their stylistic effects.

These discussions and comparisons are of the utmost importance; sentence-combining is much less useful if it is merely an at-home activity that you examine quantitatively to make certain it has been done. Ask questions in class about style, and why one version is more effective than another; talk about clause placement and organizational techniques. Encourage students to volunteer any versions they feel are better than those you have reproduced. Make certain that they are aware of their option of *not* combining if they feel they have stylistic reasons. If you see problems, or if some of the students seem to be struggling, supplement the open exercises with cued problems, and spend some time nailing down basic additions, deletions, embeddings, transformations, and punctuation changes.

The lesson of sentence-combining is simple but extremely important: as Frank O'Hare says, "writing behavior can be changed fairly rapidly and with relative ease" (*Sentence-Combining* 86). Sentence-combining is not a panacea for all writing ills; it will not turn Basic Writers into high-level students overnight; it should not be the only content in a writing class. But it is, when used with care and patience, an effective part of a complete rhetorical program.

Teaching the Paragraph

Traditional Paragraph Theory

The paragraph began to appear in the seventeenth century, as the craft of printing grew more polished. Initially, paragraphs were not indented, nor were they today's relatively small units. In manuscripts and incunabula, paragraphs were long stretches of discourse, sometimes covering several pages. Rather than being marked off by indentation, they were divided by the familiar mark in the left margin, indicating *para-graphos*—Greek for "mark outside." As printing became the method of transmission of written materials, the exigencies of the process (the size of the printing plate, the construction of the form holding the lines of type) dictated a single clean left margin. The present form of marking paragraphs by indentation came about as a result. At the same time, the stretches of discourse marked by the indentation gradually stabilized at the length we use now (Lewis 37).

All of this happened more or less as circumstance dictated, for there was no classical theory of the paragraph. None of the neo-Ciceronian or Ramist rhetoricians of the seventeenth century mention the paragraph; the three great rhetorical theorists of the eighteenth century, Adam Smith, George Campbell, and Hugh Blair, pay it little mind. In 1866, however, the Scottish logician and educator Alexander Bain formulated rules for the production of correct paragraphs in his *English Composition and Rhetoric.*[10]

Bain's "organic model" of the paragraph, in which every part contributed toward the whole of the paragraph, became immensely influential within twenty years, especially in America. Every textbook used some version of it, and it became the cornerstone of traditional paragraph theory. This theory remained unquestioned until the 1950s, when it was criticized as being reductive and prescriptive.

Though they deny the prescriptive importance of the paragraph, theorists Willis Pitkin and Paul Rodgers have established the groundwork for modern paragraph theory. They posit that discourse is not made up of either sentences or paragraphs; rather, it consists of segments that may sometimes be coterminous with paragraphs but often consist of several paragraphs.[11] Pitkin calls these segments "discourse blocs," and Rodgers, "stadia of discourse"; but they agree that blocs or stadia mark obvious ends and beginnings. The discourse bloc, according to Pitkin, is identified by *junctures,* "those moments in the meaningful continuum where we can say 'To this point we have been doing X; now we begin to do Y' " (139).

"Paragraphs are not composed; they are discovered. To compose is to create; to indent is to interpret." ("A Discourse-Centered Rhetoric" 4) These statements sum up Rodgers's beliefs about paragraphs, beliefs that are supported by our own awareness of how we write. Although formulae for the composition of paragraphs lay a measure of claim to being generative, the inductive study of real paragraphs shows that these theories of paragraph construction cover only a few types of real paragraphs. Insistence on topic sentences or levels of generality can be helpful tools in analyzing or discussing the makeup

10 For a history of the "organic paragraph" see Rodgers, "Alexander Bain and the Rise of the 'Organic Paragraph,' " 399–408.

11 See Rodgers, "A Discourse Centered Rhetoric of the Paragraph"; Pitkin, "Discourse Blocs."

of paragraphs, but they do not locate or identify the true nature of the paragraph. Every deductive formula, in other word, is reductive as well.

What, then, is the use of trying to teach any paragraph theory? Few of our students are heavy readers; as a result, most have no reliable experience of paragraph reading to rely on. If they imagine a paragraph, it will probably be a newspaper paragraph or a paragraph in an advertisement. Although our students can generate discourse, they usually have problems ordering it and breaking it into parts. With our own paragraph intuition, informed by years of reading, we can generate paragraphs that need no revision. Our students, on the other hand, may have had little experience with English prose conventions.

This section will offer techniques for helping your students order and revise rough-draft material that they generated before any awareness of paragraph theory. Throughout, this section assumes that the paragraph is a subject of revision, not of prevision, and is formed by intuition. But if these theories are incomplete, if discourse is actually composed of blocs or stadia rather than paragraphs, why do we bother at all with paragraphing, intuitive or otherwise? The roots of the answer lie in cognitive psychology, but in simple terms, we insist upon paragraphing because readers expect it. That the paragraph as we know it is a relatively recent phenomenon does not cancel out the fact that its use immediately spread until it was universal, because the paragraph developed in response to real needs of readers for breaks in written discourse. Although paragraph theories offer us ways to compose and analyze paragraphs, ultimately we use paragraphs for the reader's convenience, to guide the reader—and that is how we should teach about them.

Contending that the paragraph is mainly a device used to guide and aid readers is not to suggest that paragraphing is completely arbitrary or that the structural theorists have nothing to offer. That is far from the case. Readers have definite expectations about the content and form of paragraphs as well as about their length; the degree to which readers concur in dividing up an unbroken stretch of discourse shows that paragraph structure does play a large role in reader expectations.[12]

___

12 See Koen et al., "The Psychological Reality of the Paragraph," for work on reader expectation in paragraph structures. For useful theoretical considerations of paragraph structure, see Halliday and Hasan, *Cohesion in English*; Witte and Faigley, "Coherence, Cohesion and Writing Quality."

Students will show recurring problems in their paragraphing: paragraphs that are too short or thin in texture, that are too long and try to cover too much material, that are incoherent and mass together unrelated information.

Students who write paragraphs that are too short—that is, paragraphs that contain only one to three normal-length sentences—are often unconsciously copying in their own writing the models with which they are familiar: advertising copy and newspaper style, both of which use short paragraphs to move the reader rapidly through quickly digestible information. The paragraph structures of ads and newspapers are effective within their limited range, but are bad models for expository prose. In the hands of students, short paragraphs become choppy, interruptive, and annoying in their continual insistence on a new start even when the material doesn't warrant it.

Francis Christensen's work is most directly concerned with solving the problem of short paragraphs. A writer of short paragraphs needs to be told about levels of generality and density. In some cases, the problem is not one of underdeveloped paragraphs but of uninformed choice about where to indent. Students will then need to learn to ask themselves, in Pitkin's terms, "Am I done showing the reader X and ready to begin Y?" or "Does this indentation serve a purpose? Why is it here?"

Writers of overly long paragraphs are usually completely unaware of the traditional uses of the paragraph, and they need to be acquainted with the paragraph as both a structural and a conventional form. They may under-differentiate their paragraphs because they see their whole discourse as a rush in which they have to say something—anything. Students suffering from too-long paragraphs may need special help with other aspects of writing, particularly with invention and argumentation. If, in the essays the students write, paragraphing is one of the only problems, it is a problem that is easy to solve: showing the students how to spot topic sentences or high levels of generality will help them differentiate within their own work. If there are larger organizational problems, however, settle in for a long hard struggle to introduce conventions.

Incoherence is fairly common among freshmen: their paragraphs will skip from idea to idea, resulting in a jumbled mass of information. The traditional topic-sentence–and–development paragraph model is one way of dealing with this problem; it forces students to question the placement and purpose of each sentence in the paragraph. For those students who also have a difficult time with the "methods of development" central to the classical model, a perspective on paragraphing developed by Richard L. Larson in his article "Sentences in Action: A Technique for Analyzing Paragraphs" may be helpful. The central point of Larson's article is that every sentence in a paragraph has a function. The most common roles are: state, restate, expand, particularize, exemplify, define, describe, narrate, qualify, concede, support, refute, evaluate, identify a cause or result, compare or contrast, summarize, conclude. These are not, Larson points out, mutually exclusive roles (18). Teaching students to recognize these roles and to use them to check their sentences and paragraph development in first drafts can be a very useful way to promote coherence. Larson suggests three questions to ask about each sentence in a paragraph:

1. Is the role of each sentence in the context of the surrounding sentences evident to the reader?
2. Do the words that connect the sentence to surrounding sentences accurately characterize that role?
3. Is the role useful? That is, would the paragraph do its work as effectively without the sentence as it does with the sentence? (21)

When students learn to question the role of each sentence, the extraneous sentences gradually get pared down and transitions appear more frequently.

These, then, are the problems that the following theories can help to solve. Yet all of the paragraph theories and models in this chapter are necessarily limited; we have not yet reached the paradigmatic stage of paragraph theory. How can we be prescriptive when we know that professional writers create paragraphs that ignore all of these models?

We can because, despite the limits of these models, they do give students a structure that will create coherent paragraphs. These student paragraphs may not be professional, they may not be stylistically brilliant, but they will be understandable and will be solid bases upon which students can build. As the early paragraph theorist Helen Thomas said in 1912 about topic sentence placement, "The artist can afford to diverge from this rule. The mechanic cannot" (28). Our task is to teach mechanics who may someday become artists. Once the limiting rules are mastered they can be transcended, but only those who know the law can afford to live without it. If you are honest with your students about the limitations of the rules you set, you need never apologize for being prescriptive.

Classroom Use of Traditional Paragraph Theory

The paragraph as we know it today, with its qualities of consecutiveness and loose order of propositions, did not begin to emerge until the late seventeenth century and did not attain full codification until the eighteenth century. If there is a single ruling conception of the nature and construction of the paragraph, it is the legacy of nineteenth-century rhetorician Alexander Bain, whose systematic formulation became our traditional paragraph structure: a topic sentence, announcing the main idea of the paragraph, followed by subsidiary sentences that develop or illustrate that main idea.

Although such a paragraph form cannot easily generate material, it works well as a tool for testing and revising material already written intuitively. You *can* ask your students to generate individual paragraphs with traditional theory, but if you try to teach it as a generative form for essay writing—as many teachers for many years have done with little success—you run a real risk of hopelessly frustrating those students who try to use it. You want your students to develop an informed revision intuition, and the traditional paragraph is just one tool they can use to check their "natural" idea groupings against a concrete model.

The notion that one sentence in every paragraph should announce the topic of that paragraph was derived from the fourth law of Alexander Bain's "seven laws" for creating paragraphs, which he compiled in his 1866 *English Composition and Rhetoric* (91–134). Since Bain, the "topic sentence" has remained controversial in composition theory. Although most compositionists agree with Bain that every paragraph should have a unifying theme or purpose, not all agree that it should be announced by a topic sentence. On the one hand, in his study of professional writers, Richard Braddock found that topic sentences are used far less that we have traditionally believed; his research calls into question the value of teaching topic sentences (301). On the other hand, Frank D'Angelo argues, despite Braddock's findings, that the use of topic sentences improves the readability of a paragraph; therefore, all writers—and especially beginning writers—should use topic sentences ("The Topic Sentence"). Your beginning writers may want to heed D'Angelo's advice.

Students will need to know that the topic sentence, the master-sentence of the paragraph, has three characteristics: (1) it isolates and specifies the topic or idea of the entire paragraph: (2) it acts as a general heading for all of the other sentences; (3) it usually incorporates, at least implicitly, a transition from or to the paragraph that precedes or follows it. Often, the topic sentence is the most obvious starting place for checking a traditional paragraph for its "wholeness." The terminology used in the literature of paragraph theory to describe this "wholeness" can be confusing. For example, researchers often use the same terms (*unity, coherence, development*) to describe entire pieces of discourse as well as paragraphs; and some textbooks and articles suggest that *coherence* and *cohesion* are separate features, while others take them to mean the same thing. Therefore, you may want to introduce these elements to your students as separate entities: *unity* as a semantic concept, the paragraph's single topic; *development* as the movement in the paragraph; *coherence* as a stylistic concept, using various methods to interconnect the sentences of a paragraph; and *cohesion* as the whole-essay counterpart of unity.

After supplying your students with an essay, you may want to ask them to identify the topic of a paragraph sentence and to specify relationships between the identified topic sentence and all of the other sentences in the paragraph. Either the other sentences contribute to the main idea, making for paragraph *unity*, or they deviate from it. You may want to offer students a sample of a dis-unified paragraph as well, perhaps from a student sample.

The most common methods of paragraph *development* are *deductive*, general to specific, and *inductive*, specific to general. Traditionally, deductive reasoning has been the basis for paragraph development: the writer posits a sound general principle (major premise) and then applies that principle to specific cases, moving from general to specific. Inductive development, on the other hand, is the movement from specific cases to sound general principle. Most of us live according to inductive generalizations: we are aware of the probability that we will miss the heavy traffic if we take a particular route to school each day, that going to bed at a certain time will guarantee our awaking in the morning, that we can stay in the hot sun only so long without getting burned, that we must eat and exercise a specific amount if we are to maintain our shapes, that certain foods, animals, or plants make us itch or sneeze. But inductive and deductive reasoning almost always work together, for many of our deductions stem from inductive reasoning: morning traffic is heavy; a late night makes for a slow morning; sun burns the skin; too many calories make one fat; poison ivy causes an itchy rash.

The easiest way to explain paragraph *coherence* to your students is to demonstrate that every sentence must relate somehow, either directly or indirectly, to the sentences that surround it. If this practice is not respected, the result is a choppy and irritating prose that seems to proceed in fits and starts. Problems with incoherence can often be solved by attending to the composing process and by multiple-draft revisions. Paragraphs are rendered coherent by a large number of devices; the single most easily taught device for promoting coherence is the use of transitions and transitional markers. Of course, such words and phrases cannot by themselves create ordered relationships among sentences where there are none. Most first-year students, though, grasp the implications of these terms and thus can use them as reminders of the necessary relations their sentences must have. You might stress that transitions are used for establishing the following relationships:

1. between the topic sentence of a paragraph and the topic of the preceding paragraph
2. between the topic sentence and the sentences that develop it
3. between the developing sentences in the paragraph

You might also want to list the various transitional markers for your students:

To link related ideas between sentences or paragraphs: and, also, likewise, so, in like manner, first, secondly, again, besides, then, too, further, moreover, furthermore.

To link unrelated or opposing ideas between sentences or paragraphs: but, else, otherwise, but then, still, yet, only, nevertheless, at the same time, on the other hand, conversely, despite this fact.

To conclude or wrap up a section or essay: in short, in a word, in conclusion, to sum up, as a result, in other words.

But transitional markers are only one of the coherence devices that writers use; others include repetition (key words and important word groups), parallel structure, and pronoun reference.

To introduce the use of transitional markers or effective use of parallelism and repetition, you might want to reproduce for distribution three or four well-structured paragraphs that rely heavily on one or more of these coherence devices. If you remove the transitions, ask your students to supply words or phrases that make the paragraph more coherent, less choppy. Then ask them to compare and explain why they chose the transitions they chose. If you provide them with a full essay, ask them to identify the elements that make it coherent. But the most illuminating classroom activity will be when they go over some of their own essays, checking to see if they use coherence devices. You will want to emphasize the importance of *every* sentence to the sentences around it. If your students grow accustomed to this sentence-by-sentence testing procedure, they can improve their paragraphs.

Despite its limitations, the essential design of the Bainian organic paragraph has served to introduce generations of students to some control element against which they can measure their efforts. The traditional paragraph paradigm contains enough truth about how we control segments of discourse to give students a good deal of the guidance they need.

Francis Christensen's Generative Rhetoric of the Paragraph

Christensen's theory of the paragraph grew directly out of his work with cumulative sentences. After the success of his theory of sentences as differing levels of generality, each including a base clause and free modifiers, Christensen strove to apply a similar technique to his analysis of the paragraph. The result was "A Generative Rhetoric of the Paragraph," an important re-evaluation of paragraph form and structure. In the Christensen model and the traditional model, the paragraph is a system of related sentences organized in some way by a master sentence, usually at the beginning of the paragraph. The difference lies between models in the nature of the relationships between the sentences within the paragraph. The traditional paragraph model claims that all of the sentences must be *logically* or *semantically* related to one another, while Christensen says that the sentences in a paragraph can also be related *formally* or *structurally*, by the concept of levels of generality.

The topic sentence in a traditional paragraph is also called the subject sentence or thesis sentence. It can be in different places within the paragraph, but in strict Bainian theory it always announces the subject of the paragraph no matter where it is placed. In the Christensen model, the topic sentence is *always* the first sentence of the paragraph. It does not necessarily announce the subject, and it is defined only as the *most general* sentence in the paragraph. Like the base clause of a cumulative sentence, Christensen's topic sentence is "the sentence whose assertion is supported or whose meaning is explicated or whose parts are detailed by the sentences added to it ("A Generative Rhetoric" 146–56).

The Christensen system is based entirely on the semantic and syntactic relations between sentences, relations that exist due to different levels of generality or abstraction. A paragraph, according to Christensen, is an expanded cumulative sentence whose components are related, as are those of the sentence, by coordinate and subordinate relationships. In "A Generative Rhetoric of the Paragraph," Christensen reduced his paragraph findings to four points, similar to those describing cumulative sentences, that define the unit as he saw it.

1. *No paragraphs are possible without addition.* In expository writing one sentence cannot, under normal circumstances, be an acceptable paragraph.
2. *When a supporting sentence is added, we must see the direction of modification or movement.* Assuming the first sentence of the paragraph to fulfill the same function as the base clause of a cumulative sentence, we have to be able to see what direction the modification of it takes—whether the level of generality of a sentence is the same as or lower than that of the one before it.
3. *When sentences are added, they are usually at a lower level of generality.* This is not an absolute rule, but is usually the case; as we saw in the classical paragraph, sentences that develop a topic are usually more specific in their relation to the topic than the topic sentence.
4. *The more sentences added, the denser the texture of the paragraph.* The paragraphs we see from students too often lack density— those one-sentence paragraphs are not as rare as they should be—and one of the greatest strengths of the Christensen method of paragraphing is to get students to see this thinness when they revise their work.

The Topic Sentence For Christensen, "the topic sentence is nearly always the first sentence of the sequence" of structurally related sentences that make up the paragraph. It is the sentence from which the other sentences in the paragraph hang, so to speak, *the sentence whose level of generality cannot be exceeded without starting a new paragraph.* Unlike the thesis statement of traditional paragraphing, Christensen's topic sentence often does not state the thesis of the paragraph clearly. It may only suggest it, or it may be nothing more than a "signal sentence" that moves up to a more general level of statement than that of the previous sentence to show that a new chunk of discourse is about to begin. It may be a statement, or a fragment, or a question. The only important thing about it is that the reader gets the signal: "New level of generality; we're about to start something new."

The structure of the paragraph after the topic sentence, according to Christensen, can take a number of forms, all of which are marked by the relationships established by each sentence to the topic sentence and the other sentences. Like the relationships between clauses that Christensen identified in his cumulative sentences, the relationships he sees between sentences in a paragraph are either coordinate or subordinate.

Christensen identifies two sorts of simple sentence sequences, *simple coordinate* and *simple subordinate,* and the most common sequence, the *mixed sequence,* in which both coordination and subordination are used. Coordinate sentences are *equal* in syntactic or semantic generality, while subordinate sentences are *lower* in generality—are more specific or concrete—than the sentences that precede them. Coordinate sentences *emphasize* and *enumerate,* while subordinate sentences *clarify, exemplify,* and *comment.*

Simple Coordinate Sequence The simple coordinate sequence paragraph has only two levels: that of the topic sentence and that of the other sentences, which are coordinate with each other in terms of generality. It is the rarest and least used of all the sequence types because it usually produces a repetitive effect more common in speeches than in expository writing. In the example below, taken from R. Emmett Tyrell's *Public Nuisances,* the numbers indicate levels of generality, with the lowest number equaling the highest levels of generality:

[1] I prescribe ridicule. [2] It is an equitable response to the likes of Ralph Nader or Betty Friedan. [2] It is a soothing emollient for our peculiarly troubled national spirit. [2] Ridicule does not elevate nonsense to any higher level than that at which it is emitted. [2] It is entertaining and far more edifying to the public discourse than the facile dissimulations now rampant there. [2] Ridicule is the compliment lively intelligence pays jackassery. [2] It is a national treasure certified by Mark Twain, beloved by millions, and eschewed only at great peril.

Simple Subordinate Sequence The simple subordinate sequence introduces multiple layers—in theory, an infinite number—of semantic or syntactic generality. The notable feature of the simple subordinate sequence is that it progresses from element to element and does not return to a higher level of generality. Once again, this is not a sequence often found in nature, since it tends to introduce a large number of disparate ideas in one paragraph and does not stop to discourse on any one level. It is often found in the introductory sections of expository pieces outlining the main ideas that will be covered, like the following example:

[1] *Why Johnny Can't Read.* [2] The title is instantly familiar to thousands, perhaps millions, of people who have never read Rudolf Flesch's 1955 book about reading pedagogy. [3] Most of those people don't know that the book is an extended argument for the "phonics first" method of reading instruction and against

the "look and say" method. [4] Instead, the title has become a rallying cry for those who are interested in, or worried about, the supposed decline in the ability to read during the past two or three decades: a title like "What If Johnny Still Can't Read?" (from a Canadian business journal) illustrates the genre. [5] And it seems that as more people become worried about a "crisis" in literacy, the solutions proposed become simpler and simpler: witness the "back to basics" movement, which assumes, quite incorrectly, that the "basics" required and expected today are the same as those taught a generation or two ago. [6] This collection of essays is partially a response to the current interest in the question of literacy and illiteracy in the Western World; its aim is to provide the requisite background for informed and intelligent discussion of the many issues surrounding the question of literacy today.

(Kintgen et al. xi)

Mixed Sequence Simple paragraph sequences are not common; the simple coordinate sequence is particularly rare, and it is also rare to see a good paragraph move from element to element without stopping to return to a previous level. Most paragraphs use some form that mixes coordination and subordination, that rises and falls in its levels as the need arises. Look at the following mixed-sequence paragraph from an essay on Albert Goldman, John Lennon's controversial biographer:

[1] For years, Goldman felt like Schizoid Man, scissored down the middle between the academic drudge who taught freshman English and the cutup who engaged in comedy jam sessions with jazz-crazy characters every Saturday night at his Brooklyn pad. [2] For a time he considered becoming a professional comic. [3] "But I was just scared. [3] Many times in my life I've been defeated by my own fear. [3] I feel that's really been one of my single greatest problems. [3] What's held me back is diffidence, fear, self-doubt. [4] I didn't do it." [2] Instead he gravitated to criticism, where he found that words on the page are harder to budge than words in the air. [3] Yet he became adept. [3] He covered jazz and classical music for *The New Leader*, rock for *Life*. [3] A compilation of his riffing on rock, comedy, and jazz was briefly preserved in *Freakshow* (1971). [1] One of the best collections of pop criticism ever published, *Freakshow* showcases Goldman as that rare critic who can communicate a dizzy, complex thrill. [2] He opens up the full sensorium for Jimi Hendrix: [3] "I went home and put *The Jimi Hendrix Experience* on the turn-

table. [4] Tough, abrasive, brutally iterative, the uptake suggested the ironshod tracks of a bulldozer straining against a mountain of dirt. [4] Hendrix's program for the country blues was rural electrification. [4] The end products were futurist symphonies of industrial noise." [1] Unlike most books from rock's chesty youth, *Freakshow* hasn't faded into a dated piece of psychedelia. [2] Out of print, it may even be more apt today. [3] A doomed moonlit glamour still coats the memories of Hendrix, Joplin, Jim Morrison . . . the beautiful dead. (Wolcott 36)

Classroom Use of Christensen's Generative Rhetoric of the Paragraph

Christensen's paragraph method is essentially descriptive, not generative. It is best used—as are all other theories of the paragraph—as an after-the-fact device for editing and testing paragraphs that have already been generated intuitively. Before using this method, students must become familiar with the concepts of levels of generality and of coordination and subordination. If you have previously taught Christensen's sentence theory, that is a natural place to start; the parallels are obvious. If you have not, begin by handing out a sheet that contains examples of cumulative sentences graphed according to the Christensen method and matching paragraph structures graphed similarly. Stick with relatively simple sequences at this point—nothing long or hard to follow in its structure.

Start with the concept of the topic sentence. The topic sentence does not usually need too much stress as long as you point out that it is always first in the sequence and that it is usually a fairly general statement. Merely pointing out its existence and placement should be enough for the time being, because you have to establish its meaning contextually through an explanation of coordination and subordination before the ideal can really come to life.

The best way to explain coordination in sentences is to stress the fact that coordinate sentences "put like things in like ways," and have the same relationship to the topic sentence (*Notes Towards a New Rhetoric* 164). Your examples should include simple coordinate sequences that utilize parallel constructions, since parallelism is nearly always a sign of coordination, but make certain that you demonstrate how coordination can work without parallelism as well. Point up the fact that coordinate sentences do not comment on each other, but on previous material.

Subordination is best explained in terms of clarification or ex-emplification. A subordinate sentence is usually more specific than the one that precedes it. In a subordinate sequence, as Christensen points out, each sentence is a comment on the sentence above it, and a mixed subordinate sequence is created by "any doubling or multi-plying of examples, causes, reasons, or the like." You need not place too much stress on differentiating mixed coordinate from mixed sub-ordinate sequences, though; even Christensen admits that "it is of no great moment to settle whether a mixed sequence is coordinate or subordinate; these are just convenient terms to designate recurring configurations" (*Notes Towards a New Rhetoric* 153).

After you have explained these terms, get right down to the analysis of paragraphs. You can choose paragraphs at random from a reader, but the best initial technique is to distribute copies of paragraphs that you have chosen as not being too difficult and that il-lustrate different sorts of sequences. Begin with a simple short se-quence and work up to more complex mixed sequences. Your instructions to the students should be as simple as possible at this stage. Illustrate an analysis on the blackboard and ask the class to help by making suggestions. Try this as an approach:

First, assume that the first sentence in the paragraph is the topic sentence. It may not state the thesis or subject of the paragaph; just look at it as the signal sentence that announces a new level of generality and gets the paragraph started. Write it at the left margin of a piece of paper, numbered 1.

Now examine the second sentence. Does it *continue* the idea or structure of the first sentence or does it *comment on* the idea or struc-ture of the first sentenece? If it continues the idea or structure of the first sentence, it is parallel or coordinate with the first sentence. If, as is usually the case, it *comments* on, *refers* to, or *clarifies* the idea or structure of the first sentence, it is subordinate to the first sentence. In that case, number it 2 and indent it one half-inch when you write it down under the first sentence.

Look at the third sentence. Does it *continue* or *comment on* the first sentence? If it does not continue the idea or structure of the first sen-tence, compare it to the second very carefully. If it comments on the structure or ideas of the first sentence, ask how it relates to the second sentence. If it continues the structure or ideas of the second sentence, it is coordinate with the second sentence. Number it 2 and write it directly under the second sentence. If, however, it comments on, refers to, clarifies, etc., the structure or ideas of the second sentence, it is subordinate to the second sentence. Number it 3 and indent it a full inch when you write it down under the second.

Continue this sort of analysis with the rest of the sentences in the paragraph. The essential test will always be the question of whether the new sentence continues or comments on the sentences above it. Rmember that you must be returning to continue or comment on a level that is two or three sentences higher. Don't be afraid of getting to level 5 and then having to return to level 2. Paragraphs constantly rise and fall in levels of generality. Just make certain that you keep checking each new sentence against all the sentences that precede it.

This is a point in the course when oral discussion can help to clarify students' understanding. There will be quite a few disagreements on the numbering of sentences at first, and if you can get students arguing with each other in favor of the levels they have assigned to sentences, the whole concept will become clear to them faster than if you lecture on it for hours. There may be some sentences that are genuinely impossible to assign levels to with complete certainty, but as you go from simple to complex sequences, discussing each one, spend as much time as your students need to be able to follow the discussion. They should gradually get over their initial distrust of the novel concept of "levels of generality" and feel more comfortable with the theory.

At that point, you can turn them loose in the reader, popular magazines, handouts—anything that contains more difficult sequences. Let them apply their analyses to exposition in the rough. Occasionally you will strike a paragraph that has no topic sentence or that has introductory or transitional material in sentences at the beginning that are not part of the sequence, and at those points you need to explain that the Christensen paragraph is a theoretical model, not an absolute rule.

Finally, you should be ready to get your students to generate some paragraphs using the model. Suggest the paragraph sequences that they should follow at first by giving a list of sentence directions.[13] Start with coordinate sequence:

Write a topic sentence. (You may want to suggest one that contains a plural term such as *reasons, causes, uses,* etc.)
　　Add a sentence that supports it.
　　Add a second supporting sentence.
　　Add a third supporting sentence
　　Conclude with a final supporting sentence.

13 Paragraph sequence exercises are adapted from D'Angelo, *Process and Thought in Composition* 243.

As a sort of diagram you can put this sequence on the board in this form:

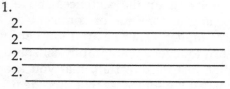

Then you can work up to a subordinate sequence:

Write a topic sentence.
   Qualify that sentence. (Write a sentence that *comments* on the first sentence.)
   Add a specific detail
   Add another detail.
   Qualify that detail.

On the board this sequence looks like:

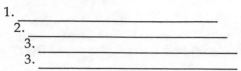

Last, try mixed sequences. These are more difficult because they require advance planning and a division of concepts. Give your students a topic sentence to work with the first time through:

Write a topic sentence that has two components.
Qualify that sentence.
Add a specific detail.
Add another detail.
Qualify the topic sentence again.
Add a detail to this qualification.
Add another detail
Qualify that detail.

This paragraph diagram looks like this:

1. _____
   2. _____
      3. _____
      3. _____

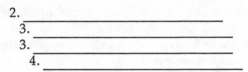

2. _____

   3. _____

   3. _____

      4. _____

If things have worked out to your satisfaction thus far, let your students create their own sequences and write their own paragraphs. A good checking exercise is to ask each student to write out his or her generated paragraph in normal form and give it to a classmate to analyze. If the analysis differs from the original plan, the students can confer and try to find out where their perceptions diverge.

Paragraph Revision Using the Christensen Model After you have reached the point at which your students are comfortable analyzing and generating discrete paragraphs—and reaching this point may take up to two weeks—you can concentrate on using the Christensen method in real writing situations, for the revision and editing of intuitively generated paragraphs. The analyses allowed by the Christensen method are extremely useful in showing students how the sentences in their paragraphs work or do not work together. Although the whole progression from analysis to generation to revision of paragraphs may not be necessary for an understanding of how to use Christensen paragraphing as an editing technique, it does guarantee a familiarity with the analytical process that makes revision easier.

The application of the Christensen model to already generated paragraphs is not difficult. The single most important step is the actual dissection of each student paragraph into coordinate or subordinate sequences. To perform this analysis, direct your students to apply these three question-types to the paragraphs they have written intuitively:

1. Is this sentence coordinate with the ones above it or subordinate to them?
2. If it is coordinate:
   A. How does it relate to the topic sentence?
   B. How does it relate to the other sentences on its level?
   C. Does this concept need further explanation with a subordinate sequence?
3. If it is subordinate:
   A. How does it relate to the level above it?
   B. How does it relate to the other sentences on its level?
   C. Is it complete as it stands or could it use further explanation with a coordinate or subordinate sentence?

Using these questions, students can pick through their intuitively generated paragraphs, weeding out sentences that are not related to the topic sentence or to coordinate sentences, and deciding whether any given sequence is fully enough developed.

Tagmemic Paragraphing

Like tagmemic invention, tagmemic paragraph theory evolved from the linguistic work of Kenneth Pike, whose theories of tagmemic linguistics became the raw material for his theories of composition. Linguistics has always been primarily a descriptive discipline, devoted to careful analysis of existing phenomena. This descriptive nature characterizes tagmemic paragraph theory as well; it was originally developed as a descriptive tool for use on "paragraph-level tagmemes." As a result, despite the fact that it can be used generatively for certain kinds of practice exercises, tagmemic paragraphing, like the other paragraph theories we have discussed, is primarily useful as an editing tool.

Tagmeme, as you will recall from Chapter 5 is the term that Kenneth Pike invented to describe the central component of his linguistic theory. Simply put, a tagmeme equals a functional *slot* to be filled plus a *class* of possible fillers of the slot. Tagmemic paragraph analysis posits an expository paragraph as a series of slots, all of which can be filled by any one of a whole class of fillers. The position of each sentence in the paragraph indicates a slot, and tagmemic paragraph theory specifies both the slots that make up the paragraph and the kinds of sentences that make up the filler classes of fillers.

Alton L. Becker, who has done most of the work using tagmemic paragraph-analysis, says in his article "A Tagmemic Approach to Paragraph Analysis" that tagmemic analysis allows an examination of the *relationship* of the parts of a paragraph as well as a mere description of the parts themselves, which is the domain of traditional paragraph analysis. He cautions, though, that tagmemic analysis as it has evolved so far cannot describe all of the content-based aspects of paragraph structure; in addition, Becker's work thus far has concentrated on expository paragraphs, excluding rigorous examination of other modes of discourse. With these caveats in mind, let us look at what tagmemic paragraph structures are.

Becker found three major patterns in expository paragraphs, two of which are closely related:

T Topic
R Restriction

I Illustration

P Problem
S Solution

Q Question
A Answer

According to Becker, these patterns can be derived inductively by giving students examples of expository paragraphs and asking them to divide them up into sections that seem significant. Becker found "a striking percentage of agreement" about the important divisions, "especially after students have partitioned enough paragraphs to recognize recurring patterns" ("A Tagmemic Approach" 238). The three patterns, in different configurations, are found in most expository paragraphs in English.

The most common expository pattern that Becker's students found was composed of some version of TRI—Topic, Restriction, and Illustration. None of these slots is absolutely limited to one sentence, but the T slot generally is filled by a single sentence, and the R slot is often also a single sentence. In its simplest form, TRI consists of a sentence that states the topic generally (T), a sentence that qualifies or restricts that general topic, narrowing down its meaning (R), and a sentence or a group of sentences in which the restricted topic is illustrated or exemplified on a more specific level (I). The following paragraph is TRI:

[T] Progress toward the kind of future depicted in the science-fiction movies of twenty and thirty years ago has been getting difficult to detect lately, and it has begun to dawn on us that the year 2000 may not deliver on all the promises that used to be made for it: world government, the colonization of outer space, backpack jet transport for the masses, robots for every imaginable form of menial labor, and the rest. [R] Certain events of the summer of 1988, however, have been running eerily close to the plot of one science-fiction movie—a movie that came out in 1961. [I] In "The Day the Earth Caught Fire," the world is visited within the space of a few weeks by floods, earthquakes, dense fog stretching from England to India (it's an English movie), and a record-setting heat wave. [I] The experts at first refuse to acknowledge a common explanation for these quirks of nature, but then word gets out that, by chance, the Soviet Union and the

United States chose the same moment for high-megaton nuclear tests, and the effect was to knock the earth out of its orbit and send it hurtling toward the sun. [I] The human species is given a life expectancy of four months.

(Lardner 4).

As in Christensen's paragraph theory, the concept of levels of generality is important in tagmemic paragraphing, since a shift from one slot to another in the TRI pattern is also usually a shift in levels of generality.

The second major pattern found by Becker is PS, Problem-Solution, of which QA, Question-Answer, is a subset. Unlike the TRI pattern, PS has only two slots: the P slot, which states the problem to be solved or the effect to be explained, and S, which provides the solution or the causes of the effect. If the S slot is lengthy or complex, it is likely to be filled by a TRI pattern of some sort; the TRI structure is generally found in some form in every paragraph of any length. Here is an example of a paragraph that uses all of the slots:

[Q]It is not difficult to envision a network of private, unsubsidized and unregulated railroads and airplanes, but could there be a system of private roads? [Q] Could such a system be at all feasible? [A] One answer is that private roads have worked admirably in the past. [P] In England before the eighteenth century, for example, roads, invariably owned and operated by local governments, were badly constructed and even more badly maintained. [P] These public roads could never have supported the mighty Industrial Revolution that England experienced in the eighteenth century, the "revolution" that ushered in the modern age. [S][T] The vital task of improving the almost impassable English roads was performed by private turnpike companies, which, beginning in 1706, organized and established the great network of roads which made England the envy of the world. [R] The owners of these private turnpike companies were generally landowners, merchants, and industrialists in the area being served by the road, and they recouped their costs by charging tolls at selected tollgates. [I] Often the collection of tolls was leased out for a year or more to individuals selected by competitive bid at auction. [I] It was these private roads that developed an internal market in England, and that greatly lowered the costs of transport of coal and other bulky material.

—Murray Rothbard, *For a New Liberty*

These, then, are the two major patterns into which expository paragraphs fall. The TRI pattern can also appear inverted into an IRT form—an inductive form that proceeds from specific to general. (Becker makes the interesting observation that students who were asked to evaluate paragraphs out of context preferred IRT paragraphs over TRI by a large margin. Perhaps it is the desire for instant gratification—having examples of narration dumped in your lap without having to work through abstractions first.)

Classroom Use of Tagmemic Paragraphing

Of the types of paragraphing discussed in this chapter, tagmemic paragraphing may be the easiest to teach, because of the limited number of concepts it employs, and the admittedly exploratory and unfinished nature of the theory itself. The result of the tentative nature of this theory is that it is both easy to absorb and incomplete.

As in the use of any model, the first step is complete familiarization of your students with the terms of tagmemic paragraphing and their meaning. Make up sheets with at least three examples of each of the common paragraph patterns—different versions of simple TRI and PS/QA patterns. Go over the handouts and analyze each of the example paragraphs orally, explaining how each slot works and how they all work together. It is probably best to stay away from the vocabulary of technical tagmemic terms at this stage of the game—you don't want your students more worried about terms rather than substance. In particular, note the relationship of the T and R slots and the fact that the I slots do not follow the T, but only the topic idea as it is restricted and defined in the R slot.

Analyzing the PS/QA patterns is easy, but make certain that your students understand that PS and QA are seldom found without some form of TRI embedded within them. Choose your examples of PS/QA carefully, making certain that they include both simple and embedded patterns.

The next sheet you hand out will be carefully chosen paragraphs that are not marked or divided, and the exercise will be a controlled duplication of Becker's original experiment: your students should be able to divide these paragraphs into TRIPSQA slots with a fair amount of consistency. Start with a simple TRI or PS pattern, then work into an embedded PSTRI pattern, and finish up with a $PS_1T_1RI_1I_2S_2T_2RI$ or something equally complicated. If your students have trouble with this exercise, keep doing similar ones until they grasp the method; it is the key to all that comes after it.

Once students recognize the slots in "tame" paragraphs, set them loose on other materials. You will have to screen the selections for this, if a selection is too narrative or argumentative it may be difficult for students to dissect. Try assigning a page rather than a specific paragraph. And ask the students to break into groups. After the paragraphs have been divided, ask for a volunteer from each group to explain their divisions. This is a good point at which to initiate a discussion, in which students can argue with each other about which slots sentences should fill. ("Look, it restricts that topic!" "No, it illustrates it. Look at the main idea . . . ." "It's a solution but also an illustration." etc.) Argument about formal properties is not always easy to elicit, but this method allows categorizations simple and real enough to be involving for students.

At this stage your students should be able to manipulate the TRIPSQA patterns fairly well, and you are ready to move on to its application to their own writing.

Tagmemic Paragraph Generation Asking for the generation of formally ordered paragraphs is not difficult. First, have the students choose a subject or an idea on a general topic—apartment or dorm living, college requirements, nuclear energy; then ask them to break into their groups and brainstorm it for a minute or so. They should not need much time; explain to them that all they have to generate is a simple proposition concerning the topic. The proposition generated will be the T slot of their paragraph.

After the T slot has been written, ask each group to write an R slot, reminding them that the R slot can be one or two sentences and that it must narrow or define the general proposition advanced in T.

Finally, ask for sentences that illustrate or develop the restricted topic. Start with paragraphs with only one or two I slots and gradually work up to more I-slot sentences.

From this simple beginning you can work into generating a simple PS/QA paragraph, an embedded PSTRI pattern, and eventually more complex patterns. Remember, though, that encouraging complexity for its own sake can discourage students, especially those who fail to grasp the ideas it embodies. Our thought processes do obey formal rules, but if form is given too much precedence over content it becomes sterile.

Tagmemic Paragraph Revision The paragraph methods we have discussed here are useful for editing the body paragraphs in an essay, not the introductory or concluding paragraphs. Make this clear to your students, because the patterns tagmemic paragraphing describes are antithetical to the usual patterns of opening and closing paragraphs. Each body paragraph in the essays they write, on the other hand, should have some identifiable agglomeration of TRIPSQA that can be analyzed sentence by sentence and labeled accordingly.

Tagmemic paragraph revision assumes that the students are familiar with the tagmemic terms. To introduce the revision process and get students acclimated to it, start by assigning a three-paragraph essay to be written in class. Ask them to choose a subject to write on, and tell them not to worry about topics or restrictions as they write, merely to draft a short essay of about three paragraphs. The writing should take about half of the class period. Collect the essays. You don't have to read them; just hang on to them. This forced disengagement from their drafts will give the students some objectivity, distancing them from the essays to a small degree (this "cold-storage" idea is used by many professional authors, over longer periods of time, of course).

Next time the class meets—ideally the interval should fall over a weekend—hand back the essays to the students who wrote them. Ask them to number each sentence in the essay and then analyze each paragraph using the TRIPSQA method, marking the number of each sentence with the slot it fills on a separate sheet of paper. If they hit a sentence that seems to fill no slot or to be extraneous or to be a part of another paragraph, it should be marked X. This process should take about fifteen minutes.

When all the students have completed their analyses, ask them to exchange essays and then do the same tagmemic analysis on each paragraph in the new essay they have received. After this task is completed, the students should return the essays to their authors and compare their analyses. Talk about this can take up the rest of the class period; there is usually a fair amount of disagreement and clarification. "But I meant . . . " "But you said . . . "

The next step is to ask your students to analyze the paragraphs in an older essay—the first one they wrote for you is the best and most illuminating to use. When they have analyzed it for paragraph structure you might offer them a chance to rewrite it for a better grade if you feel up to reading it again; if not, merely ask them to mark each sentence. What you should insist on here is not any specific pattern of slots, but a coherent approach to whatever pattern is used. Warn against the TI pattern, for instance, which is common in primitive paragraphs. Insist that PS/QA paragraphs embed a TRI to increase their density. Make certain that the I slots always refer back to the T or R slots; get the X sentences out or get them rewritten.

After going through all of these steps, you are ready to ask your students to perform tagmemic analyses on their rough drafts prior to typing them; this is the ultimate and the only really important use being made of the TRIPSQA method. Enforcing this suggestion is up to you. If you want to check to make sure it is being done, you can ask students to hand in their tagmemically analyzed rough drafts along with their typescripts. (This is also a handy way to make certain that rough drafts are being produced.)

If you have led your students through these steps you should begin to see a real improvement in the structure of their paragraphs. Short, thin paragraphs should gradually fill out, incoherent paragraphs should tighten up, and disunified paragraphs should drop their dead limbs, as what Becker calls "the organic nature of the paragraph" becomes clearer to your students. Should you be uncomfortable with the prescriptive nature of any of the approaches in this chapter, you are not alone. We all may worry that in condensing writing to discrete, mechanical formulas we are taking away more than we are giving. But be assured that with continued reading and practice in writing, your students should eventually transcend rigid, formal rules. In the final analysis, a grasp of the rules seldom ever holds anyone down and, used correctly, can help keep one up.

Works Cited *Chapter 8*

Aristotle. *Rhetoric*. Trans. Rhys Roberts. New York: Modern Library, 1954.

Bain, Alexander. *English Composition and Rhetoric*. 1866. London: Longmans, 1877.

Bateman, Donald, and Frank J. Zidonis. *The Effect of a Study of Transformational Grammar on the Writing of 9th and 10th Graders*. Research Report 6. Urbana: NCTE, 1966.

Becker, Alton L. "A Tagmemic Approach to Paragraph Analysis." *CCC* 16 (1965): 237–42.

Braddock, Richard. "The Frequency and Placement of Topic Sentences in Expository Prose." *Research in the Teaching of English* 8 (1972): 287–302.

Campbell, George. *The Philosophy of Rhetoric*. 1776. Boston: Ewer, 1823.

Chomsky, Noam. *Reflections on Language*. New York: Pantheon, 1975.

—. *Syntactic Structures*. The Hague: Mouton, 1957.

Christensen, Francis. "A Generative Rhetoric of the Paragraph." *CCC* 16 (1965): 146–56.

—. "A Generative Rhetoric of the Sentence." *CCC* 14 (1963): 155–61.

—. *Notes Toward a New Rhetoric: Six Essays for Teachers*. New York: Harper, 1967.

—. "The Course in Advanced Composition for Teachers." *CCC* 24 (1973): 163–70.

—, and Bonniejean Christensen. *A New Rhetoric.* New York: Harper, 1975.

Coe, Richard. *Toward a Grammar of Passages.* Carbondale: Southern Illinois UP, 1987.

Combs, Warren E. "Sentence-Combining Practice: Do Gains in Judgments of Writing 'Quality' Persist?" *Journal of Educational Research* 10 (1977):

Cooper, Charles. "An Outline for Writing Sentence-Combining Problems." Graves 118–28.

Daiker, Donald, Andrew Kerek, and Max Morenberg, eds. *Sentence-Combining: A Rhetorical Perspective.* Carbondale: Southern Illinois UP, 1985.

—. "Sentence-Combining and Syntactic Maturity in Freshman English." *CCC* 29 (1978): 36–41.

—. *Sentence-Combining and the Teaching of Writing.* Conway, AK: L&S, 1979.

—. *The Writer's Options: College Sentence-Combining.* New York: Harper, 1979.

D'Angelo, Frank. *Process and Thought in Composition.* Cambridge, MA: Winthrop, 1977.

—. "The Topic Sentence Revisited." *CE* 37 (1986): 431–41.

Faigley, Lester. "Problems in Analyzing Maturity in College and Adult Writing." *Sentence-Combining and the Teaching of Writing.* Ed. Donald A. Daiker et al. 94–100.

Genung, John F. *The Practical Elements of Rhetoric.* Boston: Ginn, 1886.

Graves, Richard L., ed. *Rhetoric and Composition: A Sourcebook for Teachers.* Rochelle Park, NJ: Hayden, 1976.

Halliday, M.A.K., and Ruquaiya Hasan. *Cohesion in English.* London: Longmans, 1976.

Hunt, Kellogg W. *Grammatical Structures Written at Three Grade Levels.* Urbana: NCTE, 1965.

—. "A Synopsis of Clause-to-Sentence Length Factors." Graves 110–17.

—. "Anybody Can Teach English." *Sentence-Combining and the Teaching of Writing.* Ed. Donald Daiker et al. 149–56.

Kane, Thomas S. "The Shape and Ring of Sentences: A Neglected Aspect of Composition." *CCC* 28 (1977): 38–42.

Kerek, Andrew, Donald A. Daiker, and Max Morenberg. "Sentence-Combining and College Composition." *Perceptual and Motor Skills* 51 (1980): 1059–157.

—. "The Effects of Intensive Sentence-Combining on the Writing Ability of College Freshmen." *The Territory of Language.* Ed. Donald McQuade. Carbondale: Southern Illinois UP, 1986.

Kintgen, Eugene, Barry M. Kroll, and Michael Rose. *Perspectives on Literacy.* Carbondale: Southern Illinois UP, 1988.

Koen, Frank, Alton L. Becker, and Richard Young. "The Psychological Reality of the Paragraph." *Journal of Verbal Learning and Verbal Behavior* 8 (1969): 49–53.

Lardner, James. "Notes and Comments." *The New Yorker Magazine* (August 29, 1988).

Larson, Richard. "Sentences in Action: A Technique for Analyzing Paragraphs." *CCC* 8 (1967): 16–22.

Lewis, Edwin H. *A History of the English Paragraph.* Chicago: U. of Chicago P., 1894.

Markels, Robin B. *A New Perspective on Cohesion in Expository Paragraphs.* Carbondale: Southern Illinois UP, 1984.

Mellon, John. "Issues in the Theory and Practice of Sentence-Combining: A Twenty-Year Perspective." *Sentence-Combining and the Teaching of Writing.* Ed. Donald Daiker et al. 1–38.

—. *Transformational Sentence-Combining: A Method for Enhancing the Development of Syntactic Fluency in English Composition.* Urbana: NCTE, 1969.

Memering, Dean, and Frank O'Hare. *The Writer's Work.* Englewood Cliffs, NJ: Prentice-Hall, 1980.

Miller, B.D., and J.W. Ney. "The Effect of Systematic Oral Exercises on the Writing of Fourth-Grade Students." *Research in the Training of English* 1 (1968): 44–61.

Minto, William. *A Manual of English Prose Literature.* Boston: Ginn, 1892.

Morenberg, Max, Donald A. Daiker, and Andrew Kerek. "Sentence-Combining at the College Level: An Experimental Study." *Research in the Training of English* 12 (1978): 245–56.

Ney, James. "The Hazards of the Course: Sentence-Combining in Freshman English." *The English Record* 27 (1976): 70–77.

O'Hare, Frank. *Sentence-Combining: Improving Student Writing without Formal Grammar Instruction.* Urbana: NCTE 1973.

—. *Sentencecraft: A Course in Sentence-Combining.* Lexington, MA: Ginn, 1985.

Pike, Kenneth L. "A Linguistic Contribution to Composition." *CCC* 15 (1965): 237–42.

Pitkin, Willis L., Jr. "Discourse Blocs." *CCC* 20 (1966): 138–48.

Rodgers, Paul C., Jr. "A Discourse-Centered Rhetoric of the Paragraph." *CCC* 17 (1966): 2–11.

—. "Alexander Bain and the Rise of the 'Organic Paragraph.'" *Quarterly Journal of Speech* 51 (1965): 399–408.

Strong, William. *Sentence-Combining: A Composing Book.* New York: Random, 1973.

—. *Sentence-Combining and Paragraph Building.* New York: Random, 1981.

Thomas, Helen. *A Study of the Paragraph.* New York: American, 1912.

Whately, Richard. *Elements of Rhetoric.* 1828 London: Fellowes, 1841.

Witte, Stephen P., and Lester Faigley. "Coherence, Cohesion, and Writing Quality." *CCC* 32 (1981): 189–204.

—. "Topical Structure and Revision: An Exploratory Study." *CCC* 34 (1983): 313–41.

Wolcott, James. "The Lives of Albert Goldman." *Vanity Fair* 51 (October 1988): 36.

Young, Richard E., and Alton L. Becker. "Toward a Modern Theory of Rhetoric: A Tagmemic Contribution." *Harvard Educational Review* 35 (1965): 465.

Invitation to Further Study

If the test of theory comes when we put it into practice, the reverse holds true as well. All classroom practices need to be reexamined continually in the light of contemporary scholarly discussions. Beginning teachers are often interested to find out why certain theories translate well into practice, while others, seemingly worthwhile and sensible, refuse such adaptation. And after a year in the classroom, though they recognize certain successes, teachers cannot explain those successes in terms of their theoretical base. Fortunately for those interested in the theory and practice of rhetoric and composition, scholarly discussions are not hard to find.

In particular, professional organizations such as the Conference on College Composition and Communication (CCCC), the Modern Language Association (MLA), the Rhetoric Society of American (RSA), the International Society for the History of Rhetoric (ISHR), the National Council of Teachers of English (NCTE), and state and local organizations offer a wide arena for activity and stimulation for growth. Many teachers of writing feel that attendance at one of these national or state meetings provides the excitement of learning and professional sharing that sustains them through a hard year of work. The NCTE is the most broad–based of these organizations, for its membership comprises language arts, literature, and writing teachers–pre K through college. For college-level writing teachers, perhaps the most stimulating and useful of professional meetings is the annual CCCC convention held in March. Over a three-day period, the CCCC offers over 250 sessions that balance pedagogy, theory, and research. And like most other organizations, the CCCC offers special membership and conference rates to graduate students.

Some of these organizations have their own journals—*College Composition and Communication (CCC)*, *College English (CE)*, *English Journal (EJ)*, *Rhetoric Society Quarterly (RSQ)*—which are included in the membership. *CCC* remains the showcase for contemporary lines of research, theoretical debates, and reexamination of both composition theory and *praxis*. In the last fifteen years, however, a number of new journals devoted to scholarship in rhetoric and composition have appeared: *Rhetoric Review (RR)*, *The Writing Instructor (TWI)*, *Written Communication*, *Journal of Advanced Composition (JAC)*, *Pre/Text*, *Freshman English News (FEN)*, *Rhetorica*. Taken together, these journals provide ample opportunity for publication in the field as well as a means of keeping up with the latest issues and concerns. *TWI*, published by the rhetoric and composition graduate students at University of Southern California, is especially interested in featuring the work of other graduate students.

NCTE also sponsors (and University of Southern Illinois Press publishes) a series of moderately priced monographs expressly for CCCC, "Studies in Writing and Rhetoric," the latest work by the best researchers in our field. And in response to a call for collaboration between colleges and secondary schools, the State University of New York Press (Albany) has launched *Essays on the Teaching of English in the Secondary School*, edited by Gail Hawisher and Anna Soter. What you will soon realize is the comfortable give-and-take between each organization and its publications—and among the authors and subscribers.

What are the issues that most concern theorists and practitioners today? Of the many we might cite, let us examine three that seem to be particularly crucial. The first, a difficult question which runs across all levels of education, is that of evaluation. Who are we testing, and for whose purposes are we doing so? While we as a nation seem completely devoted to assessing and testing, the reasons for doing so are far from clear. Even more troubling is the fact that our theory of testing (like most of the tests themselves) rests on an outmoded epistemology, one that views knowledge as exterior and statistically verifiable. Such a view has been under attack for most of the century in almost every field, but it still underlies our entire testing effort. Because these tests are so important to our students' lives, we must take the lead in developing a more contemporary and complex theory of testing and then applying that theory in our testing practices.

Most pressing for the classroom teacher is the question of how best to measure the success of student writing. Gone are the days when a C+ at the top of a student's paper would speak for itself; today, most teachers want to help, not merely evaluate, their students. Yet we find ourselves sensitive to and critical of the less-than-ideal aspects— shortcomings in content, organization, mechanics—of our students' papers. We are all English majors, educated in reading the most difficult, the most tortuous, the vaguest of prose, who feel satisfied and smug after we have wrung the meaning from an especially runic passage of *Ulysses* or a soliloquy in *Hamlet* or a creative spelling in a medieval manuscript. Why is it then that we feel miffed if we stumble over a violation of correlative conjunctions in any of our students' papers? Several compositionists are working toward tentative answers to questions of responding to student papers. In "Students'

Rights to Their Own Texts: A Model for Teacher Response," Lillian Brannon and C.H. Knoblauch argue that while we are willing to give experienced writers authority over their own texts, we are unwilling to give student writers the same courtesy: "[I]n classroom writing situations, the reader assumes primary control of the choices that writers make, feeling perfectly free to 'correct' those choices any time an apprentice deviates from the teacher-reader's conception of what the developing text ought to look like or ought to be doing" (158).

Brannon, Knoblauch, and Nancy Sommers all express concern that in our attempt to tell the writers how to do a better job than they could do alone, we in effect "appropriate the writers' texts" (Brannon and Knoblauch; Sommers 149–51). In addition, their research has shown that although our purpose is to help student writers communicate their ideas successfully, our theory falls short of its mark. We comment on their papers to dramatize the presence of a reader, to help them become that questioning reader themselves, and to create a motive for revising. But our comments seem to be especially useless when so many of us mark the final product, so their writing will be better *next* time.

Recent theorists have provided us with several alternatives to the traditional approach to responding to student writing; pervasive in all of the alternatives is the idea that responding supportively to student writing does not have to limited to writing comments on it. In "The Process of Teaching" (*Learning by Teaching*), Donald Murray tells us that we can *listen* to our students instead. The listening teacher waits, reads, and listens (152). In Murray's portfolio method of evaluation, students submit only their best work when they are ready to be evaluated. Peter Elbow offers other alternatives to the traditional method of responding to student writing. In *Writing Without Teachers*, he tells us how to move the responsibility for responding from the teacher to the students as a group. In the process of learning how to respond to the writing of their peers, they also develop the ability to respond to their own texts. Elbow's *Writing with Power* shows us how to use collaboration; he spurs writers to take responsibility themselves for seeking out collaborators who will provide two kinds of feedback: criterion-based feedback and reader-based feedback. There are other alternatives to responding to student writing as well. Richard Haswell published the benefits he sees in "minimal marking," his use of checks in the margin to alert the student writer of a problem in that line of the text. Besides being a quick way to mark papers, minimal marking reduces the amount of teacher comment on the page and puts the responsibility of editing back on the student writer. In *Evaluating Writing: Describing, Measuring, Judging*, Charles R. Cooper and Lee Odell explain current techniques for assessing student writing, including measures of syntactic complexity, holistic evaluation, and primary-trait scoring. Perhaps the most comprehensive yet easily understandable coverage of holistic grading is Edward M. White's *Teaching and Assessing Writing*. White suggests that holistic evaluation creates an "interpretive community" of readers in which evaluation is properly categorized and goes on to offer much commonsense advice on testing, organizing holistic tests, and using testing and evaluation in teaching.

After exploring the question of measuring the success of individual papers, teachers are often interested in measuring the success of their entire writing program. Fortunately, there are several good sources for such a quest. In *Evaluating College Writing Programs*, Stephen P. Witte and Lester Faigley tell us that outside evaluators often confuse description with evaluation and that the quantitative approach often rests on faulty assumptions about the goals or administrative structure of a writing program. Charles Cooper has edited *The Nature and Measurement of Competency in English*, a collection particularly useful for administrators and their assistants, which includes his own essay on the political and cultural implications of state-mandated testing.

A second major issue confronting scholars of rhetoric and composition is the relationship between individual cognition and social ways of knowing. Researchers have most recently begun to pay close attention to what the writer does while writing, and their work attempts to answer this twofold question: where do a writer's ideas come from and how are such ideas formulated into writing? Such a question demands a new focus on *invention*, discussed in works of Janice Lauer, Richard Larson, Richard Young, Linda Flower, John Hayes, Stephen Witte, John Daly, and Mike Rose, many of which are cited in Chapter 5. This renewed interest in student writers has led in another powerful direction as well, notably in the work of Ken Macrorie (*Telling Writing*) and, more pervasively, of Peter Elbow. Elbow is interested in how writers establish unique voices and realize individual selves in discourse, and his work with students presents dramatic evidence of such activity.

This relationship between individual cognition and social ways of knowing is being explored in many fields, particularly psychology, as researchers seek to understand the ways language mediates between self and society. In rhetoric and composition, the larger body of work on cognitive processes has traditionally concentrated on individual writers, seeking to map the ways in which they represent tasks, make plans, and choose strategies that will lead to text. Kenneth Bruffee is probably the best-known composition theorist who argues that knowledge is constructed socially, and his work is related to a large body of research on collaborative writing, reading, and learning. Tori

Haring-Smith bases arguments for writing-across-the-curriculum efforts on such a collaborative foundation. More recently, a group of researchers at Purdue University (Meg Morgan, Nancy Allen, Teresa Moore, Dianne Atkinson, and Craig Snow, "Collaborative Writing in the Classroom") has studied collaborative reading, writing, and learning in a number of settings, using differing research methodologies; they are attempting to understand the ways in which knowledge—and even texts—are constructed socially. In addition, the work of Andrea Lunsford and Lisa Ede ("Collaborative Learning: Lessons from the World of Work"; "Let Them Write—Together"; "Why Write . . . Together?") demonstrates that this contextual element—collaboration—characterizes a great deal of writing and reading done on the job. Thus far, however, these two important strands of research have not been systematically linked—or approved—either in theory or in practice. Doing so holds out the promise of much exciting theoretical and practical work.

A final issue is of great concern to teachers and researchers of composition everywhere. In what ways are issues of gender, race, and class related to success or failure in writing, to the dynamics of the classroom, to ways of knowing in general? Here we are at the earliest stages of investigation and understanding. Recent publications span the entire range of questions: Paula S. Rothenberg's *Racism and Sexism*, a collection of essays exploring the permutations and ramifications of race, class, and gender in American institutions; Elizabeth Abel's *Writing and Sexual Difference*; Elizabeth Flynn and Patrocinio Schweickart's *Gender and Reading*; Cynthia Caywood and Gillian Overing's *Teaching Writing: Pedagogy, Gender, and Equality*; and Mary Field Belenky et al., *Women's Ways of Knowing*. All of these questions have been articulated clearly and persuasively in David Bleich's *The Double Perspective: Language, Literacy, and Social Relations*. Bleich argues for recognizing and implementing the "double perspective" that comes from acknowledging the simultaneous presence and interaction of biology, psychology, society, and culture on the way we use language to read, write, think, and react.

For most of our history, teachers of writing have treated students pretty much as all alike, but that convenient fiction is no longer feasible. Our students come to us with different native tongues and different levels of fluency in edited American English, from different socioeconomic classes and different sectors of society. And now more than ever before, there is a huge range in their ages and life experiences. Their entrance into the academy has made us suddenly aware of our inattention to these differences, which is reflected in our subsequent neglect of our curricula, and the (a)political agenda of our (mostly pale male) educational institutions.

What lesson, then, can we learn from the recent and compelling work of Rothenberg, Abel, Flynn and Schweikart, Caywood and Overing, Belenky et al., and Bleich? It should not be surprising that the lesson we learn from these books is a grammatical one, for structures of hierarchy and power are inscribed in our language in the ways we talk about gender, race, class, and clan, in the ways we read, write, think, and respond. Language study is part of a complex grammatical structure. Unless we learn this lesson, we may have listened in class and read the books, but we will not have learned from them. The time has come for us to respect those differences in our classroom and make them central to our pedagogy.

Works Cited — *Invitation to Further Study*

Abel, Elizabeth. *Writing and Sexual Difference.* Chicago: U. of Chicago P., 1982.

Belenky, Mary Field, et al. *Women's Ways of Knowing.* New York: Basic, 1986.

Bleich, David. *The Double Perspective: Language, Literacy, and Social Relations.* New York: Oxford UP, forthcoming.

Brannon, Lillian, and L.H. Knoblauch. "Students' Rights to Their Own Texts: A Model for Teacher Response." CCC 33 (1982): 157–66.

Bruffee, Kenneth. "The Brooklyn Plan: Attaining Intellectual Growth through Peer-Group Tutoring." *Liberal Education* 64 (1978): 447–69.

—. "Collaborative Learning: Some Practical Models." CE 34 (1973): 634–43.

—. "Collaborative Learning and the 'Conversation of Mankind.'" CE 46 (1984): 635–52.

Caywood, Cynthia, and Gillian Overing. *Teaching Writing: Pedagogy, Gender, and Equity.* Albany: SUNY P, 1987.

Cooper, Charles R., ed., *The Nature and Measurement of Competency in English.* Urbana: NCTE, 1981.

Cooper, Charles R., and Lee Odell. *Evaluating Writing: Describing, Measuring, Judging.* Urbana: NCTE, 1977.

Elbow, Peter, *Writing Without Teachers.* New York: Oxford UP, 1973.

—. *Writing with Power.* New York: Oxford UP, 1981.

Flynn, Elizabeth, and Patrocinio Schweickart. *Gender and Reading.* Baltimore: Johns Hopkins UP, 1986.

Haring-Smith, Tori, ed. *A Guide to Writing Programs, Writing Centers, Peer Tutoring Programs, and Writing Across the Curriculum.* Glenview: Scott, 1985.

Haswell, Richard. "Minimal Marking" CE 45 (1983): 600–04.

Hawisher, Gail, and Anna Soter, eds. *Essays on the Teaching of English in the Secondary School.* Albany: SUNY P, 1989.

Lunsford, Andrea, and Lisa Ede. "Collaborative Learning: Lessons from the World of Work." *Writing Program Administrators* 9 (1986): 17–26.

—. "Let Them Write—Together." *English Quarterly* 18 (1985): 119–27.

—. "Why Write—Together?" *English Quarterly* (1985): 119–27.

Macrorie, Ken. *Telling Writing.* Rochelle Park, NJ: Hayden, 1970.

Morgan, Meg, et al. "Collaborative Writing in the Classroom." *The Bulletin* (Sept. 1987): 20–26.

Murray, Donald. *Learning By Teaching.* Upper Montclair, NJ: Boynton, 1982.

Rothenberg, Paula S. *Racism and Sexism.* New York: St. Martin's Press, 1988.

Sommers, Nancy. "Responding to Student Writing." *CCC* 33 (1982): 149–51.

White, Edward M. *Teaching and Assessing Writing.* San Francisco: Jossey-Bass, 1985.

Witte, Stephen P., and Lester Faigley. *Evaluating College Writing Programs.* Carbondale: Southern Illinois UP, 1983.

Suggested Readings for Composition Teachers

Bibliographies

Bizzell, Patricia, and Bruce Herzberg. *The Bedford Bibliography for Teachers of Writing.* 1987 ed. Boston: Bedford, 1987.

Braddock, Richard, Richard Lloyd-Jones, and Lowell Schoer. *Research in Written Composition.* Urbana, IL: NCTE, 1963.

Cooper, Charles R., and Lee Odell, eds. *Points of Departure.* Urbana, IL: NCTE, 1978.

Lindemann, Erika. *Longman Bibliography of Composition and Rhetoric.* New York: Longman, 1984–85, 1986–87.

Tate, Gary, ed. *Teaching Composition: Twelve Bibliographical Essays.* Fort Worth: Texas Christian UP, 1987.

Collections

Beach, Richard, and Lillian S. Bridwell, eds. *New Directions in Composition Research.* New York: Guilford, 1984.

Connors, Robert J., Lisa S. Ede, and Andrea A. Lunsford, eds. *Essays on Classical Rhetoric and Modern Discourse.* Carbondale: Southern Illinois UP, 1984.

Enos, Theresa, ed. *A Sourcebook for Basic Writing Teachers.* New York: Random House, 1987. Includes articles on literacy, cognitive development, peer collaboration.

Graves, Richard, ed. *Rhetoric and Composition.* 2nd ed. Upper Montclair, NJ: Boynton/Cook, 1984.

McClelland, Ben W., and Timothy Donavan, eds. *Perspectives on Research and Scholarship in Composition.* New York: MLA, 1985.

McQuade, Donald A., ed. *The Territory of Language.* Carbondale: Southern Illinois UP, 1986.

Newkirk, Thomas, ed. *Only Connect.* Upper Montclair, NJ: Boynton/Cook, 1986.

Rose, Mike, ed. *When a Writer Can't Write.* New York: Guilford P, 1985.

Tate, Gary, and Edward P.J. Corbett, eds. *The Writing Teacher's Sourcebook.* 2nd ed. New York: Oxford UP, 1988.

Books

Applebee, Arthur, et al. *A Study of Writing in the Secondary Schools*. Urbana, IL: NCTE, 1974.

Bartholomae, David, and Anthony Petrosky. *Facts, Artifacts, and Counterfacts*. Upper Montclair, NJ: Boynton/Cook, 1986.

Beale, Walter. *A Pragmatic Theory of Rhetoric*. Carbondale: Southern Illinois UP, 1987.

Berlin, James. *Rhetoric and Reality: Writing Instruction in American Colleges, 1900–1985*. Southern Illinois (NCTE/CCCC), 1987.

—. *Writing Instructions in Nineteenth Century American Colleges*. Southern Illinois (NCTE/CCCC), 1984.

Berthoff, Ann E. *The Making of Meaning*. Upper Montclair, NJ: Boynton/Cook, 1987.

Brannon, Lillian, Melinda Knight, and Vara Neverow-Turk. *Writers Writing*. Upper Montclair, NJ: Boynton/Cook, 1983.

Britton, James, et al. *The Development of Writing Abilities, 11–18*. London: Macmillan Education, 1975.

Bruner, Jerome. *The Process of Education*. New York: Vintage Books, 1960.

Cooper, Charles, and Lee Odell. *Evaluating Writing: Describing, Measuring, and Judging*. Urbana, IL: NCTE, 1977.

Elbow, Peter. *Embracing Contraries*. New York: Oxford UP, 1986.

—. *Writing With Power*. New York: Oxford UP, 1981.

—. *Writing Without Teachers*. New York: Oxford UP, 1973.

Emig, Janet. *The Composing Process of Twelfth Graders*. Research Report No. 13. Urbana, IL: NCTE, 1971.

—. *The Web of Meaning*. Upper Montclair, NJ: Boynton/Cook, 1983.

Halliday, M.A.K., and R. Hasan. *Cohesion in English*. White Plains, NY: Longman, 1976.

Hirsch, E.D. *the Philosophy of Composition*. Chicago: U of Chicago P, 1977.

Hunt, Kellogg. *Grammatical Structures Written at Three Grade Levels*. Urbana, NJ: NCTE, 1965.

Kinneavy, James L. *A Theory of Discourse*. Englewood Cliffs, NJ: Prentice-Hall, 1971. Rpt. Norton, 1980.

Kitzhaber, Albert R. *Themes, Theories, and Therapy: The Teaching of Writing in College*. New York: McGraw, 1963.

Labov, William. *The Study of Nonstandard English*. Urbana, IL: NCTE, 1970.

Lanham, Richard A. *Literacy and the Survival of Humanism*. New Haven: Yale UP, 1983.

Lauer, Janice, and William Asher. *Composition Research: Empirical Designs*. New York: Oxford UP, 1988.

LeFevre, Karen. *Invention as a Social Act.* Carbondale: Southern Illinois UP, 1987.

Lindemann, Erika. *A Rhetoric for Writing Teachers.* 2nd ed. New York: Oxford UP, 1987.

Loban, Walter. *Language Development: Kindergarten through Grade Twelve.* Urbana, IL: NCTE, 1976.

Macrorie, Ken. *Telling Writing.* Rochelle Park, NJ: Hayden, 1970.

—. *Uptaught.* Rochelle Park, NJ: Hayden, 1970.

Mellon, John C. *Transformational Sentence-Combining: A Method for Enhancing the Development of Syntactic Fluency in English Composition.* Urbana, IL: NCTE, 1967.

Moffett, James. *Coming on Center.* Upper Montclair, NJ: Boynton/Cook, 1981.

—. *A Student-Centered Language Arts and Reading, K–13.* Boston: Houghton, 1968.

—. *Teaching the Universe of Discourse.* Boston: Houghton, 1968.

Murray, Donald. *A Writer Teaches Writing.* 2nd ed. Boston: Houghton, 1985.

Neel, Jasper. *Plato, Derrida, and Writing.* Carbondale: Southern Illinois UP, 1988.

Odell, Lee, and Dixie Goswami. *Writing in Non-Academic Settings.* New York: Guilford P, 1985.

O'Hare, Frank, *Sentence-Combining: Improving Student Writing Without Formal Grammar Instruction.* Urbana, IL: NCTE, 1973.

Rose, Mike. *Writer's Block: The Cognitive Dimension.* Carbondale: Southern Illinois UP, 1984.

Shaughnessy, Mina. *Errors and Expectations.* New York: Oxford UP, 1977.

Smith, Frank. *Understanding Reading.* 2nd ed. New York: Holt, 1978.

Vygotsky, L.S. *Mind and Society.* Boston: Harvard UP, 1978.

—. *Thought and Language.* Trans. Eugenia Hanfman and Gertrude Vakar. Boston: MIT P, 1962.

White, Edward. *Teaching and Assessing Writing.* San Francisco: Jossey Bass, 1985.

Winterowd, Ross. *Contemporary Rhetoric.* New York: Harcourt, 1975.

Witte, Stephen, and Lester Faigley. *Evaluating College Writing Programs.* Carbondale: Southern Illinois UP, 1983.

Young, Richard E., Alton L. Becker, and Kenneth L. Pike. *Rhetoric: Discovery and Change.* New York: Harcourt, 1970.

Articles

Modern Rhetorical Theory

Connors, Robert, "Composition Studies and Science." *College English* 45 (1983): 1–20.

Emig, Janet. "Writing as a Mode of Learning." *CCC* 33 (May 1977): 122–28. Rpt. *Web of Meaning.* Tate and Corbett.

Hairston, Maxine. "The Winds of Change: Thomas Kuhn and the Revolution in the Teaching of Writing." *CCC* 33 (1982): 76–86. Rpt. Graves, *Rhetoric and Composition.*

Kinneavy, James. "The Basic Aims of Discourse." *CCC* 20 Dec. 1969): 297–304.

Knoblauch, Cy, and Lilian Brannon. Chapters 1 and 2. *Rhetorical Tradition and the Teaching of Writing.* Upper Montclair, NJ: Boynton/Cook, 1984.

McCrimmon, James. "Writing as a Way of Knowing." The Promise of English: NCTE 1970 Distinguished Lectures. Carbondale, IL: NCTE, 1970. Rpt. Graves, *Rhetoric and Composition.*

The Composing Process

Flower, Linda. "Interpretive Acts: Cognition and the Construction of Discourse." *Poetics* 16 (1987).

Graves, Donald. "An Examination of the Writing Process of Seven–Year–Old Children." *RTE* 9 (1975): 227–41.

Macrorie, Ken. "To Be Read." *English Journal* 57 (May 1968): 686–92. Rpt. Graves.

Murray, Donald. "Teach Writing as a Process, not Product." *The Leaflet* (Nov. 1972): 11–14. Rpt. Graves.

Perl, Sondra. "The Composing Process of Unskilled College Writers." *RTE* 13 (1979): 317–36.

---. "Understanding Composing." *CCC* 31 (Dec. 1980): 363–69. Rpt. Graves.

Pianko, Sharon. "A Description of the Composing Process of College Freshman Writers." *RTE* 13 (1979): 5–22.

Stallard, Charles. "An Analysis of the Writing Behavior of Good Student Writers." *RTE* 8 (Summer 1974): 206–18.

Voss, Ralph. "Janet Emig's *The Composing Process of Twelfth Graders:* A Reassessment." *CCC* 34 (1983): 278–83.

Witte, Stephen. "Pre-Text and Composing." *CCC* 38 (December 1987): 397–425.

Revision

Berthoff, Ann E. "Recognition, Representation, and Revision." *Journal of Basic Writing* 3 (Fall-Winter 1981): 19–32.

Flower, Linda. "Writer-Based Prose: A Cognitive Basis for Problems in Writing." *CE* 41 (September 1979): 19–37.

Sommers, Nancy. "Revision Strategies of Student Writers and Experienced Adult Writers." *CCC* 31 (December 1980): 378–88. Rpt. Graves.

Witte, Stephen. "Topical Structure and Revision: An Exploratory Study." *CCC* 34 (1983): 313–41.

Basic Writing

Bartholomae, David. "The Study of Error." *CCC* 31 (October 1980): 253–69.

Lunsford, Andrea. "Cognitive Development and the Basic Writer." *CE* 41 (September 1979): 38–46.

—. "The Content of Basic Writers' Essays." *CCC* 31 (October 1980): 278–90.